FOUNDATIONS
OF INDUCTIVE LOGIC

Books by Roy Harrod

THE LIFE OF JOHN MAYNARD KEYNES

TOWARDS A DYNAMIC ECONOMICS

ECONOMIC ESSAYS

THE DOLLAR

FOUNDATIONS
OF
INDUCTIVE LOGIC

BY

ROY HARROD
STUDENT OF CHRIST CHURCH
FORMERLY SENIOR CENSOR

HARCOURT, BRACE AND COMPANY
NEW YORK

PRINTED IN GREAT BRITAIN

PREFACE

Apology is due from one who, with few credentials, comes
forward and claims to make a major contribution in a difficult
subject. I have acute and painful feelings of diffidence in the
presence of learned colleagues in the academic field, including
men of great distinction who have devoted their whole lives
to philosophy. I console myself with this thought : it is
commonly agreed that in philosophy the prime method of research is neither the study of the printed word nor the conduct
of experiments, but reflexion. To the subjects dealt with in
this volume I have devoted concentrated and arduous reflexion for numerous periods in the last twenty years ; and
they have been of interest to me over a longer stretch of time.
I am well acquainted with all the agonies of frustration when,
again and again, hopeful lines of approach have to be abandoned. I have not failed to pay in arduous toil what may be
deemed a proper price for venturing to publish my conclusions.

I should not be frank if I did not express the belief that
these conclusions are of great importance. Only that belief
could give me face with myself in being so bold as to publish,
although a layman in the field. On my first introduction to
philosophy I appreciated that the theory of induction was in
an unsatisfactory condition. Nineteenth-century attempts to
vindicate it had been discredited. During my lifetime the
hope of doing so has been largely abandoned. Distinguished
philosophers have lapsed into feeble forms of pragmatism.
Some have sought refuge from the uncomfortable sense of
failure in this field in a comforting dogma, which claims not
only that induction cannot be vindicated, but that any attempt
to vindicate it would entail some kind of self-contradiction.
Yet it is on the face of it strange that there should be no
means of vindicating on general principles those methods
of thought that have led man forward to so many intellectual triumphs. I claim to be setting out in this volume,

v

although only in the roughest outline and without finish, what the essential principles of induction are, and to show that these principles are co-equal in validity and authority and certainty with the principles of deduction.

In the past it has been thought that the validity of induction depended on the prior acceptance of such principles as the Law of Universal Causation and the Uniformity of Nature. More recently it has been claimed that we have to assume initial prior probabilities for certain beliefs. All such prior postulates have been totally dispensed with here. If induction is to be vindicated, it must be vindicated without any prior assumptions about the nature of the universe whatever. In this I subject myself to Hume, the great master. Starting from his basic principles I have, I would claim, rebutted his sceptical conclusions. Indeed one way of characterizing this volume would be as the refutation of Hume. My hope is that no future Keynes, reviewing the progress of inductive theory, may be able to say 'Hitherto Hume has been the master, only to be refuted in the manner of Diogenes or Dr. Johnson'.

Being concerned with induction, this book is also necessarily a treatise on probability. This has been the subject of fully developed mathematical theory. It is clear that the doctrines that I have set out should be given mathematical expression. I lack the qualifications to do this, but believe that this is not fatal to my work, which, to use an old-fashioned word, may be regarded as the prolegomena to the theory of probability. It would naturally be a source of pride if it inspired a mathematical treatment and development of its central concepts. I would only add one ungracious word of warning. I have the impression that there is a rather considerable gulf between the logical faculty and the purely mathematical faculty. This may have tended to be obscured by recent developments of symbolic logic, which are of the first importance in their own way. The mathematician is largely concerned with the manipulation of symbols. His quality does not of course show itself merely in the correctness of his manipulation, but in his genius in discerning how to devise, by a use of symbols, a correct movement of thought from one point to another : for example, in finding the proof of a given theorem. The symbols constitute a safeguard.

Logicians, perhaps inspired by mathematics, have believed it their task to set up a system of symbols and of rules for their use which would provide similar safeguards in proving logical theorems. This has become prominent in symbolic logic, but the tendency dates from Aristotle's syllogism. Misconceptions are involved here ; the proper task of logic is to criticize and interpret any set of symbols or rules, and, when that criticism and interpretation have been achieved, the task of logic proper ends. Thus 'symbolic logic' should only be an appendix to logic proper.

Logic is concerned with the relation known as 'entailment'. It has been traditionally divided into deductive logic and inductive logic. There has recently been some tendency to claim that any considerations concerning entailment belong to deductive logic ; this leaves the status of inductive logic, considered as a normative discipline, somewhat obscure. It will be contended in this volume that deduction and induction are co-equal branches of the general theory of entailment.

If the doctrines here set out are correct, much, perhaps most, current thought about induction is wrong. The theory of induction should take on a new lease of life. If this is true, it can hardly be denied to be of some philosophical importance. I would even venture further. In modern times philosophy has become very specialized, and the thoughtful members of the community have felt less qualified to take an interest in it than they did in the nineteenth century. This may be inevitable, but it is unfortunate. Although people of this type now feel somewhat cut off from the details of the subject, they are yet aware that at the very heart of modern philosophy there is an extreme degree of scepticism. In this way treatises that are fully understood only by a handful may yet have a very wide influence, and I have the idea that this influence may be harmful and discouraging to strong resolve and high determination in relation to human progress. The great belief in progress of the nineteenth century is often derided, but there is a sense in which we still live on the capital created by that belief ; the great movements of amelioration which are yielding ever more abundant fruits to-day had their original impetus in nineteenth-century hopefulness. That hopefulness was not unconnected with a certain self-confidence among philosophers. We now see flaws in their reasoning, which lie at the very basis of their thought. Twentieth-century philosophers, aware of those flaws, appear to have capitulated. We are not now creating a new capital of hopefulness. It is my conviction that the surrender and the resort to the easy paths of pragmatism or scepticism have been made too readily. The problems involved are difficult, but to judge them insoluble is a sign of complacency. For these reasons I claim, although I am aware that this is almost painfully presumptuous, that a reconstruction of inductive logic is not only of professional philosophical interest, but of wide-reaching importance for the good of society.

It is usual in a preface to provide a list of acknowledgements. Owing to the peculiar circumstances of my case, perhaps I may be forgiven for a brief resumé which is more biographical than bibliographical in character. In boyhood my great debt was to J. S. Mill, always to be relied on to kindle enthusiasm in the adolescent mind. I also became acquainted with some of the work of Bertrand Russell, and went to Oxford full of a brimming enthusiasm to learn what modern thought could rescue from Mill, and to get a deeper understanding of the exciting developments initiated by Russell. My hopes were utterly disappointed. I found in Oxford no one who was interested in the things that had interested me, no one even who seemed to have the faintest comprehension of why such things could possibly interest anyone. The prevailing school of philosophy at that time, based ultimately on the thought of the Ancients, had been given a special twist by Professor J. Cook-Wilson and perhaps could be described as a kind of common-sense realism. And there was a minority school which still derived inspiration from Kant and belonged to the tradition of T. H. Green and Bradley. These preoccupations, however, were consistent with an instruction to pupils to read, in addition to the Ancients, the original texts of Locke, Berkeley and Hume, and that was a great gain. I remain unrepentant in the view that this group of British philosophers has not been matched by any other, ancient or modern. But in general the Oxford experience was one of complete frustration. The arguments that seemed good and valid in Oxford struck me as invalid, and the arguments I sought to bring forward struck my mentors as invalid. But my mentors were far more skilled in argument than I ; and the result of the whole experience was total discouragement.

I add by way of digression that the Oxford philosophical scene has since changed out of recognition, and good foreign judges have informed me that Oxford now stands high in world regard for the vitality of its philosophical thinking. A notable contribution to the transition was made by Professor H. H. Price who, while much influenced by the Cook-Wilson school, developed independent and important lines of thinking of his own. In early days we had philosophical walks together, until he outpaced me, physically as well as mentally. A larger change was made some ten years later when Professor Ayer appeared on the scene. Bringing to the task a fiery zeal, masterly lucidity of exposition, dialectic skill, lightning riposte, and philosophical quality of the highest order, he made a devastating onslaught on established positions. He showed great moral courage. Examiners took his deviation to be due merely to lack of intellectual capacity. But when he came into open debate and entered into controversy without restraint, they had to take him a little more seriously, and were displeased. So strong was the hold of orthodoxy that he would not have received academic appointment in Oxford but for a series of happy accidents. But he had sown the seed ; younger men listened, and his disciples were soon established in teaching positions. The Oxford philosophical scene had been transformed. In this connexion it is proper to record that his tutor, who was Professor Gilbert Ryle, had already, albeit by slower steps, proceeded far from the old Oxford orthodoxy towards those positions which he has since made famous by his writing.

To return to the main narrative, my own profound philosophical disappointment ten years earlier was relieved by some faint rays of hope. I had known the Whitehead family from schoolboy days ; I often visited them until Alfred Whitehead's departure for Harvard, and found in many talks with him a support for the view that I might not be altogether wrong in my discontent with Oxford philosophy. In 1922 I went to Cambridge for a period in quest of economic wisdom. There I found among the undergraduates Frank Ramsey, Professor

R. A. Braithwaite and Mr. J. S. Bentwich, with whom I had enlightening talks. Ramsey's prestige was already great owing to the high esteem in which Bertrand Russell and Keynes were known to hold him, and the interest he showed in his delightfully easy style of philosophical conversation gave me further moral support. We maintained an occasional interchange of visits until his premature and tragic death. During the 'twenties, I had many long sessions of discussion with Lord Cherwell, largely in the early hours of the morning. His mind is wide-ranging and has great penetration wherever it chooses to alight on a subject of interest. Some parts of philosophy were comprehended in this interest, and here again I found support for the view that in my disagreement with Oxford orthodoxy I might not be altogether in the wrong.

During what I may call my fallow period in philosophy, the book that impressed me most was J. Nicod's *Foundations of Geometry and Induction*. The clarity and beauty of his thought, his power of selecting and concentrating upon central points of philosophic interest, and the remorselessness with which he pressed his reasoning to its logical conclusion, yet always against a background of tentativeness in relation to larger issues, have seemed to me to give him a rank in philosophy which it would be hard to match in the twentieth century. I came back to these essays after twenty-five years (but I had re-read the one on induction while engaged on writing the *Life of Keynes*), and was as delighted as before ; and indeed I had the feeling that his thought had been working in me at an unconscious level throughout the period. The essay on induction is slight ; he had the conviction, which he was not yet able to justify by explicit argument, that induction by simple enumeration was more fundamental than induction by methods of elimination. That is the standpoint of this volume.

At some time late in the 'thirties I went to a meeting of an Oxford philosophical society to which G. E. Moore read a paper, either on the subject of, or anyhow mainly concerned with, memory. It was a characteristic production ; he used his tremendous power of persuasion to recommend the view that we were talking the utmost nonsense if we put forward any doubt about whether our clear memories were true.

Bertrand Russell was in the audience ; in a few words he put forward a sensible and timely plea for scepticism ; after all, we were sometimes deceived in what seemed to be very clear memories indeed. I do not know if he entertained more constructive views upon the subject of memory ; if he did, he did not vouchsafe them on that occasion. I returned to my rooms, my brain on fire. Here I had just been listening to two men who might well be ranked as the two most distinguished philosophers of our time, and between them they had said on the central and all-important topic of the validity of memory nothing to the point at all. Yet trust in memory is necessary for almost all our thinking. There had been no hint whatever that we are entitled to trust memory simply because our general experience gives us inductive reasons for doing so. A strong inner voice said that it was intolerable to let the matter stand like that, and I resolved to give it my thought.

It very soon became evident that nothing could be done for memory unless one was standing on sure ground in holding induction to be valid. That brought one back to the old, old question. I wrestled with this problem for a long time, and, to my joy, was able to convince myself that the problem was soluble. During the early months of the late war I found an opportunity for setting out my views in the form of an article on memory. It appeared in *Mind* (January 1942), and I give the following extract from it :

'May it not be that the inductive hypothesis can be accepted *a priori* not merely as a working hypothesis but as a truth ? The proposition is that *if* certain things have been found to remain stable for some time, they are likely to continue to do so for a little longer. This proposition is conditional. It is not claimed that stable elements have been found, for the memory hypothesis is still subject to inquiry.

'It may be feared that I am endeavouring to reintroduce the principle of the uniformity of nature in new phraseology. But this is by no means so. I am only claiming a uniformity limited in space and time and scope of application, and I am only claiming probability, not certainty. The general uniformity of nature appears to me a wild and somewhat disreputable speculation of philosophers.

'The principle for which I argue can only be established by reference to the general nature of the universe. Of this in a certain sense we know nothing *a priori*. It might be a Heracleitean flux through and through, or it might be uniform through and through, or it might be any form of admixture. But suppose it were possible to discover by experience that it was not Heracleitean through and through, would anything follow ? Let us suppose that by experience it was discovered to have certain stable elements in some part of it. Experience only vouches with certainty for that part of it which constitutes the experience. Accepting the experience and turning to review the general constitution of the universe, it would be possible to say of it that it has in a certain part of it stable elements. Now, if contact has been made with certain stable fragments, it is improbable at any time that one is on the extreme edge of those fragments. Whatever their size, it is much more probable that one is at some distance from the edge.

'To say that anything is as likely to happen as anything else at a given moment despite experience, is to affirm that immediately outside experience the universe is entirely Heracleitean. If it has not been so within experience, then one must just have finished exploring the whole of a specialised fragment, and this, though possible, is *a priori* improbable.

'The principle stated is related to the theory of sampling, and it is suggested that it should stand at the basis of all logic. Of course, as is well known, a sample may be entirely misleading ; and this is recognised when it is admitted that the universe may at the next instant dissolve and leave not a wrack behind. In the absence of knowledge to the contrary the sample may be accepted as a guide to what is likely to be in the vicinity.

'It is important to emphasise that this principle is not based on experience ; only if its validity is independently established, shall we be able to tap the findings of past experience. Within a present, however, we have experience of one kind of continuity—spatial. In reflecting upon this, we may contemplate an example of an application of the principle. A room commonly contains smooth surfaces of various shapes and sizes. Suppose a man's vision, reduced to a pin-point, to move for a pre-determined finite length over a surface, or alternatively the finger of some one blindfolded. It is improbable that at the end of the time it would rest on the edge of the surface. This proposition is independent of the sizes of the objects and of the distribution of their sizes. There is no assumption of an equally probable chance of each size or of a distribution according to any law. The room may be filled with a chance collection of heterogeneous objects; the probability is valid, however improbable—according to some other principle—is the distribution of sizes; and of course it is assumed that this is entirely unknown. The meaning of this probability principle may here be interpreted in terms of frequency. If a large number of experiments are made, the eye or hand will come to rest on the edge of a surface much less often than at some point a finite distance from the edge.

'It may be objected that the experiment will take time to perform. But no experiment is necessary. The truth may be apprehended *a priori* within a given present. No doubt, if the experiment is made, the principle will be verified. But, as in the case of some more sophisticated probability propositions, the experiment would be entirely bogus; if carried out, it would only serve to establish the propriety of the conditions, namely that the parties to it had acted in good faith, and not the truth of the probability proposition itself.

'There need be no hesitation in passing from spatial to temporal continuities, for the spatial character of the surface plays no part in aiding the mind to apprehend the probability law.'

Soon the facts of war wrapped us more tightly in their embrace, but I devoted all my spare time for a number of months to a resolve to master Quine's *Mathematical Logic*.

In the attempt to formulate the principle of probability implicit in the foregoing paragraphs, I realized that if one considered a multiplicity of occasions of being upon a surface, one would require some fair sampling postulate. It accordingly seemed that one needed to get a set of occasions within which a probability relation could be established from experience on a single surface. When I showed a rough draft to my learned colleague, Professor J. O. Urmson, he pointed out that my solution was unsatisfactory because in the estimate of probability at a particular point the judgements already made on the journey over the surface were past and done with and no longer relevant to an estimation of probability, and yet my estimate of probability had to include them within the class. In consideration of this difficulty, I came to apprehend the relation set out in the square diagram on page 56. This constitutes the foundation of my theory; all else depends on and follows from it. It at once struck me that publication was desirable, and, after a lapse of some years, an article setting out the point appeared in *Philosophy* (January 1951).[1]

Once this central position was established, other doctrines fell into place fairly easily—the basic theory of simple enumeration, the possibility of dispensing with the fair sampling postulate, the justification of argument by analogy, of the single crucial experiment, and of the preference for simple over complex laws as scientific explanations. As a result of some discussion, Professor A. J. Ayer invited me to give five lectures to his class in London in the autumn of 1954. I there had the benefit of comments by himself and members of the staff.

In recent years, I have tried to enrich my knowledge by reading a number of treatises that have appeared recently, as well as the older classics. While I hope I have derived philosophic strength from such reading and have become acquainted with the current treatment of a wide range of problems, the main conclusions of this volume have been reached independently, and are the fruit of consecutive thinking for many years.

It was only when the main part of my task was finished that I read Professor Broad's well-known articles on induction and probability (*Mind*, 1918 and 1920). In the second of these

---

[1] I am afraid that my philosophy was at that time so rusty that I actually referred to the 'method of agreement' when I meant to refer to the 'method of simple enumeration'.

he approaches positions that are very similar to mine. But he falters, and, in my judgement, falls into confusion. The result is inconclusive.

Still later certain references caused me to read Professor D. Williams's *The Ground of Induction.* I am in substantial agreement with that volume. There are many matters which he does not take up. His inductive system really depends upon a single point (explained on pages 93-104). But that point is correct and all important. Professor Williams appears to write as one who feels himself to be *solus contra mundum.* He alone in the present age believes that the validity of induction can be demonstrated without prior assumptions. I am in complete accord. It strikes me as painful and a bad symptom that his work has not already had a more widespread influence.

It remains to express gratitude to those who have given me direct assistance. First and foremost I must mention Professor H. H. Price, who read the greater part of my manuscript and took the trouble to write out a very extensive commentary, which has been of great value to me. Professor A. J. Ayer has continued to give me encouragement ; he also arranged for the course of lectures in University College, London, to which reference has already been made. Professor J. Sprott read certain sections ; he gave me the benefit of his opinions and also the opportunity of ventilating mine in Nottingham. Mr. Handel Davies, my mathematical colleague in Christ Church, looked over those sections where the text touches on the fringe of mathematical problems and made some helpful criticisms. I must express my deep appreciation to Mr. O. P. Wood, also of Christ Church, who made time in the course of a busy term to study my galley sheets. While expressing no views about the validity of my arguments, on a number of points he made observations which were so pertinent that I felt impelled to alter my text in almost every passage on which they bore. Mr. John Sparrow, an unfailing source of sage advice on all literary questions, has read through this preface, except for this paragraph of it. I am grateful to my wife for helping in the laborious task of making an index.

R. F. H.

CHRIST CHURCH
June 1956

CONTENTS

CONTENTS

CHAPTER I

INTRODUCTORY

DEDUCTION and induction have traditionally been the two kinds of inference studied in logic. In this tradition deduction consisted in argument from a general premise, while inductive argument proceeded from particulars.

The question may be asked whether it is possible for us to acquire knowledge about the universe in which we live by the method of deduction alone. I will forbear to probe into the logical tenets of ancient and mediaeval logicians ; a negative answer to this question was provided by Locke when he gave reasons for holding that we are born into this world without 'innate ideas' ; his great treatise remains the classic exposition of this subject. According to this view, everything we know about nature we have had to learn from experience. Locke's position has been accepted by many philosophers and has certainly been implicit in the researches of all the different kinds of scientists ever since. They have enquired into nature in an open-minded spirit, that is without supposing that by mere thought they could, prior to investigation, furnish themselves with independent knowledge of how it really works. It is assumed in this book that Locke's view is correct.

Accordingly, since experience consists in a mass of particular events, no further progress in knowledge can be made unless there is some valid form of argument from particulars. This means that knowledge cannot be extended by deduction save with the aid of induction.

In the last half-century a vast development in the theory of deduction has occurred. This volume is concerned with induction only. But it would be a proper and convenient procedure to summarize at the outset the current findings of deductive theory, so as to have the scope of deduction securely defined and docketed. Unhappily this is not possible. The present phase of deductive theory is such that any attempt at summary, even of the barest and most cursory kind, would involve a lengthy and controversial disquisition. It is painful to have to introduce a treatise that aims at simplicity and clarity with a passage that will inevitably be somewhat obscure.

There can be no doubt that the general tendency of the recent development of deductive logic has been to pare down and whittle away the power of deduction to extend our knowledge of the facts of life. It has tended to re-enforce the view, which may be expressed in old-fashioned terminology by saying, that whatever is in the conclusion of a deduction is already present in the premises.

The following sentences may overstate the detachment of modern deductive logic from the real world. That logic sets forth certain symbols. It frames rules for the transformation of expressions by the substitution of symbols for one another. Beginning with an appropriate grouping of symbols and applying the rules laid down, we find it possible to derive, or deduce, the commonly accepted principles of deductive logic and the whole of mathematics. This is an astonishing fact, and the intellectual ingenuity of the pioneers of this system has been rightly admired. The original impetus to the work appears to have been given by the observation of a structural similarity between certain logical principles and the basic theorems of algebra.

The devising of symbols and the framing of rules is, in this system, in a certain sense free. This contrasts with the older theories of deduction in which the basic axioms were subject to the requirement that they must be self-evident and thus constitute intellectual intuitions. The modern tendency has been to suspect, and even to reject, the notion of self-evidence. This removes the old criterion for the selection, out of possible groupings of symbols and transformation rules, of a unique set which shall specify correct logical principles. The selection may accordingly be made, either with the view that in certain circumstances they would express a true movement of thought, or without regard to this. I believe that there is still difference of opinion as to how far in the initial stages of the construction of the symbolic system, self-evidence continues to exert some implicit control.

It seems clear, however, that whether one adopts a radical or modified version of what has happened, the change throws an additional burden on to induction. For if the initial choice of symbols and rules is in some sense arbitrary, as in the invention of a game, it has to be ascertained by some independent process whether the resulting principles of argument are in fact applicable to our world. So long as all the principles of deductive logic could be taken to be self-evident, or to be derivable by a self-evident process of inference from self-evident axioms, it would be safe to apply these to any universe whatever. But if this cannot be assumed, then a check-up has to be made, to ascertain whether our world is of such a character that reasoning about it on the lines laid down gives correct answers. By what principles is the check-up made ? Some kind of inductive reasoning is evidently involved. The particular events that constitute our experience have to be examined from this point of view.

The fate of geometry provides an analogy. At one time it was taken to be self-evident that we lived in a space which was accurately specified by Euclidean geometry. By itself this geometry could give no guidance as to the development of events ; presumably to live in an empty space — whatever that may be — is to have no experience whatever ; there must also be events or bodies and the separate (empirical) discipline of physics is required to give guidance as to their behaviour. But the fact that the properties of our empty space could be deemed to be accurately and certainly specified by Euclidean geometry was an aid to making deductions from certain hypotheses of physics. In due course other geometries were developed, and the question was raised whether it was after all so certain that we do live in a Euclidean space. Perhaps some other geometry more accurately specified the spatial properties of our world. How discover ? It is clear that only experience can settle (or tend to settle) this question ; thus an extra load is put upon our capacity to argue from experience. Instead of the kind of space we live in being determined for certain *a priori*, we have to question our experience to ascertain what kind of space it is.

In a similar way, if the basic principles of deduction are not self-evident, but constitute some freely chosen rules like those of a game (or of a geometry), we have to seek for guidance from experience as to whether the particular set of rules chosen is applicable to it. The mode for obtaining this guidance is not included in the formulations of deductive logic itself. It therefore has to be provided by some other kind of logic — presumably by induction.

I should not be frank, did I not express a considerable degree of uneasiness as regards the present condition of the theory of deduction. This uneasiness will re-appear at various places in this volume. It generates in turn a considerable degree of confidence that another half-century will see a very great development in our thinking in this field. I believe that no adequate account has yet been given of the philosophical, and indeed of the logical, significance of the modern reconstruction of deductive theory. It has been in essence a *technical* achievement of superlative excellence. Logicians have been so glamorized by it that they have not yet taken breath and stood back and given it a critical examination, or assessed its logical bearings.

Furthermore it has caused an altogether undue importance to be attached to the study of written symbols. Logic, as I understand it, is concerned primarily with the movement of thought and only secondarily with the written symbols that give a more or less adequate expression to that thought. In certain passages I shall venture to contrast 'logic proper' with 'symbolic logic'. I do not deny, but, on the contrary, contend, that symbolism plays a vital part in our thought processes. But the most important symbols of all are often not written symbols, but internal illiterate symbols which it would be impossible to represent accurately by a squiggle on paper.[1]

Language, as ordinarily written and spoken, is no doubt from a logical point of view gravely inadequate, and the endeavour to provide symbols which shall represent the vital elements in thinking more accurately is wholly praiseworthy. I do not question the immense value of the system of symbols which is becoming conventionalized in modern symbolic logic, though one may be allowed to hope that in due course it will become a little more elegant. But it must be recognized that in the main the development of a system of symbols can only

[1] Cp. p. 172 below.

follow in the train of the development of logic itself. It is important that the symbolism should not, so to speak, take charge.

Written symbols are an especially valuable aid to thinking, when there is a lengthy chain of argument. But in logic itself, that is in thought about thought, some of the most important movements are of one step only. There the written symbol is not likely to be of great assistance.

It was refreshing to find that a distinguished physicist, Professor H. Margenau,[1] in commenting upon modern logic, has issued a similar caveat. 'The physicist thinks . . . that he is more at home with experiments and ideas than with linguistic or any other kind of symbols. . . . Sudden recognitions break through unbaptized, ideas are born before they are named. Sometimes the results of a complicated theory are foreseen in general outline even before a word is spoken or a mathematical symbol is put on paper.' A layman will readily accept that this is true of physics ; it is certainly true of logic itself.[2]

While the tendency in the modern theory of deduction has thus been to attenuate its power to extend knowledge about the world of fact, there has been an opposite trend in the thought of those who study scientific method. Deduction has been booming. Indeed there is perceptible a tendency to overthrow the traditional dichotomy of deduction and induction in favour of a new canonical scheme, constituted by the trinity of hypothesis, deduction and verification. Within this totality deduction has to play an important rôle.[3] There is no need to doubt that this scheme gives a fair description of

[1] *The Nature of Physical Reality*, p. 231 (1950). While the philosophical sections of this notable work are not altogether satisfying, the insight into the *philosophical* implications of the modern developments of physics appears far more profound than what is to be found in the books by scientists of well-known names that one was bidden to read in the 'thirties.

[2] Professor Margenau proceeds to a quotation from Professor C. I. Lewis to that effect. 'Linguistic expression of what is meant and what is apprehended is the dependent and derivative phenomenon : it is meaning and apprehension themselves which are the fundamental cognitive phenomena, and those are independent of any formulation in language'.

[3] This tendency is illustrated in R. Braithwaite, *Scientific Explanation*, and J. O. Wisdom, *Foundations of Inference in Natural Science*. The stress laid by the latter on the falsification of hypotheses is analogous to that laid by theorists' of induction on methods of elimination. This is discussed later.

the actual processes in advanced disciplines, such as physics or genetics. Indeed, reasons will later be given for supposing this a natural development after a subject of study has progressed a certain way. None the less any claim that this scheme has canonical authority must be challenged.

The progress of deductive theory has been triumphal, although unhelpful ; in the same period the theory of induction has been a shambles, as will presently be explained. It may be that those who recommend the tri-une scheme of scientific method have been actuated by the hope that we may thereby evade the problems of induction that have proved so baffling. But that is an illusion.

All turns on the third member—verification. This is constituted by one or more particular pieces of experience. An observable or group of observables is found on one occasion or on several occasions to have the characteristics which according to the deductive argument it should have, if the hypothesis is true. That is satisfactory so far as it goes. But the hypothesis has wider ambit. Its truth, if it is true, implies not only that this particular set of observables shall have the specified characteristics, but that other sets of unobserved observables in similar circumstances have them. Furthermore, if the hypothesis is linked to the observables in question by a deductive process, some variation in the content of the deduction could show that the hypothesis implied certain characteristics in other sets of unobserved observables differently circumstanced, and, if those other sets of observables do not in fact have the required characteristics, then the hypothesis is after all false. Reference to the three members of the total process leaves out the most vital element, namely assessment of the logical force that the verification in question has in establishing the truth of the hypothesis. It is here that the principles of induction come into play. The word 'verification' merely signifies that the observables observed conform to the specification that issues from the hypothesis and the deduction. Assessment of the logical significance of this conformity and of its tendency to establish the truth of the hypothesis is a separate process and involves inductive argument.

It may well be that the reason why this fourth process has sometimes tended to slip out of the catalogue, is that it often seems very obvious that the verification does tend to establish the hypothesis (with extremely high probability), so that the assessment is implicitly taken for granted and may not even come into the consciousness of the scientist bent on a particular enquiry. It is none the less an essential part of the process and the logician must insist on a thorough and exhaustive analysis of the principles that govern it. In certain cases a single verification may endow the hypothesis with high probability — the most optimistic scientist, provided that he has the smallest smattering of logical knowledge, will not claim certainty. In other cases a large number of verifications will only endow the hypothesis with low probability. Inductive theory is required to elucidate the principles that underlie this difference. And, at a deeper level, it is required to show why a verification does endow the hypothesis with any probability whatever ; to hold that it does so implies that the fact that certain observables before us have a certain character renders it probable that a whole host of other unobserved observables have certain characteristics determined by the hypothesis and the various possible deductions from it. This is a momentous claim. For logicians to hold that this does not require the strictest examination and vindication would be to fail in their most central duty. Logic might then be deemed a dead subject.

There may be another reason for the recent tendency to minimize the rôle of induction. It may be thought that induction consists essentially in the generalization from a number of observed similarities. Thus B may have been frequently observed to follow or accompany A, and the essence of induction is thought to consist in inferring quite simply that B probably always follows or accompanies A. This is not wrong. But actual processes of modern scientific enquiry seem so far removed from this simple scheme, that it is too hastily assumed that some novel method of reasoning has been discovered that renders induction obsolete. This is a superficial view. As enquiry progresses and knowledge accumulates, it is not surprising that the forms of argument explicitly used become more complex. Primitive simplicities are overlaid. Explicit processes of reasoning become more elaborate, and will no doubt continue to do so. Unhappily the most elementary processes of empirical argument have not yet been elucidated by inductive logicians ; until this is done, it is not likely that they will have success in coping with modern complications.

Another point may be made in this connexion. Too simple a view of induction may have suggested to some the idea that it is supposed to specify the methods which we ought to use in framing hypotheses. Thus, to take the former example, the experience that whenever A has been observed B has always followed it, may suggest the hypothesis — thereafter to serve as the premise of various deductions subject to further verification — that B always follows A. Certainly a hypothesis might be suggested in this way. But this mode of coming to hypotheses is indeed far removed from that normally employed in modern science. A hypothesis may consist in positing that there exists some unobserved and unobservable kind of entity endowed with specified characteristics. It must be emphasized that inductive logic does not purport to consist of a set of rules for suggesting hypotheses ; its rules, if and when we can formulate them, should determine whether all the evidence, including the so-called verifications, tends, and in what degree, to establish the truth of the hypothesis. In the forming of hypotheses we are free ; the acid test of logic comes when we collect all available evidence and assess its bearing on the probability of the hypothesis. The formation of hypotheses gives scope for the play of the creative imagination ; it is in that activity that scientific genius can show its cunning. Science would rapidly come to a standstill if scientists were told that in essaying to form hypotheses they must always look up a book of logical rules, to discover what hypotheses are indicated by the observations so far to hand. The rules come in not during the process of searching the mind for an appropriate hypothesis, but in the *ex-post* assessment whether in the light of all the evidence the hypothesis is probably correct. The contrast between the free scope for genius in the quest for hypotheses and the fixed rules for an ex-post assessment of their probability is not special to empirical enquiry. In mathematics the proof of a theorem once set forth is either right or wrong ; it is subject to stringent logical test. But the activity of the mind in seeking the proof or indeed in formulating the theorem is not subject to fixed rules.

Professor Carnap has an excellent passage to this effect. 'The mathematician . . . cannot find fruitful and interesting new theorems, say, in geometry, in algebra, in the infinitesimal calculus, by computation or any other effective procedure. He has to find them by an activity in which rational and intuitive factors are combined. This activity is not guided by fixed rules ; it requires a creative ability.' Turning to inductive logic, he adds : 'There is no effective procedure for solving these problems' [*i.e.* finding an appropriate hypothesis]. '. . . However, we see now that this feature is by no means characteristic of inductive thinking ; it holds in just the same way for the corresponding deductive problems.' [1] Confusion between the methods used in devising hypotheses and those required for assessing their probability may have contributed to the recent tendency to underestimate the importance of induction.

Thus we see that on the one hand the experts in the theory of deduction have taken a standpoint which minimizes the power of deduction unaided to extend our knowledge about the world of facts. On the other hand deduction is coming to play an ever greater rôle in the more mature sciences, and students of scientific method have been tending to make large claims for it. They make deduction play a major part, aided only by a 'verification', the logic credentials of which they scarcely deign to analyse. This is not a satisfactory position. We must now turn to a brief retrospect on the fate of inductive theory.

We have already mentioned Locke's rejection of 'innate ideas'. This rejection may be re-phrased as a denial that we have knowledge, prior to experience, that any feature A in nature is necessarily, or always, or usually, connected with some other feature B. Consequently if we are to have any knowledge about nature there must be some valid method of arguing from particulars, since our experience of nature consists only of particulars. But about the methods available for conducting such argument Locke said little. We may pass straight to Hume.

If one may be allowed a confession of faith, I would aver that for strictly logical faculty Hume strikes me as *sans pareil*

[1] *Logical Foundation of Probability*, pp. 194-5.

in the history of thought. It is intriguing to recall that he used no symbolism except that of conversational English. His achievement was to set out the essentials of the problem. The correctness of his presuppositions and premises are taken for granted in the arguments of this book. His error lay in his sceptical conclusions. Perhaps he would have got beyond them, had he not broken off so young to devote himself to subjects of more interest to the eighteenth-century intelligentzia.[1] He was a genial, and not a dogmatic, sceptic. One would like to summon up his shade and give an assurance : 'Your point of departure and methods were correct ; using them it turns out that one can after all justify many common-sense beliefs'.

Logicians of the nineteenth century, like J. S. Mill, who were determined, despite the havoc wrought by Hume, to justify an empirical approach, had resort to the postulates of the Uniformity of Nature and the Law of Universal Causation. I believe that these principles have never been satisfactorily defined. Even, however, if the concepts are a little woolly, one can see how they can be brought into service to aid the inductive process. If one is certain, to begin with, that an event of a given type must have a cause, one may hope to identify that cause by applying a process of elimination to members of a class of cases of the same kind (Mill's Methods of Agreement and Difference). By the Uniformity of Nature the same cause must be operating in all members of the class of cases. Professor von Wright has well shown that even on rather favourable assumptions these methods of elimination are much weaker than one would suppose at first blush.[2] None the less it will be admitted that, if one is entitled to assume certain uniformity axioms, this should give some assistance to the task of arguing from particulars.

But the trouble is that the uniformity axioms, if assumed from the outset, would constitute 'innate ideas' ; their assumption would not be analogous to some postulate at the base of a pure deductive system ; the axioms purport to describe, and

---

[1] A current issue of the *Illustrated London News* (20 August 1955) carries a photograph of a house in Edinburgh which it describes as formerly the home 'of David Hume, the historian'.

[2] Vide *The Logical Problem of Induction*, pp. 71-99. Also Nicod, *Foundations of Geometry and Induction*, pp. 222-65.

must describe if they are to be useful in empirical enquiries, the characteristics of the empirical world. There might be a world of events or bodies which showed no uniformity whatever. Therefore to assume these axioms from the outset would be a gross violation of the empirical method. Mill recognized this, and he sought escape from the difficulty by arguing that the uniformity of nature can itself be established by an inductive argument. If we proceed with our observations and make generalizations by induction from them, we soon find that nature is uniform. Thus uniformity, he argued, can be accepted as a basic axiom because much experience, perhaps all experience, provides evidence for it. This type of argument is irretrievably circular. If no mode of induction can be found that is valid without the support of any uniformity axiom, then we have no grounds for those very generalizations which purport to provide the empirical evidence for a general uniformity of nature. Therefore, if we are to make any progress out of our initial state of nescience, which is due to our birth into the world without innate ideas, there must be some mode of induction that is independent of any uniformity axiom.

Despite this circularity Mill's view does seem to have great plausibility, and it embodies elements of truth. It can hardly be denied that by analysing and organizing our experiences, we have discovered much uniformity in nature ; it would certainly be wrong to hold that the degree of uniformity that we now tend to take for granted has merely been an assumption constantly present from the outset ; we are right to think that we have discovered it, unearthed it. Also it can hardly be denied that in many branches of science there is prior assumption of uniformity which plays some part in scientific arguments ; save for this prior assumption scientists would require to take vast samples and make endless repetitions of experiments, instead of resting content, as they often do, with a small number. There is great plausibility for both arms of the following belief : experience has taught us that nature has much uniformity, and in many cases where we try to learn from experience we make a prior assumption that there is uniformity. It is possible to reconcile these two beliefs, but not in the way that Mill did. They are reconcilable if the following three stages in the advance of knowledge are clearly demarcated and kept rigidly apart.

1. By induction we argue directly from observed similarities in experience to wider generalizations implying much uniformity among certain kinds of phenomena. 2. By induction we argue from the uniformities established in the first stage that in the case of these kinds of phenomena there is likely [1] to be much uniformity among the relations between them that have not yet been examined, and that there is likely to be much uniformity in the behaviour of unexamined phenomena of a *similar kind*. 3. By induction, and also by using the probability in favour of uniformity in certain spheres established in the second stage, which at the third stage may be designated a prior probability, we argue from further observations to further generalizations. The prior probability in favour of uniformity that can be assumed in the third stage greatly reduces the number of favourable observations required to establish a given degree of probability for the generalizations reached at that stage.

It is to be noted that in neither of the first two stages can any prior probability that there is uniformity be assumed. In both these stages we must be able to make a number of valid inductions if we are ever to proceed to the type of argument that becomes available in the third stage. Consequently it is necessary to show that there are valid forms of induction which are *not* supported by the prior assumption that nature is uniform or that any parts or aspects of nature exhibit uniformity.

In our day most of the researches of the more mature sciences lie in the third stage. This was also true of Mill's day. Consequently it was natural for him to exhibit methods of induction the validity of which depends on nature being uniform. It was also natural for him to assume, since it is true, that it is experience that has taught us that nature has much uniformity. His mistake lay in not making a clear separation of the stages. Accordingly he failed to see that methods of induction which do presuppose the uniformity of nature — we should say presuppose the probability of uni-

---

[1] No distinction is made in this volume between likelihood and probability. This distinction has been too much associated with points of view here held to be fallacious.

formity in certain aspects of nature, but Mill was not strong on probability — are only valid if there also exist other methods of induction which are valid independently of any presupposition of uniformity. Consequently he had nothing to say about such other methods. This volume is mainly concerned with the first stage, although some hints will be given (in Chapter V) in regard to the later stages. Our task is to show that there are forms of fully valid inductive argument that require no support from any presupposition as regards uniformity nor indeed as regards any characteristics of nature whatever. Whoever achieves this task knows more of the philosophy of Logic than the wisest of our nineteenth-century empiricists.

Meanwhile an independent development of thought had long since been proceeding, which is highly relevant to our theme. In the foregoing paragraph a reference was made to probability ; it is now universally and rightly held that probability only, and not certainty, can be claimed for the conclusions of inductive arguments. The word 'probability' requires definition and our second chapter is devoted to the task of defining it. A common-sense appreciation of its rough meaning will suffice for this brief historical resumé.

An important development of the theory of probability on mathematical lines had already occurred in the eighteenth century, and is largely associated with the name Bernouilli. It has to be observed that the greater part of this theory, which consists in the theory of 'direct' probability, belongs to the domain of deduction. This is a paradox, since deduction is usually conceived as being concerned with certain and immutable verities, while the world of dubiety, probability and improbability is that of empirical study. The paradox involved may have accounted for some confusion of thought. In the theory of direct probability an ascription of probability occurs in the initial premises of an argument. On the basis of this ascription it is possible to make certain predictions and this appears to bring the subject within the realm of empirical study. But this is in appearance only and not really so. The predictions concern the probable frequency of certain events, probable deviations, the tendency to limits, etc. But all this is entailed by the ascription of probability in the original premise. The theory has nothing to say about why such a probability should be ascribed in the first instance. It must presumably be conceded that if the course of events jars sufficiently with the predictions, this will have the negative effect of tending to discredit the original ascription of probability. This is an inductive argument. But just as direct probability theory has nothing to say about why it is ever right or proper to make the initial ascription, so by itself it provides no apparatus for determining the amount by which that ascription is undermined. Direct probability theory is concerned with the consequences of a probability ascription *within* the hypothesis ; it has nothing to say, *ex ante* or *ex post*, about the degree of probability *of* the hypothesis. Thus the theory of direct probability provides no apparatus for enabling particular observations to enlarge our knowledge and accordingly it does not belong to the sphere of induction.

Probability theory has won great réclame in recent years by being brought into service, first in statistical mechanics and then in quantum mechanics, and the problems of physics have stimulated further developments of it. If I understand the matter rightly, the probability theory there used is a branch of deductive theory. A hypothesis is framed that certain entities defined in physics obey statistical laws in their behaviour. Statistical theory is then used in a deductive process which traces out the consequences of the hypothesis, those consequences including a specification of what should be observed in defined circumstances if the hypothesis is true. As before, if observations jar, and subject to the accuracy of the deduction being carefully checked, the hypothesis will come up for revision. But it seems that the work done by the probability theory is inside the deductive member of the trinity of hypothesis, deduction and verification.

There was another strand in the early thinking about probability, which has been known as 'inverse' probability theory ; with this we enter the field of induction. The formulations of the basic inverse principle, as set out in standard treatises, stem from a theorem of Bayes as developed by Laplace. Let it be possible to enumerate two or more hypotheses, which between them exhaust the possibilities of the case, so that one or other must be true. Let it be possible to assign a definite prior probability to each of the hypotheses.

Let it also be possible, assuming in turn that each separate hypothesis is true, to assign in each case a definite probability for the occurrence of an event X in certain defined circumstances. Then if X does occur (or does not occur) in the circumstances in question this enables us to assign new probabilities to the original hypotheses.[1] This is certainly a form of induction. For the occurrence of a particular event X in our experience enlarges our knowledge about the probabilities of the hypotheses, each of which has much wider ambit than its bearing on the occurrence of the particular event in question. It may in certain cases be possible to find an appropriate X such that, if it occurs, it will raise the probability of one or other of the hypotheses to practical certainty. This is eminently satisfactory.

It may be useful to give a very simple example of an application of the Bayes theorem. Let there be a manufacturer of dice — it is painful to mention thus early those little pieces which have done so much to bedevil logic — who has done honest trade but also entered into contracts with fraudulent customers for biased dice. Let it be known that ordinary dice, defined as true dice, show a six on average once in every six throws. Let the biased dice be cunningly devised so that on a run of throws the six will show on average once in every two throws. This may be a difficult requirement, but we assume that the technical problem has been satisfactorily solved. Let the fraudulent customers be put in prison before the contracts are fulfilled, and let a careless assistant have muddled the boxes, so that it is impossible to distinguish between the true and biased dice. Let it be known that a hundred times as many of the former as of the latter have been produced. Let them all be sold across the counter. Let them all have the maker's mark (improbable in the circumstances!),

---

[1] I give the most readily intelligible formulation of the inverse theorem. Let there be two alternative and exhaustive hypotheses and let p_1 be the prior probability that one is true and p_2 the prior probability that the other is true. Let q_1 be the probability that X will occur if the former is true and q_2 the probability that X will occur if the latter is true. Then if X does occur the probability that the former is true is $\dfrac{p_1 q_1}{p_1 q_1 + p_2 q_2}$ and the probability that the latter is true is $\dfrac{p_2 q_2}{p_1 q_1 + p_2 q_2}$. If X does not occur we substitute $(1 - q_1)$ and $(1 - q_2)$ for q_1 and q_2 in these expressions.

C

so that his dice can be distinguished from all others. I own one of these dice. There are two hypotheses that between them cover the ground, one that the die is true, the other that it is biased. The prior odds in favour of the hypothesis that the die is true are a hundred to one, since there are a hundred times as many true dice as biased dice in circulation. In the real world these prior odds could not be affirmed with certainty, since there would be all sorts of other possibilities, such as that a second maker forged the trade mark of the one in question and many other more recondite ways by which I might be deceived; these are waived for the purpose of the illustration. Since we have not yet defined probability, this statement of odds must beg many questions; but a rough and ready notion will suffice to make plain the bearing of the inverse theorem. Let the die be tossed and show a six. By the formula the odds are still in favour (100 : 3) of the die being true. Let sixes appear continuously on further throws. The odds continue to be in favour of the die being true till the fifth throw when they turn in favour of the die being biased (100 : 243). By continuing the tossing — this is an illustration of 'finding an appropriate X' as required in the last paragraph — the density of sixes may be such as to give tremendous odds, amounting to 'practical certainty' that the die is one of those biased. This is a genuine induction. It is to be noted that the knowledge gained by the series of tosses is not simply that constituted by the events themselves. We move outwards from those events and believe it probable that on many other occasions, whenever this die is used, there will be an undue proportion of sixes; we may indeed turn fraudulent ourselves and put the knowledge to lucrative use among the unwary.

The importance of this theorem, which seems on the face of it rather specialized, is that it is the only fundamental theorem that has been rigidly proved, which enables the occurrence of a particular fact to extend our knowledge beyond the realm of that fact. I cannot assess the extent to which this theorem has been used, implicitly or otherwise, in the advance of scientific knowledge.

It has been observed that the scene set for the application of this inverse (Bayes-type) theorem implies a good deal of prior information, as appeared in our illustration. There must be two sets of previously known probabilities. The second set, the q's, need not give serious trouble, since they may be implicit in the initial hypotheses ; for instance the probability of $\frac{1}{6}$ for a six showing on a toss was entailed by the definition of a true die. But the probabilities pertaining to the hypotheses themselves require some prior knowledge, and often, as in our example, a great deal. If the preliminaries of our illustration seemed a little far-fetched, it may be that one has to go a long way to find a suitable instance. Let us suppose that all the information about the makers and the markings did not exist, and that there was no relevant information about the prior probability of bias. What would then be the significance of a run of sixes ? One might take the extreme case of its being literally inconceivable that anyone should be so base (or careless) as to make a biased die. Then a run of sixes would have no tendency to establish bias. (There is of course the question of whether a perfectly made die, however perfection may be defined, is not as likely as not to show a preponderant proportion of sixes.) Suppose that a biased die is not literally inconceivable, but almost so. How long a run of sixes is significant? Of this the Bayes-type theorem can say nothing.

Two points must be made. First there is the doubt whether in the ordinary run of general experience or science we often have information by virtue of which exhaustive alternative hypotheses can be framed with the prior probabilities of each nicely docketed. Secondly, and far more important, it is clear that on the threshold of knowledge, where we have no prior information, we lack evidence for any such docketing. The Bayes-type theorem has been the sole rigidly proved theorem in probability theory for making particular facts yield wider knowledge. If it cannot be used without prior information, then it was not available as a tool for getting induction going in the first instance. Therefore, if induction generally is valid, there must be some valid form of induction, *other than* that expressed in the Bayes-type theorem, to rescue us from our initial nescience.

At this point in thinking a grand departure was made, giving rise to the highest hopes. It was held that if it is possible — as it clearly is sometimes — to frame alternative hypotheses that exhaust the possibilities of the case, and if no information whatever is available for assigning them prior probabilities, it is in general proper to assign to each an equal prior probability. This would certainly get things going well — indeed too well. It would make the path of science very much easier than it has proved to be. This proposal has had various names — 'The Principle of Indifference', or the 'Equal Distribution of Ignorance'. It is totally unacceptable.

It has been shown many times that, anyhow in its crude form, it entails violent contradictions, and nothing more on that score need be said here. It is possible, however — and attempts have been made — that such severe restrictions could be put upon its use, as to avoid the contradictions, and yet leave the Principle capable of rendering some assistance. There are further grave objections.

The first and foremost is that this ascription of equal initial prior probabilities is entirely unwarranted. It involves assumptions about nature that we have no right to make. I do not believe that its more sober defenders have any good reasons to recommend it, but rather have adopted it as a counsel of despair. They have felt deeply, and as I contend rightly, that induction must be valid, and have clutched at this principle as the only available resource for vindicating it. But that is not good enough in logic ; we must be patient and think again.

Furthermore, it is inconsistent with the proper definition of probability, by which probability only occurs when there is inference and serves to relate a conclusion to premises. In the case of initial prior probabilities, there are no premises, so that the word 'probability' is used inappropriately, and the ascription of an initial prior probability, when there are no premises whatever, is in the strictest sense meaningless. It is true that there are other views as to the meaning of probability, on which that would not be so. In due course I shall argue that such views are unacceptable, if we are to develop a rational account of the nature of probability.

The case is even worse. At the most crucial stage of the argument that vindicates induction,[1] an uncritical use of the Principle of Indifference would frustrate the argument. Thus the Principle is to be condemned not only as unwarrantable

[1] See pp. 60-3 below.

in itself and liable to raise false hopes, but as capable of obscuring the true principles of induction.

Some writers in the nineteenth century did good work in showing that probability theory and the traditional theory of induction should be welded together. But as the logical foundations of both were weak, the results were not satisfactory.

When Keynes attacked the problem afresh, he believed that it was necessary to show that we are entitled to posit initial prior probabilities. This belief was no doubt due to the predominant, indeed monopolistic, position of the Bayes-type formulation of inverse probability theory. So long as one accepts that position, it is indeed the case that one can make no advance unless one can postulate initial prior probabilities. Keynes did not accept the Principle of Indifference in its crude form ; indeed he made most caustic and effective criticisms of it. He thought that the required initial prior probabilities would issue from the postulate that there are only a finite number of generator properties in our universe. This postulate is not unacceptable. It will later be contended that our knowledge, including that of low probability only, does not extend beyond a finite range ; within such a range there certainly cannot be more than a finite number of generator properties. Keynes only gives a sketch of how the limitation in the number of properties may establish finite probabilities in favour of particular hypotheses ; but it is not necessary to discuss this here. The crucial question is how large this finite number is. If it approaches in magnitude the number of atoms within our range of observation, the initial prior probability in favour of the operation of any one generator property (or combination of properties ?) will be so low as to be incapable of aiding induction to conclusions of interesting probability. But if it is necessary to postulate a number of properties that shall not only be finite, but also conveniently small by comparison with the number of atoms in the universe, then we are clearly being asked to make an unwarrantable and indefensible postulate.

Keynes's lack of success has been followed by a period of great defeatism. The task of vindicating induction appears to have been abandoned in despair. Shallow doctrines of a pragmatic kind have been in vogue. It has been suggested that the cogency of an argument consists simply in its inducing a state of belief in its conclusion, the degree of belief being capable of being measured by the behavioural reaction of the believer. Alternatively it is suggested that the task of the inductive logician is merely to catalogue without criticism the types of argument actually used by scientists ; science being so successful, it can be assumed that their methods are to be recommended. The question of their validity just does not arise. This negative attitude has been carried to even greater extremes. It is suggested that the attempt to provide a logical vindication of induction was a mistake from the beginning ; that it is only in deduction that we expect a logical vindication ; that to provide a vindication for certain types of allegedly inductive argument would merely be to transfer them to the domain of deduction. Thus it seems that there are to be two types of argument, those which can be shown to be valid, namely the deductive, and the rest, which we may call inductive if we wish. It is unfortunate that all our knowledge about the world in which we live depends on arguments which belong to the latter character. It must further be noted that according to modern deductive theory the part played by deduction in scientific enquiry is itself of dubious validity, if we do not ascertain by some *other* type of argument that the field of application is appropriate to the mode of deduction proposed for use.[1]

I have used the word 'defeatism' ; I am emboldened to add the word 'escapism', which betokens unwillingness to admit defeat and the human frailty of *amour propre*. Such a charge may be brought without at all impugning the intellectual eminence and probity of the persons concerned. 'We are very clever people ; any problem that you bring us we can solve ; if we seem to be failing to solve the problem of induction, that is merely because it is a bogus problem.' This book is conceived as a protest against and a refutation of views of this type.

Mention must be made, however, of an exception to the tendency to regard induction as altogether inferior to deduction in respect of the validity of its arguments. In his formidable, but fascinating, volume on the *Logical Foundations of*

---

[1] See above, pp. 3-4.

Probability Professor Carnap appears, if my interpretation is correct, to be claiming parity of esteem in this respect for deduction and induction.[1] It is to be feared, however, that this parity is not established mainly by an up-grading of induction — although he shows a certain tendency in that direction — but rather by his implicit recognition without fuss that deduction has already been irretrievably down-graded. None the less his recognition that the validity of the two types of argument is of the same general character is an important advance and likely to have a beneficial influence on future work.

With his central position, however, I am not in agreement. It appears that he is seeking to establish, or, to be in conformity with his thinking, I ought to say to 'rationalize', induction, by accepting in an immensely refined form the Principle of Indifference and initial prior probabilities. His main effort is directed to choosing the alternatives, between which the equality of initial prior probability should be deemed to lie. He does not seek a logical justification for the choice, in the old-fashioned sense and in my sense ; that would be out of accord with his general position. The justification, such as it is, consists partly of rather vague recommendations of seemliness and simplicity and partly that he hopes to make it yield a set of inductive principles in conformity with those in general use.

I have only been privileged to see Volume One of this treatise ; consequently any comment must be subject to reservation. Furthermore it seems almost heinous to attempt to summarize, in two or three loosely worded sentences, ideas to the formulation of which Carnap has devoted some six hundred closely reasoned pages displaying the finest expertise. We take a universe consisting of individuals, to which in principle proper names could be assigned, and of primitive predicates. We then have a vast host of logically possible alternatives. A specification of which primitive predicates each named individual has or lacks constitutes a 'state description' of the universe. Before we have any knowledge about the construction of the universe there are as many possible state descriptions as there are possible ways of combining every possible condition of each named individual, as regards its

[1] *Vide*, especially pp. 30-3 and pp. 180-90.

having or lacking each of the primitive predicates, with every possible condition of each other individual. But some of these state descriptions are isomorphic, that is they differ from one another only in respect of which of the named individuals have any given combination of primitive predicates and not in the number of individuals which have any given combination. The isomorphic state descriptions may be lumped together and what they have in common constitutes a structural description. It is to all possible structural descriptions that equal initial prior probabilities are assigned.

For the probability of a statement for which there is no evidence whatever, Carnap uses in general the symbol c_o; when the probability is based on the assumption characterized in the foregoing paragraph he uses the symbol $c_o{}^*$. This probability existing in the absence of evidence is correlated with a symmetrical 'regular measure function' which belongs to statements taken in isolation; it is called in general an m-function. When the assumption characterized above is made, it is called the m^* function. Since probability is rightly defined as a relation between evidence and a conclusion, and since the m value belongs to statements taken in isolation, the m value is not *called* a probability. But in its logical aspect, that is, in terms of thought and not of symbols, this m^* function is an initial prior probability.

It would be premature and unfair to raise the doubt at this stage whether the postulate of equal initial prior probabilities for every structural description would enable the inverse theorem to yield factual probabilities of interesting value; there would be terrific factorial numbers in the denominator of the initial prior probability. But that is precisely a matter on which it is proper to await satisfaction in Volume Two. Professor Carnap's scheme is unacceptable, because his use of the Principle of Indifference even in this refined form is unwarranted. There is nothing more to be said.

Professor Carnap would no doubt argue that the idea of a warrant for the initial basic assumption is meaningless. Logic consists, I judge that he would hold, in the elaboration of a system of reasoning from a basic assumption which is itself arbitrary. The opposite view is taken in this volume. It is contended that the validity of induction can be established without making any basic assumption whatever about probabilities in nature. If this is correct, it involves an up-grading of inductive logic by comparison with Professor Carnap's view of it, and by comparison also with deductive logic in its present state. Whether this points to the need for a revision of the theory of deductive logic it is not for me to judge.

Mention is made elsewhere of my agreement with the views that Professor Donald Williams has been developing. His treatment is very slight by comparison with that of Carnap, but it has the advantage of having the heart of the matter in it.

The task before us is simple, but arduous. It is required to show that there can be valid inductions about nature without any prior assumption about the characteristics of nature whatever. There must be no prior assumption that nature is uniform in whole or in part, or that causes operate. The Principle of Indifference must not be used in any form whatever. No initial prior probabilities must be postulated. We must remain totally open-minded until the accumulation of evidence from experience begins to give guidance. The trouble is that so far logicians have been unable to specify any valid principle or principles justifying argument directly from experience without the aid of some prior assumption.

The question may be raised as to the meaning of the word 'validity'. A preliminary answer might be that a type of argument is valid if the conclusions of arguments of this type are invariably true. In induction, however, we are only concerned with conclusions that are probable; in that case what should be 'invariably' true is the degree of probability assigned to the conclusion. The meaning of this must await the definition of probability provided in the next chapter.

It is not enough, however, that the conclusion should in fact invariably be true; it is needful also that the form of argument should vouchsafe knowledge that it is true. Then a definition of knowledge is required This is supplied in the seventh chapter.

CHAPTER II

PROBABILITY

Iт is widely agreed among various schools of philosophy
that we should abandon the quest for certainty in regard to
all empirical matters, that is in regard to all matters of fact,
whether particular facts or generalizations. This covers the
whole ground both of what may be called common-sense
knowledge and of scientific knowledge. Here on the threshold
we may pause to ask what exactly this certainty of knowledge
that we reject is. Formerly one would have thrown light by
pointing to the generalizations of logic itself, or of mathematics ; that expedient is not available for the reasons already
indicated.

Alternatively one might point to the kind of knowledge
one has about the objects of direct observation, and add that
the kind of certainty there found cannot be obtained when it
is a question of arguing from the observations in question to
other matters outside our direct experience. It is to be noted,
however, that within the field of direct observation we have
certainty only to the extent that its subject matter is not interpreted ; certainty may be ascribed to the statement 'I feel a
pain in my gum', but not to the statement 'I feel an abscess
in my gum', to the statement 'I am seeing certain coloured
patches', but not to the statement that 'I am seeing certain
chairs and tables' — unless the words 'chairs and tables' are
regarded as synonymous for certain 'coloured patches', and
not as referring to objects supposed to have lasting properties.
This greatly pares down the realm of certainty even within
the field of direct observation. And it may be doubted, for
reasons which will be discussed later, whether it is appropriate
to apply the word knowledge to states of mind described by
such phrases as 'I feel a pain' or 'I am seeing certain coloured
patches'. To do so would seem to make the sphere of knowledge coterminous with that of experience itself, and this is

surely inappropriate; knowledge should rather be regarded as a specific kind of experience.

Failing any help from analogy, one might approach the matter directly. Some experience gives ground for belief in a fact or facts outside that experience. Let us call this kind of experience 'evidential experience'; for example, the ground is wet, and we infer that it has been raining. We may put the negative point by saying that we do not think that evidential experience is ever of such a kind as to give logical justification for the belief that something outside the experience is certainly the case. Here, however, we still have the word 'certainly', which is what has to be explained. We might be tempted to find a way out of this difficulty by saying that there is no evidential experience of such a kind that, when it occurs, certain beliefs about matters lying outside the experience are always true. That would be to go much too far; it may well be the case that, whenever certain types of experience occur, other specific things lying outside that experience also always occur, so that, if, when we had this kind of experience, we had certain appropriate beliefs, these beliefs would always be true. Rather what we want to say is that there is no kind of experience such that we *know*, in virtue of it, that certain beliefs about something else are true. But this is merely to bring us back to our previous dilemma, and to make what is sometimes called a higher order statement comprising the word 'know', corresponding to the lower order statement that there is no kind of evidential experience justifying the belief that something outside the experience is certainly the case. There are undoubtedly obstacles in the way of defining what it is we are denying when we deny certainty of knowledge in empirical matters.

Without resolving the problem at this stage, we may seek more precision about the nature of the denial. Are we simply denying that we have ever come across any experience on the basis of which we are logically justified in holding that something outside the experience is certainly the case? Are we denying that we can imagine any experience of the kind? Or are we going further and denying that there can possibly be any experience of such a kind? Are we in fact holding that experience of such a kind would be self-contradictory, or entail something self-contradictory? Such a tenet would certainly be a very bold one, and even appear on the face of it to be self-contradictory itself. For it appears to involve the impossibility of a certain kind of experience, and the word 'impossible' implies that there is certain (negative) knowledge anyhow in regard to one aspect of the nature of experience. We may indeed find rescue from this apparent contradiction by saying that the tenet in question does not concern empirical matters directly, but concerns knowledge about empirical matters, in fine that it is a higher order tenet; some may suspect, however, that the possibilities of knowledge in regard to empirical matters must depend in part upon the nature of the empirical matters. We shall return to this problem at a much later stage of our enquiry.

Meanwhile we shall abandon further consideration of this denial, and approach the subject in a positive way — namely by analysing the nature of the evidence and the valid grounds for belief that arise in the empirical sphere. When we have gone through this arduous process, we shall have a much better understanding of the view that certainty of knowledge about matters of fact cannot be obtained by inference.

If we accept this view we have to move over to the realm of probability. Probability is a notion that occurs in common-sense thought about things; the layman has some idea of what he means, but would be hard put to define it. So we may turn to the experts. If among laymen we find some haziness and obscurity, among the experts we find dense fog and violent contradictions. The search for clarity in this subject seems to baffle writers of the highest philosophical distinction. Their basic ideas clash and jar with one another. This is indeed a remarkable thing. If we reject certainty, then the theory of probability covers all the thinking of ordinary mortals about the common-sense affairs of life and the most remote researches of scientists. If at the outset we lack agreement among experts about the very meaning of probability, we may say that logic itself has barely made a beginning. That, I fear, is not far from the truth.

It should be laid down at the outset that probability is essentially a relation between a premise or premises and a conclusion. It is a concept that relates to the logic of inference.

This view may be thought to be widely accepted by the best logicians. In common speech we often refer to the conclusion of an argument as being probable without reference to its premise. But it would be generally agreed that this merely represents an economy of effort. One cannot be at pains to refer to the evidence, or even to the existence of evidence, every time that reference is made to the probability of something. The reference is implied, and it would be pedantic to object to this elliptic form of speech.

Some logicians, however, have postulated the existence of an initial prior probability for certain opinions. This is, on the face of it, in flagrant violation of the characterization of probability as a relation between premises and a conclusion. If this characterization is proper, there is no meaning in holding something to be probable in and by itself ; and no meaning therefore in postulating an initial prior probability; by such a postulate the elliptical usage of popular speech is taken over, and treated as though it were not elliptical. The ascription of initial prior probability is often made to play a prime and indispensable rôle in the whole logical process even by those who define probability as a relation between premises and conclusion. One can hardly have a stronger example of confusion of thought. Keynes is careful at the outset of his treatise to define probability as a relation between evidence and conclusion ; yet he postulates initial prior probability. Carnap assigns low probability in cases where there is 'no confirmation'.[1] This is based on an m-function which was referred to in the last chapter. In regard to it Carnap is careful not to use the word 'probable'. Yet it seems clear that this m-function is destined to do similar work in his system to that done by initial prior probability itself in the more sketchy system of Keynes. While this m-function is, so to speak, anonymous, it can be given no meaning nor made to play any part in a logical model purporting to be applicable to the actual processes of human thought in empirical enquiries, unless it is regarded as a structural counterpart of this very notion of initial prior probability that we have been discussing. The true nature of the function cannot be disguised by anonymity.

A relation may be regarded as an attribute of each of its

[1] See also below, p. 59.

terms. As the word probability has been requisitioned in ordinary speech to be an attribute of the conclusion, we need a corresponding attribute for the premise or premises, and I shall use 'evidential value' for such an attribute. 'Evidential value' and 'probability' refer to one and the same relation, as do 'father' and 'son'.

We have next to consider the specific nature of this relation. We should be guided in formulating our doctrine by what people generally have in mind when they entertain the idea of probability or use the word. The necessarily rather vague and fluctuating, but not on that account meaningless, popular notion of probability has been conveniently called by Carnap an explicandum, while the logician's more precise definition he calls the explicatum.[1] But for correct linguistics the latter term should be, not 'explicatum', but 'explicant'. The popular notion may be put as follows. It does not often happen that one both gets evidence of a certain kind in favour of a something being the case and finds that that something is not the case. That is what we mean when, having evidence of such a kind before us, we say that the something to which the evidence points is 'probably' the case. It is recognized — at least by careful people — that despite the apparently cogent nature of the evidence, this something may, after all, not be the case. But it is held that it would be a very rare coincidence to have evidence pointing so strongly to something and have that something not be so. In the great majority of cases when evidence of such a kind is before us, the thing is so. This popular phrasing is unsatisfactory, because the words 'evidence' and 'in favour of' beg the question. Accordingly the definition must be reconstituted. We must, however, embody in the improved definition the key words in the popular account, which are 'it does not often happen' or 'in the great majority of cases'. (When I refer in these passages to something being the case, I mean either that an event has occurred, is occurring or will occur, or that a number of events have occurred, are occurring or will occur on types of occasion specified. The language of 'being the case' is used here to dispense with circumlocutions needed to deal with the various tenses and to comprise both particular events and groups of events. The

[1] Carnap, *op. cit.* p. 3.

word 'fact' is used in a similar way.)

We are at this point concerned with the meaning of the probability relation, not with why or when it occurs. That is dealt with later. An event is said to have evidential value if it belongs to a class of events all having a certain character in common, which we may call A. This character A is such that it does not often happen that an event having that character occurs, and some other event of a kind determined by the specific nature of the A event does not occur. A is a generic character, qualifying every one of a class of events, which may severally be called M, N, O, etc. To each member of this class belongs a logical correlate, which may be called X_m, X_n, X_o, etc. If each member of the class of events M, N, . . . Z has the character A, this is taken to mean that it does not often happen that M or N or O, etc., occurs without the correlate appropriate to each, viz. X_m or X_n or X_o, etc., also occurring. What the X's (that is all things deemed probable) have in common is simply the property of being logically correlated to events all of which have the common property A. If we are confronted with an event N belonging to the A class, we say that X_n is probable. N entails X_n means that it follows from N being what it is that, if N is the case, X_n is also the case. N is evidentially favourable to X_n means that N belongs to a class called A which is such that it seldom happens that a member of it is the case and its correlate is not the case. X_n is probable means that X_n is correlated to a member of class A which is the case.

This account, however, does not quite exhaust the matter. It is not enough for it to be true that it does not often happen for an A to be the case and its correlated X not to be the case. It is also necessary, if we are to have a valid opinion about whether an X is the case or not, to *know* that there is this kind of link between the A and the X. This brings the theory of probability within the ambit of the logic of entailment. To have good grounds for believing X to be the case means to *know* that X is probable ; a belief that X is probable without good grounds for the belief has no logical status. If having A before us is to justify us in holding X to be probable, it is not enough that the observed nature of A is such that among the occasions on which A is the case X is seldom not the case ;

it is also necessary that the observed nature of A be such as to entail that among the occasions on which A is the case X is seldom not the case.

I suggest that this definition of probability has the double merit of conforming to the common-sense idea of it and being logically clear. Our central problem does not lie in the provision of such a definition, but in elucidating when and how and why there can ever be facts having the character A. It has doubtless been the very difficulty in seeing how there can be such facts, that has prevented the convergence by logicians on the kind of definition that I have provided ; instead they have strayed into quite different definitions poles apart from one another. The main task that I have set myself in this volume is to show how there can be facts having the character A. It is my submission not only that there are such facts, but that they occur in sufficient abundance to account for and justify most ordinary common-sense beliefs as well as the conclusions of scientists. In my view the analysis of why certain facts have the character A is the main task of logic. I have the impression that the fascinations and thrills of modern symbolic logic — and I do not underrate these — have deflected the attention of our eminent contemporary logicians from their central task.

So far I have characterized A by the rather vague words 'not often', and 'seldom'. In due course we shall have to consider A as a group of classes to each of which separately some quantitative expression much more precise than 'seldom' can be applied. Still confining ourselves to general terms, there may be occasions when we can say a correlate is 'very seldom' not the case, or 'very, very seldom'. If there are grounds for holding the 'seldom-ness' to be very extreme, we regard ourselves as having practical certainty. In such cases common sense claims absolute certainty, although logic does not allow this. If the favourable probability is as high as a billion to one or 10^{50} to one, common sense brushes aside the alternative possibility ; it may even indignantly insist that there is complete certainty in such a situation and regard scepticism as pedantic and absurd, a mere logistical trifling.

Of course, the probability is not always strong. Common sense and logic are also concerned with low probabilities. The

sub-class of A, to which N belongs, may be such as to entail
that, when a member is the case, its correlate is occasionally
the case ; in that event the presence of N would entail a low
probability in favour of X_n. A slight divergence between
logical speech and popular speech occurs on this kind of
occasion. In logic we say that X_n has low probability ; but
in popular speech we tend to apply the word probable to X_n
only if we deem it more probable than not. Otherwise we
content ourselves with saying that there is some evidence in
favour of X_n. This difference of usage presents no difficulty.

But a difficulty presents itself in connexion with the popular
use of the word 'improbable', which makes it necessary to
mention in anticipation some matters of the most far-reaching
importance. *When we frame a hypothesis* that there is a
specific probability, for instance, one chance in six, or one-
sixth, in favour of X, we usually simultaneously make the
hypothesis that the probability of X *not* being the case is
five-sixths. These fractions add up to 1, which stands for
certainty, and this gives expression to what is undoubtedly
true that it is certain that X is either the case or not the case.
Logical speech then says that X has a positive probability equal
to one-sixth, but popular speech says that X is 'improbable',
since it is more probable than not that X is not the case.

But when we are dealing with a probability that flows from
certain empirical evidence we are in a totally different situation. The evidence may establish a low probability — say one
well below a half on the above notation — in favour of X ;
it by no means follows that this same evidence establishes a
correspondingly high probability — above a half — in favour
of X not being the case. On the contrary there may be no
evidence at all in favour of X not being the case. For instance
we may be interested in the probability of an hypothesis on
the basis of some rather slender evidence ; thus the probability
vouchsafed by the evidence may be rather low. But there may
be no evidence at all against the hypothesis ; *all* the available
relevant evidence may be favourable, but happen not to be
very strong. In these circumstances it would be grossly fallacious to argue that there is a high probability that the hypothesis is false.

The fallacy arises from the following apparently safe

D

inference. Since the evidence in favour of X can only establish a low probability, well below a half, and since there is certainty (=1) either that X or that not-X is the case, it is argued that there must by simple subtraction be a probability of more than a half that X is not the case. It is for this reason that when in a hypothesis, which is to be the premise of an argument, we assign a probability of, say, one-sixth for X being the case, we often deem it that this entails a probability of five-sixths for X not being the case.

When, on the other hand, we are considering the probability which empirical evidence justifies us in assigning to a hypothesis, it is usually found — and I would be inclined, but for the danger of a universal generalization, to say that it is always found — that the probability justified is expressed by saying that it is *at least*, say, one-sixth. The evidence does not provide a precise probability of neither more nor less but a minimum probability. This being so, nothing can be argued from the evidence in question about the probability of X not being the case. We cannot subtract the ascribed probability from one and ascribe the remainder to the probability of not-X.

It follows from the foregoing that in any development of probability theory the words 'at least' should play an important part throughout. In my examination of standard treatises I have not found these key words in great evidence. The reason no doubt is that these treatises are concerned with developing the consequences of hypotheses in which probabilities are assigned to X and not-X that add up to one. This means that these treatises are not concerned with the basic principles of probability that govern induction. And this may account for the failures of inductive logicians to weld together probability theory with inductive theory. Traditional probability theory does not provide material of the right kind.

When, therefore, the empirical evidence provides a low probability of X, popular speech is quite correct in confining itself to asserting that there is some evidence in favour of X and refusing altogether to say that X is improbable. It only consents to say that X is improbable, if there is positive evidence for the view that it is more probable than not that X is not the case.

In the foregoing definition the words 'not often', 'seldom', 'very seldom' were used. These are vague quantitative expressions. The question may be raised whether for such a term as 'seldom' we can usually, or always, substitute a precise number. The overwhelmingly preponderating answer given to this by men of common sense will be that it is very rarely or never possible to make such a substitution. Some writers have taken the line that it ought usually, or always, to be possible to state a number when we affirm a probability relation. Yet, as soon as we begin to cite any of the multifarious cases of actual opinions in probability, some claiming practical certainty, others lower degrees of probability, it seems quite absurd to suggest that we could insert, with any pretensions to validity, some particular numbers such as odds of a million to one, or of ten to one, in favour. The fact that we usually seek a minimum probability does not make the provision of a precise number easier. Keynes, with many of whose general views on probability I am in strong disagreement, has subjected the claim that it should always be possible to insert a precise number to a devastating criticism.[1] He suggests that what these logicians are really implying is that, if only we had a little more knowledge, we could insert a precise number. If this means we have no right to claim a valid judgement of probability unless or until we obtain that little bit of extra knowledge, this would rule out as invalid almost all the opinions of everyday life and science. This requirement for a little more knowledge offends against the essential nature of probability, which is a relation between the limited knowledge that we actually have and a proposed conclusion. Knowledge that we do not have has nothing to do with the case. Further knowledge might alter the situation completely. In probability we are concerned with the evidential value of the facts before us, not of some other facts of which we might get cognizance by further investigation. If the facts before us do not allow the insertion of a precise number, then we must rest content with a probability relation that can be defined only by vague quantitative terms, such as 'not often'. Furthermore, if we subsequently obtain additional evidence relating to a conclusion previously regarded as probable, it usually happens that this serves to raise the

[1] *A Treatise of Probability*, chap. 3.

probability, but not to make the number expressing the degree of probability any more precise than it was before.

So far the argument suggests that on this point Keynes is altogether in the right. Nevertheless I believe that there is an element of truth in the views against which he was contending. This can only be made fully plain after the types of situation giving rise to the probability relation have been thoroughly analysed. But it is expedient to anticipate in order to fill out the concept of probability that will be used in the following pages. What is said must appear dogmatic, pending a detailed investigation of probability situations. I believe that on every occasion where a probability relation arises there is a precise minimum number, although this may be unknown to us; I would add that the evidence capable of providing this number is in a different category from other possible evidence that is outside our ken. We may elucidate this by way of analogy. Let us suppose that I examine a cistern to see how full it is. When cross-questioned, I may say that the cistern is 'fairly full'. I may be further cross-questioned : 'How full is it exactly ?' 'Well, it is certainly more than two-thirds full.' 'Was it nine-tenths full ?' 'No, not as much as that.' 'Well, was it three-quarters full ?' 'I am afraid that I cannot say, I could not judge.' I could not have observed that it was more than two-thirds and less than nine-tenths full — and it is assumed that I did correctly observe that — unless it had in fact had a precise degree of fullness. I could not judge this with precision because my vision was not sufficiently accurate, or because I did not have a measuring rod with me. The fact that the cistern was fairly full of water entails — assuming our ordinary notions about physical objects — that there existed a perfectly precise fraction constituting its fullness. It is true that I do not know what this fraction is, but the knowledge that I have could not exist unless such a precise fraction also existed. In my statement about the fullness of the tank this precise fraction is not present in my knowledge ; but the relation of the knowledge that I have to this unknown fraction is much more intimate than its relation to other pieces of evidence that one might bring to bear upon the problem of how full the tank is — such as knowledge that water has been flowing into it for a certain time at a certain rate, together with the dimensions of the tank, knowledge that no one has been near it to remove water, and knowledge about the rate of evaporation.

Or, to take another example, I may observe a great flight of starlings and be quite sure — subject to the normal deceptions of sense — that there were many hundreds. I cannot give the precise number of starlings, because I just did not have time to count. But the fact that I observed a particular flight of starlings — again assuming this not to have been an hallucination — entails that there were at that time a perfectly precise number of starlings flying across the sky. Here again, although the precise number is not part of my knowledge about the flight of starlings, the kind of knowledge I have entails that a precise number of starlings flew.

I suggest similarly that observations giving valid grounds for probability judgements always entail a precise number. The reason why we cannot specify the number is simply that we have not had time, nor, perhaps, inclination, to make the counts that would be required for an evaluation of the probability number. As a result of our observations, which give rough limits to the values of certain numbers, we may be able to affirm that the probability in question is very high. But since we have been unable to make the relevant counts — for instance to count the number of the items in a sample — we do not know what the precise probability number is. We can validly say that it is high, and that is the limit of our knowledge in this matter ; we cannot name a precise number. But the number is always there, so to speak, in the background ; the facts that give rise to our notion about probability always entail the existence of such a number ; this number pertains to the observations we have actually made, although we do not know what it is, and has nothing to do with quite different observations that we might relevantly make, but have not in fact made. Thus although the evidence before us has not been counted or sifted so as to yield a precise probability number, this number may be thought of as intimately connected with the evidence before us — it would be available if only that evidence had been properly sifted and counted. This lack of proper sifting and counting of the evidence we have is in an altogether different category from the lack of other evidence lying outside the field of the observations at our disposal.

It may seem surprising that, if a precise number is indeed always there in the background, we so seldom ascertain it. There are two distinct reasons for this. One is that the matters about which we have common-sense opinions are so numerous that, if we were to endeavour to substantiate them by means of precise numbers, we should at any time be having to make thousands of simultaneous counts of great and impracticable rapidity. We have common-sense opinions about the stability of physical objects, and all these are the results of inductive inferences, namely inferences of a sampling kind. It would be literally impossible to make even a minute fraction of the counts necessary to insert precise numbers into all our opinions of this sort.

A second and distinct reason for the absence of counting is that in a great many of our common-sense opinions, and also in the findings of scientists, the probabilities are very high. This will become apparent later. If on a minimum estimate of the value of our evidence we have favourable odds of the order of a billion to one, a count which would make these odds more precise would be a waste of time. We shall not get certainty in any case. A successful experiment in the 'harder' sciences often establishes the case in the favour of a law with enormously high probability, so that the scientist, for all his caution, regards the law as certain within fine limits of tolerance.[1]

In the case of 'softer' sciences, where probabilities in favour of generalizations are often much lower, the counting needed to establish the precise number of the probability becomes important, and is often in fact carried out. It is largely within the field of biological science that it has been found necessary to develop a fully articulated theory of sampling; here we find precise numbers actually provided for the probability relations; the reason why counts are carefully made in these cases is that, when the probability is not exceedingly high, it becomes much more interesting to know exactly what it is. Similarly sampling methods involving counts may be valuable

---

[1] The probability theory that has recently come into prominence in physics is not, I believe, a form of sampling theory, but a branch of direct probability theory (see above, p. 14).

in relation to certain engineering problems, where we are dealing with rough working generalizations of relatively low probability, and not with the exact laws of physics and chemistry proper. In the case of the last-named laws, the probabilities usually being exceedingly high, precise evaluation of them would be redundant. In the realm of everyday life there are unhappily very many cases where the probabilities are low ; there we have to remain in doubtful ignorance ; the counts needed to establish precision would be far too numerous to be made ; we cannot usually see in advance which among the many millions of possible counts might later prove serviceable to solve a doubtful point. In everyday life most opinion is based on data observed in the past and remembered. All this will become plain when we see what kind of actual situations give rise to a probability relation.

In probability theory a conventional notation has grown up by which the proportion of occasions on which an X is expected to be the case is expressed as a fraction of all occasions on which an A is the case. While this notation is needed for a mathematical development of probability theory, it will often be sufficient in the following discussions, which are concerned with foundations, to express probabilities in the more popular style of odds in favour or against. In the conventional notation the number 1 stands for the case of 'whenever A then X', or 'if A, then it is certain that X', and this case may be ruled out as being incapable of being established in empirical enquiries. There may, none the less, be occasions when the number 1 appears in empirical calculations, as when we are considering a finite number of alternative hypotheses that exhaust the range of possibility ; if precise probability numbers can be assigned to each of these, they must add up to 1.

The traditional notation has one grave defect. In many, I believe most, treatises on probability theory, 'probability equals 0', is made to stand for impossibility; thus we should write 0 if the conclusion was self-contradictory or contradicted the premise, or entailed something self-contradictory. If the probability is represented by a number above 0, however small, this implies, in accordance with the conventions, that the premises have some evidential value, however low, in favour of the conclusion. But what of the case where the premises have no evidential value whatever in favour of a proposed conclusion, and yet the conclusion is not inherently impossible nor rendered impossible by the premises? It is surprising that this hallowed and universally adopted notation has no simple means of expressing so important a logical relation. After all, the case of no evidential value is the most common of all. The symbol zero being earmarked for 'impossibility', there is nothing left for 'no evidential value', or, in other words, 'no probability'. This is clearly a very serious gap, and I have the impression that it may be worse — that it may have had a deceptive influence leading to serious aberrations by writers on this subject.

In Keynes's notation zero stands explicitly for impossibility. He is able to express 'no evidential value' in a roundabout way. If the probability of a conclusion on evidence h is equal to that on evidence h and a, then a is 'irrelevant', $i.e.$ has no evidential value.[1] It is unsatisfactory that so simple an idea should have to be expressed in this indirect manner. Furthermore how can it be expressed if no h can be found, that is, if nothing can be found which has a positive evidential value in favour of the conclusion in question? It is well known that Keynes holds that there are certain initial prior probabilities. I do not know if his doctrine entails that every conceivable conclusion of an argument in probability has some prior probability. If it does, his notation is comprehensive, but if it does not, then there is a lacuna. In order to save the idea that probability is essentially a relation between premises and conclusion, Keynes regularly inserts the symbol h to stand for all or part of the premises, where h signifies the general circumstances other than the specific evidence under consideration. He does this whether there is any evidence specifically bearing upon the conclusion or not. Thus where a belief is not impossible, either inherently or in view of the evidence, but where there is no specific evidence in favour of the belief, we can ascribe to the belief some probability above zero (which would betoken impossibility), and at the same time represent this probability as flowing from evidence by writing down h (the general circumstances) as the evidence. These general circumstances may be taken to include the

[1] *Treatise of Probability*, p. 120.

reasons that impel us to assign initial prior probabilities in appropriate cases. I suggest that this saves the idea that probability is essentially a relation between premises and conclusion in form, but not in substance.

In Carnap zero stands for 'impossible'; zero is inserted when the conclusion or premise is in his language 'L-false'.[1] I am not sure whether zero is explicitly and exclusively reserved for this case in his system. On page 287 the following sentence occurs : 'To attribute to an arbitrary state-description the probability zero . . . without any knowledge of facts, would be an *a priori* decision not to reckon with the occurrence of this possible case'. This seems to imply that if zero is assigned, the case is written off as impossible. The alternative which he adopts is to attribute to the state-description in question, although we are 'without any knowledge of facts', some low positive probability. This is objectionable. What one would think we need to do is to put the state-description in question into suspense so long as we are 'without any knowledge of facts', assigning it no probability, but holding it available to be brought in as a conclusion with positive probability, if and when we discover some facts pointing in that direction. Carnap appreciates that this attribution of a positive probability when there is no confirmatory evidence is an important step. 'The concept of null-confirmation is very important in inductive logic' (page 308). The arguments he brings in favour of doing so are not, however, very convincing.

Carnap too seeks to save the principle that probability is a relation between premise and conclusion. To do this in the case where we are without knowledge of any relevant facts, he writes in a tautology as the premise. This is a more barefaced device than that of Keynes. The latter could at least claim that the general considerations (*h*) in favour of assigning initial prior probabilities to beliefs were a kind of evidence for them, but a mere tautology cannot be evidentially favourable to any belief about an empirical fact. It is hard to resist the suspicion that the exigencies of notation have had some slight

[1] I shall use Carnap's convenient terms L-true and L-false from time to time. A sentence is L-true 'if it would be true under any conceivable circumstances, in other words, in any possible case'. See *Logical Foundations of Probability*, p. 83.

influence in inclining these distinguished authors to the attribution of initial prior probabilities, however low.

That same reason that we cited in the last chapter as impelling thinkers to seek grounds for assigning initial prior probabilities has probably been responsible for the absence of rebellion against this gravely defective — and indeed, we may say, if we give the matter explicit scrutiny, quite absurd — notation. It is the fact that the Bayes-type formulation of the inverse principle has been the sole valid method in probability theory for arguing from particulars. If prior probabilities, however low, belong to any hypothesis that one seeks to establish as a conclusion from empirical evidence, the absence of notation for stating that the matters alleged to be evidence do nothing towards establishing the hypothesis is not a felt want, since one can always leave the hypothesis with the probability it had before the alleged evidence was adduced — unless the evidence is inconsistent with the hypothesis, in which case the symbol zero is available. But if, as I propose to show, there are arguments in inverse probability that do not stem from the Bayes-type theorem and do not imply prior probabilities for the hypotheses, then the absence of any symbol for conveying that the alleged evidence considered has no tendency to establish the hypothesis will be a great inconvenience. It is not my purpose to propose a new system of symbolism. But I have the idea that if the experts in symbolism made a manful effort to repair this grave defect in traditional notation, it would necessitate a fruitful and welcome revolution in probability theory.

A preliminary definition of probability having been set out, it may be well to consider other views. Keynes, herein followed by Professor Jeffreys, holds probability to be an indefinable relation. This is unacceptable. We should always be chary of allowing the claim that something is indefinable — that is too easy a way out of difficulties. To safeguard ourselves we should adhere to the doctrine of Hume, which has not in my judgement been refuted. That doctrine only permits an idea to be indefinable, if it is a replica of some element in our sensible experience — external or internal. Such elements are the various colours — in the visual sense of colour — small numbers, the relations of between, of greater

than, of before and after in time. It will later be argued that
the relations of truth and belief may also be included in this
list.[1] In regard to the ideas that are replicas of these elements
we should hold, not only that they need not be defined, but also
that they must not be defined — otherwise than 'ostensively'.
For other ideas definitions are necessary, the predicates of the
definitions being either ideas that have already been defined,
or indefinables, that is replicas of elements in sensible experience. It could hardly be claimed that probability is the
replica of an element in sensible experience. Accordingly it
requires a definition.

It may, however, serve to rebut the claims of those who
would regard probability as indefinable if we can find a definition which accords with common usage and is logically
acceptable.

There is another type of approach which it is more difficult
to characterize and deal with. This regards the probabilities
that occur in logic as based upon, or reflections of, statistical
frequencies in nature. Carnap holds that this may be a legitimate sense of 'probability' and designates it 'probability $_2$'.
His work is concerned with a different kind of probability,
designated 'probability $_1$'. This work also is concerned with
probability $_1$. It is doubtful whether it is desirable to sanction
the usage in our language of probability in the sense of 'probability $_2$'; 'statistical frequency' might suffice for the relation
in question. Recent developments in physics, however, where
probability has become prominent, probably render the hope
of such a terminological reform vain, and we shall have to put
up with the linguistic ambiguity.

There are indeed some who would like to expunge probability $_1$ from the language. These are the logicians who are
floundering in a sea of confusion as regards the meaning of
probability $_1$; in desperation they recommend a direct passage
from observations to degrees of belief, denying that there are
any logical or objective 'probability $_1$' relations which, if only
they existed, might mediate between the observations and the
beliefs. Happily the use of 'probable' in the sense of probability $_1$ is so deeply entrenched in ordinary speech that there
is not the remotest danger of this linguistic reform being

[1] See Chapter VII.

carried into effect. Here is a case where the common man with his common-sense language holds the fort, while logicians are passing through a phase of rout and demoralization.

It need not be denied that statistical frequencies in nature, to the extent that there are grounds for believing them to exist, may give rise to a rich progeny of logical probabilities. If it is possible to assign a precise number to a statistical frequency in nature, then the logical probabilities generated by the number representing the frequency will have the advantage of themselves embodying precise numbers. If one seeks to elaborate a mathematical theory of logical probability, it is important to be able to take as instances cases where precise numbers are present. We shall proceed farther and faster if our premises contain precise numbers than if they merely contain such vague quantitative expressions as 'often' or 'very often'. This may well be the reason why probability theorists have been so much concerned with the cases of logical probability that spring from hypotheses asserting statistical frequencies in nature. (Nature may be deemed to include artefacts such as well constructed dice.) The amount of attention given in probability theory to this class of cases is by no means in proportion to its importance in the whole field of empirical inference — and we must always remember that probability theory is concerned with that whole field. The objections to seeking in statistical frequency for the key to logical probability are two.

1. Statistical frequencies in nature are never known to be the case for certain. Consequently any conclusion in probability, the premise of which is a statistical frequency in nature, is infected by the probability that attaches to the hypothesis of this statistical frequency itself. In fact there are two probabilities involved, the probability of the hypothesis and the probability of some event, if that hypothesis is true ; the conclusion about the event is infected by both probabilities. There is no opinion in probability derived from the hypothesis of a statistical frequency in nature that is not also subject to a probability derived from another source.

The two probabilities, the probability of the hypothesis of a statistical frequency in nature (including the behaviour of artefacts), and the probability of the event if that hypothesis is true, are both strictly 'probabilities $_1$'. But the value of the second probability $_1$ is equal to that of the probability $_2$, since it is governed by the alleged statistical frequency in nature (including the behaviour of artefacts). If it so happens that the former probability $_1$ is a near certainty, and may be regarded for practical purposes as a certainty, i.e. as equal to one, then the whole development of the argument is concerned with the second probability $_1$, and, as this is equal in value to a certain probability $_2$, we appear to be dealing directly with this probability $_2$ and with its consequences. The most frequent use of direct probability theory is in the demonstration of the consequences in this type of case. As the direct theory is the mathematically developed part of probability theory, we may lapse into the idea that probability theory is primarily concerned with probability $_2$. This accounts for the obscuration in some logical writings of the fact that the fundamental logical concept is probability $_1$, and that we are only able to develop an argument from a premise that appears to be asserting a probability $_2$ because in the special circumstances the value of the probability $_2$ in question can be taken for practical purposes as equal to that of a probability $_1$.

2. The greater part of induction, all of which rests on some kind of probability theory, is concerned not with statistical frequency in nature, but with (a) alleged uniformities in nature or (b) particular facts which have no specific connexion with any alleged statistical frequency.

We may dwell briefly on these two objections, and in doing so may bring out one or two facts that have not been sufficiently observed in probability theory. On the first point take the case of an 'unbiased' die. An unbiased die may be defined as one which on a large number of throws will show each facet a roughly equal number of times. It would be in accord with our definition of probability that, if we accept the premise that a given die is in fact unbiased, the probability of its showing a six on a given throw is about one-sixth. But of course we can never know for certain that any particular die is in fact unbiased. We must assemble our evidence for that hypothesis. This may consist of (1) a lengthy experiment in tossing the die itself, (2) a careful physical examination of it, (3) some knowledge of the maker and his reputation for honesty

and accurate workmanship. At best we can only hope for a
probability in favour of the die being unbiased within certain
limits of tolerance, but these limits may be sufficiently fine
for us to ignore them. Let us suppose that in consequence
of our investigations — the logical aspects of which are to be
discussed in later chapters — we can show that there are 999
odds to 1 in favour of the die being unbiased within limits
of tolerance so fine as to be negligible. While we may get a
precise number in consequence of our investigation under (1),
it is very unlikely that we should do so under (2) or (3) ; but
let that be. Let us for the sake of argument suppose a precise
number. Then in virtue of the multiplication principle, we
can say that the probability of the die showing a six on the
next toss is *at least* $\frac{999}{1000} \times \frac{1}{6}$. The probability of its showing
one or other of the other numbers *at least* $\frac{999}{1000} \times \frac{5}{6}$. It is to
be observed that these two probability numbers do not add
up to 1 but to $\frac{5994}{6000}$. But — assuming that the die will not
stand poised on one corner — it is certain that it will show
one or other of the facets ; this suggests that the alternative
probabilities ought to add up to 1. It will be noted, however, that my two statements in regard to the two probabilities
both contain the words 'at least'. These were inserted to
allow for the fact that, even if the die was biased, it must still
show either a six, or one of the numbers other than six, and
might show either.

There might be a temptation among some to argue that
the difference between 1 and $\frac{5994}{6000}$ should be split equi-
proportionally between the six facets, on the ground that, if
the die is biased, it is just as likely to be biased one way as
another. If this argument were accepted the probability of a
six would be precisely $\frac{1}{6}$, but in fact the argument is fallacious.
The hypothesis that the die is unbiased is assigned a probability on the basis of the various observations enumerated
above. The more extensive these observations, the higher,
supposing that they all support the hypothesis, will be the
probability that can validly be assigned to that hypothesis.
Splitting the difference, on the contrary, would be on a basis
of no evidence at all. It could only be justified by the Principle
of Indifference, which is unacceptable and responsible for
many fallacies in inductive logic. Of course, it may be that

we are not entirely ignorant in regard to the bias of dice generally. It may be that we have knowledge about their manufacture pointing to the hypothesis that defects will be equi-proportionately dispersed as between facets among all the dice produced ; such a conclusion could not be reached without considerable knowledge about the general nature of the process of manufacture ; it would be based on similar empirical considerations to those which lead us to believe that a large class of dice, namely the so-called unbiased dice, will show various facets a roughly equal number of times. Any hypothesis of this kind can be applied to the chance (1 in 1000) that the die before us is biased. But this further knowledge and this further hypothesis will still not suffice to close the gap ; the probability of a six computed in the light of the additional knowledge and the probability of not-six similarly computed will still not add up to 1. If the gap were to be closed, it would have to be on the basis of the Principle of Indifference, which is unacceptable. Accordingly the gap must be left unclosed and represents what may be called an area of total nescience.

If it were legitimate to rely on the Principle of Indifference to close the gap, it would have been legitimate to have relied on it from the beginning, seeing that the die must fall onto one of its six sides ; on this principle one could have said prior to investigation that the probability of the die showing a six was $\frac{1}{6}$. Thus all our elaborate investigations would have, on this view, been a pure waste of time ; which is absurd. The right statement is that prior to all investigation we are in a state of total nescience ; that after investigation the probability that the die will show a six is *at least p*, the probability that it will show some other number is *at least q* and the area of total nescience is $(1 - p - q)$. Opinion, if it is to be justified by logic, can go no further. The effect of extending the investigations, to the extent that they all continue to favour the hypothesis of lack of bias is to raise both p and q, so that $(p + q)$ tends in the direction of 1. But it remains in the end a finite distance away from 1. The formal requirement that the probabilities of alternative hypotheses that are logically exhaustive must add up to 1 is satisfied by the inclusion of 'at least' before each probability number.

Where the area of total nescience is small, we may be under the temptation to split the difference between the alternative possibilities. It may be convenient to eliminate this area with a view to further calculations. So long as it is recognized that this procedure has no foundation in logic, that it is adopted merely as a matter of convenience and that the consequential probabilities written down contain this margin of error, there is no harm in it. The difference may be split in various ways, for example in the proportion of p to q or half and half, or the whole may be assigned to one or the other hypothesis. No one of these methods is logically superior to the others ; there may be an urge to use the $p : q$ ratio, but this is mere pedantry of no intellectual value. In these circumstances it would be a wise maxim, since the procedure is for convenience only, to split the difference, that is the area of total nescience, in such a way as to get the roundest numbers for the probabilities of the two hypotheses. If this procedure were standardized and regarded as mandatory, it might be a safeguard against any tendency to fall a prey to the fallacy of the Principle of Indifference.

In regard to hypotheses about uniformities in nature it will very frequently be found that a statement of the probability should include the words 'at least'. As further favourable evidence is accumulated this does not show a tendency towards entitling us to withdraw these words or towards concentration upon a particular number, but rather to the raising of the number, with the words 'at least' still present. It is to be emphasized that this quest for uniformities gives a much wider sphere for the application of arguments in probability than the quest for statistical frequencies. In the latter case special techniques are required and used ; these techniques do lead, in cases where there is a regular frequency in nature, to a progressive concentration upon a particular number. But in the wider sphere of probability argument there is no such tendency to concentration. This alone may suffice to suggest that logical probability theory in its general form is not derived from, nor a reflection of, statistical frequency in nature.

The point may perhaps be made clearer by reference to our original definition. When we are dealing with statistical frequencies in nature, the members of the larger class of

events, to which we refer a particular event in order to assess
a probability, usually have *material* similarity. Thus we may
be expecting a birth ; we refer this event to the class of all
expectations of births ; about this larger class we entertain
the belief, for whatever reason, that a certain proportion of
these expectations are followed by the birth of a boy ; and
we deduce a certain probability for a boy being born on this
occasion. This argument is good enough, subject to the reservation, already explained, that it is only probable that the
alleged frequency of boy births actually obtains among births
not already on the record. But this type of argument is only
a special case. In far the greater number of cases when we
refer a particular event to a larger class, in order to determine
the probability of a correlated event, the character that the
members of this larger class have in common, which we have
called A, does not constitute *material* similarity at all, but
consists solely in a *logical* similarity. Thus the event before
us (our N) may consist of a sample of a certain size, all members of which have two features conjoined. The larger class
to which we refer this, in order to establish a probability for
X_n, may be simply all samples of that size, all members of
each of which have two features conjoined. The common A
character consists solely of being a sample of that size with
two features uniformly conjoined in all its members. These
various samples, having A in common, may consist of totally
different things and have nothing at all in common save their
logical structure.

There has been a tendency to divide probability theorists
into those who hold a 'frequency theory' and those who do
not. How should the foregoing definition of probability be
classified ? If by frequency theory is meant a theory that
regards probability numbers as derived from or reflexions of
statistical frequencies in nature (Carnap's 'probability $_2$'), my
theory is emphatically not a frequency theory. On the other
hand probability on my theory is defined in terms of frequency.
'X is probable', is said to mean that the evidence for X is of
such a character that it seldom happens both that evidence of
that character is the case, and that the conclusion to which
it points is not the case. The probability relation is thus essentially and by definition a relation of frequency. According

E

to my understanding, when the whole system of Carnap is expounded, it will prove to be a frequency theory in this sense. On page 172 he writes 'the common probability $_1$ value of several hypotheses can be interpreted as the estimate of the relative frequency of truth among them'. This is encouraging.

Some theorists have held that probability is indefinable. I reject their view. Those, on the other hand, who have attempted to define it, have all, to my understanding, defined it in terms of frequency in some form. It is among the latter group that I class myself.

I conclude this preliminary account by stating one axiom, which is of the utmost importance for the development of the system that is to be expounded, and should therefore be looked at with the most careful scrutiny.

Axiom : If it is the case that B is true if, and only if, A is true, whatever probability pertains to A pertains to B also.

CHAPTER III

THE PRINCIPLE OF EXPERIENCE

When Locke attacked the doctrine of innate ideas and the view that one could deduce the nature of the external world from certain first principles to be accepted *a priori*, he offered an alternative aid to the advancement of knowledge — experience. It is my understanding that he held that reliance on experience constituted a positive principle to be used in inference. Yet as things have turned out, those, who claiming to be empiricists have endeavoured to develop a system of inductive logic, have, oddly enough, not relied much, or at all, on this principle itself; they have not made it do work in the process of inference. Hume made a formidable attack on the validity of the principle. Nineteenth-century logicians tended to look elsewhere for the major premises of inductive reasoning. They brought into play the principles of Universal Causation and the Uniformity of Nature. But this was quite a different mode of approach. If every cause must have its unique effect and every event must have one of a limited number of causes, it was held that by a careful scrutiny of certain phenomena and by using methods of elimination, one could establish that an event (B) was certainly an effect of an event (A) in a class of cases; then, by applying the principle of the Uniformity of Nature, one could generalize and hold that an event of character A would invariably be followed by an event of character B. Reference has already been made to weaknesses in the method of elimination; what it is important for our present purpose to observe is that the use of methods of elimination by the aid of uniformity axioms is not essentially an application of the principle of experience; it fails to make the principle of experience as such do logical work in the argument. Empiricism might be said to be saved in systems of this kind only to the extent that the major premises

(Universal Causation and Uniformity of Nature) are themselves generalizations from experience. But all attempts to show them to be such involve circular reasoning, unless we have in the first instance other methods of inductive argument at our disposal.

The inductive logicians who relied on inference by inverse probability may have come a little nearer to bringing experience into play. But their logical foundations are so uncertain, that it is difficult to assess how far experience as such is doing work in their systems.

What is this principle of experience? I suggest that it must be taken, as a minimum, to mean that the mere fact that things have been found in experience to be thus and thus gives, in and by itself, a valid reason for holding that they will continue to be thus and thus for the time being. If, with Hume, we hold that there is no valid reason for this, it follows without more ado that experience as such is not a pointer to the enlargement of knowledge. This is the issue that we have to face. Empiricists would not, of course, claim that the fact that things have been thus and thus allows us to infer with certainty that they will continue to be so ; that would clearly be an excessive claim, which would soon be disproved. Empiricism only holds that experience gives a pointer, provides a good reason for holding that a continuance is likely. Of all the countless things that might happen next, in the sense that they are logically possible, we should deem a continuance of what has gone before to be more likely than the other possibilities. The fact that things have been thus and thus entitles us to give some weight to the possibility that they will continue in that shape as against the myriads of other possibilities. Thus the principle of experience plants us right at the outset in the realm of probability theory. Discouraged by Hume, logicians have tended not to face this issue fairly and squarely, but to run off in other directions. It is the purpose of this chapter to show that the principle of experience is valid and is part of the logic of entailment.

In the preceding chapter it was claimed, with a view to defining probability, that there can exist a certain character A such as to entail that, out of all the times that things having that character are the case, something else, X, is also often the case. It must be understood that it was not intended to imply that the facts of nature are connected by an inner necessity of the same kind of character as the necessity of logical entailment ; the necessity in question is not, so to speak, inside nature, but results from our own sorting out of the phenomena in question and our own selection of the right kind of conclusion to be derived therefrom. The necessity arises from our own method of procedure. It might be said, and has been said, that if we seem able to conjure up a necessity of this sort, when there is no necessity in nature, this must be by some kind of trickery. In a certain sense a 'trick' is indeed involved ; but this is not a disparagement. What is the whole of mathematics but a trick ? The development of modern symbolic logic goes to reinforce the view that in mathematics we are confronted with a piece of trickery on a heroic scale. It should not be inferred from the analysis of the symbolic logicians that it is in principle impossible for mathematics to be of any service in extending the frontiers of knowledge. In this case the human mind has shown that it is able, by devising its own method of model building and by its selection and arrangement of phenomena, to achieve an enlargement of its knowledge. The trouble about mathematics and, more broadly, about deduction, is not that it does nothing for us at all, but that it does not suffice to extend knowledge by itself ; it needs general propositions for premises ; it cannot begin with mere particulars in the form of bits of experience or observations. Yet that is what we humans have to begin with *faute de mieux*. To advance from these bits and pieces, it is, and has long been, recognized that we need a complementary inductive process. It is this process that has never been properly analysed. If there is to be a successful analysis, one ought to expect that it will show that induction contains tricks, in precisely the same sense that deduction has been shown to be a great galaxy of tricks. Why should such procedures be appropriate in one part of the total process that advances our knowledge and yet be ruled out in the other part of the process ? Indeed I would go so far as to say that unless the analysis of induction brings to the surface something in the nature of a trick, one might suspect that the analysis has not got to the root of the matter.

May I suggest an analogy with a simple situation in mechanics ? Yonder weight is manifestly too heavy for any human being to lift. A conjurer comes forward and, by an arrangement of looking glasses, makes it appear that he is lifting the weight. This is trickery in a bad sense ; the weight is not being lifted at all in fact. But let someone else come and arrange a series of pulleys, and, lo and behold, the weight is lifted by one man. It is really lifted, despite the fact that it is beyond the power of anyone to lift it in the ordinary way. It is the second kind of trick that is analogous to what we do in induction and in deduction.

The task before us is to justify the Principle of Experience. We require, in order to do this, to show that experience as such entails there being a class of cases in all of which the premises have a specific kind of quality called 'A'. This is the kind of quality to which we referred in the definition of probability. It is a quality such as to entail that within the whole class of cases in which it occurs, something else, X, is often the case.

We are starting, as we must in a fundamental analysis of induction, from a condition of total nescience. Before having made any inductions, man could know nothing whatever, except what is under his nose. Consider a journey by such a nescient man along a continuity. The continuity may consist of a uniform colour, texture or sound, or of a repeated pattern, where the pattern is easily cognizable at a glance, this uniformity being in contrast with a heterogeneous background. The set of premises of the class of arguments in probability that he can develop are constituted by the facts that successively arise as he proceeds. The common quality A is the fact of travel on *this* particular continuity, *e.g.* this particular strip of uniform colour. Note that at this stage we are concerned with one continuity only, not with a class of continuities. Some memory is required for this experience. We need, therefore, a vindication of the informative nature of memory ; this is fully elaborated in a later chapter. It is to be noted that, as the journey proceeds, the premises change in detail. To have travelled for a minute over this continuity is not the same as to have travelled for two minutes : but throughout the journey these premises retain the same quality A, which consists of being travel on this continuity, viz. on this

strip of uniform colour. Let a conclusion be proposed that
this continuity will continue for a length constituting at least
one-tenth of the length for which it has already proceeded.
In more general terms we may suppose a belief in a continuance for at least $1/x$ of the length for which it has already
proceeded. If we entertain the belief of at least one-tenth,
which is the conclusion of our argument, continuously from
the beginning to the end of the journey, it is quite certain
that we shall be right ten times for every once that we are
wrong. We shall be right during the first ten-elevenths of
the journey and wrong during the last eleventh. If we entertain the belief of continuance for at least $1/x$, it is quite
certain we shall be right x times for every once that we are
wrong. This, in accordance with the traditional notation,
gives a probability of being correct of $x/x + 1$. The probability
of the belief in continuance will be higher, the more modest
the extrapolation.

It is to be observed that we have here a precise probability
number. It can be entertained with absolute certainty. Subsequent verification will invariably prove it correct. It is to be
noted also that the achievement of this number as a matter of
strict entailment depends simply on our arrangement of the
data. All that nature contributes to the argument is a continuity. That is innocent enough in all conscience ! It cannot
be said that when we postulate that there is a continuity in
nature — from the dawn of experience we have myriads of
examples of continuities — we are thereby postulating some
inner necessity in nature or making a prior assumption about
nature. Yet this existence of the continuity gives rise to a
situation in which premises can be found which yield, as a
strict logical entailment, a conclusion in probability, in the
sense defined. The entailment arises through our own choice
of the class of cases within which the probability is to be
established, namely the whole class of successive positions on
a given journey. The 'journey' is defined simply as the continuation of a specific uniform feature — colour, pattern or
what not. We have been careful also in the selection of our
proposed conclusion, namely the belief in further continuance for a fraction of the length already achieved. Here at
the outset of our enquiry we have an instance of a class of

premises all members of which have a property A (in this case simply 'being in the course of this journey') which is such that the conclusion X (viz. that the continuity will continue for at least $1/x$ of the time for which it has already lasted) is true a precise proportion of all the times that the premises are true ; we have in fact a precise probability number. By making the extrapolation sufficiently modest, we can make the probability number as near 1 as we like.

We now proceed to the next stage of our argument. It may be objected that this probability number would not have relevance to any actual situation where someone was striving to enlarge his knowledge, and so would not serve to enlarge significant knowledge. The ground of the objection is that, out of the total number of true answers, namely ten true answers for every one false answer, some out of the total of true answers have already been given and verified at any point of the journey. (By 'answer' here and in what follows is meant an affirmative answer to the question whether the continuity will proceed further for such and such a proportion of the antecedent length.) Some of the beliefs that the continuity will proceed for at least one-tenth of its former length have already been entertained and proved correct. But the traveller is interested in what lies ahead, and will therefore not deem this probability number to be relevant to his case. Even those answers already made that have not yet been proved correct, viz. the last one-eleventh of them, must be assumed for his purposes to have been correct if he is to assign to a further continuance of one-tenth any positive probability at all ; for if any of the answers already made are false, the answer that he gives now and all future answers must be false also.

It is to be emphasized that no precise analogy to the case we are considering can be found from the type of cases so dear to probability theorists, where it is a question of drawing black or white balls from a bag. A true answer in the case before us might indeed be taken as analogous to a white ball and a false one to a black ball ; but there are fatal differences between our case and any case of that type. One is that it is not known whether any answer is true or false until the very end of the journey ; that would mean, by analogy, that we should not know whether any ball was white or black until all the balls had been drawn out. The other is that no answer in our case is false until all the true answers are exhausted — no black balls would be drawn until all the white balls had already been taken out. None the less there is an analogy in this respect, namely that at any given point on the journey some of the true answers have already been given ; that would correspond to the case of some white balls having been drawn out *and not replaced*. That is a fact that has to be taken into account in the estimating of a probability number during the course of the journey.

At first sight this may seem to present an insurmountable difficulty. It is essential for the probability estimate that we make our predictions in terms of a fraction of the length travelled ; in order to subtract the answers already given — on the analogy of subtracting the white balls drawn out and not replaced in estimating probabilities for future drawings — we should need to be able to measure the number of these answers in terms of the total length of the line or some fraction thereof. But so long as the journey lasts, the traveller is in total ignorance of the ratio of the length already travelled to the total length of the line. Consequently his knowledge that some part of the journey has already been made cannot be brought directly into relation with the probability number that he is seeking to assess. Actually this difficulty can be overcome.

The total series of answers, namely predictions that the continuity will continue for at least $1/x$ of the length already traversed, may be represented by a straight line of $(x + 1)$ units ; the x units, representing the length over which the predictions will be true, may be shown on the left part of the line and the 1 unit where the answers will be false on the right part. The traveller is assumed to advance from left to right. The use of the notation 1 does not of course imply that there is only one answer in this latter part ; both the x and the 1 must be multiplied by some common coefficient (n) representing the rate at which answers are occurring per unit of length. All terms in the formulae we are discussing are to be multiplied by this coefficient, which accordingly cancels out and may be omitted.

The next step is to consider this series from every point

of view, namely from the point of view of every position on the
line. The total array of answers, namely the series of answers
considered in turn from every point of view, may be represented by a square, each side of which has $(x + 1)$ units. The
horizontal side of the square is simply the series of answers ;
the vertical side of the square represents the number of times
that this series has to be surveyed, if it is surveyed from every
point of the journey.

Draw a diagonal across the square, as in the figure adjoining.
Let P be a point on the left-hand side of the square at a distance y_p from the left-hand bottom corner. From P draw a

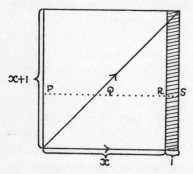

line PS parallel to the base
of the square, intersecting
the diagonal at Q. PQ
measures the answers already
past and QS those still to
come, when the traveller has
proceeded a distance y_p.
Similar computations may be
made for all values of y
between o and $(x + 1)$. Consequently the whole area on
the left-hand side of the diagonal represents, within the total
array of answers, all the answers that have already been given
considered from every point of view ; the area on the right-
hand side represents the answers still to come. Taking the
journey as a whole and surveying it successively from every
point of view during the course of the journey, it is clear that
half the total array of answers belong to the past. In order to
get a probability that will be relevant to a traveller in the course
of the journey, it is necessary to subtract answers already given.
Therefore, in estimating this probability we should concern
ourselves only with the answers on the right-hand side of the
diagonal.

It is to be noted that in the total array of answers, equal
weight is given to each of the series as surveyed from each point
of view. This implies that the traveller is equally likely to be
at one point as at any other point of his journey. This is *not*
an application of the Principle of Indifference. It is by definition quite certain that the traveller will be an equal time in

each sector of the line where a sector is defined as an equal aliquot part of the line ; this should be made as small as possible. The construction of the diagonal implies the reduction of the 'sector' to an infinitesimal.

In the figure an area on the right-hand side of the square has been shaded. This is a rectangle equal to one-eleventh part of the whole square. Within this rectangle all the answers are false ; in the remainder of the square all the answers are true. If we take the answers as surveyed from the beginning, viz. the series represented by the base of the square, $1/x + 1$ will be false and $x/x + 1$ true. To assess the probability for a traveller, who has already proceeded part of the way — he knows not what proportion — we must subtract answers already given. This can be done by subtracting all answers to the left of the diagonal from the total array of answers. That leaves the answers to the right of the diagonal. The probability of being correct in the prediction of continuance for at least $1/x$ is represented by the ratio of the unshaded area on the right of the diagonal to the whole area on the right of the diagonal. It will be remembered that the ratio of true answers to all answers as surveyed at the starting-point is $x/(x + 1)$; the ratio of true answers to all answers, after subtracting answers already given as surveyed from every point of view, is seen to be $x^2/(x + 1)^2$.

The diagonal across the square may be thought of as representing the traveller's journey. Its lateral movement represents his movement along the continuity, its upward movement represents the shift in the point of view at which, actually but unknowingly, he is placed in relation to the total series of answers. If we take any point on the diagonal and draw a horizontal line to the right-hand side of the square, the ratio of the length of this line in the unshaded area to its whole length is equal to the ratio of true future answers to all future answers (QR : QS in the figure). This ratio must not be taken to rank as a probability number. The traveller is always ignorant of his position on the diagonal, and consequently this number would never be known to him. The probability is simply the ratio of all true to all false answers in the array, after all answers in the array that have already been given have been subtracted. The figure shows how this subtraction can be correctly executed. For an *ex-post* verification of the probability, however, the ratio of true future answers to all future answers should be observed as from every point on the journey and the unweighted arithmetic average taken.

The only special property of this probability number, as compared with others that we shall have to consider, consists in the provision of a special mechanism for subtracting answers already given.

The general principle noted earlier, that the more modest the extrapolation the higher the probability, applies to the formula adjusted for answers already given as well as to the unadjusted formula. It is also true that one can make the probability number approach 1 by reducing the extrapolation sufficiently.

It is interesting to observe an analogy with the mechanical 'trick' already mentioned. In that operation, the heavier the weight, the less the distance that it will be lifted by a given pull on the part of the individual. To the weight of the physical object corresponds, in probability theory, the weight of probability that it is desired to assign to a given prediction ; to the amount of force an individual can exert corresponds the length of his experience to date ; in both cases this quantity has to be taken as fixed and given. If the individual wants to lift a heavy weight (or achieve a heavy weight of probability), he has to acquiesce in his own force (the length of his experience) lifting the weight through a proportionately smaller distance (justifying extrapolation of a proportionately smaller fraction of length already travelled). Thus the analogy is complete.

The theory just outlined breaks down for very short distances. If a continuity has proceeded for one minimum sensibile, the rule states that the prediction of at least one more minimum sensibile, namely a length equal to that already travelled, has a probability of a quarter. But the continuity may cease after the first minimum sensibile, so that the sole prediction fails. Similar discrepancies will continue. The reason for the error is plain ; it is due to the existence of a minimum sensibile. If throughout the length of the first minimum sensibile it had been possible to make a long chain of predictions, the ratio of true to false answers would have corresponded to that given by the formula, even if the continuity had terminated at the end of the first minimum sensibile.

In fact the error is due to our inability to break down every minimum sensibile, however small, into still smaller parts. The error due to this fact becomes negligible when we are considering lengths of substantial size compared with a minimum sensibile.

In this connexion it is interesting to observe that our formula bears some family resemblance to the much abused Law of Succession. It must by no means be confused with that law, as its logical basis is totally different. The Law of Succession is derived from assigning equal prior probabilities to members of a class of alternative possibilities; thus the Law of Succession makes use of the Principle of Indifference. Our formula, by contrast, in no way implies the Principle of Indifference, and owes nothing to any assumption of prior probabilities. For instance, it requires no assumption in regard to the frequency distribution of the lengths of the various continuities in our universe; it would hold in every case, however erratic, that frequency distribution might be; it has no implication that the continuity being examined is as likely to be of one length as of any other. Arguments brought against the Law of Succession will therefore have no application to our formula. None the less the family resemblance is undeniable. Now in regard to the Law of Succession, it has been generally felt that in its application to long runs it has a certain plausibility; it has been thought that, despite its faults, it must have some relation, albeit one that no one has been able to define or justify precisely, to the truth. It is also to be noticed that the gross and flagrant fallacies to which the application of the Law of Succession leads, all arise in the case of short runs, namely one or two or three observations. If the principles by which the Law of Succession is derived were correct, then it ought to apply to very short runs, as well as to longer runs; no one, to my knowledge, has shown why on these principles this should not be so. By contrast, it can be shown quite clearly why our formula, which is based on totally different principles, does not apply to very short runs; thus the exception proves the rule. I suggest that the plausibility of the Law of Succession arises precisely because of its family resemblance to our formula; to the extent that it resembles it, it has truth.

Before proceeding it is necessary to give warning against a very strong temptation that must be resisted. It is a fact that, as the traveller proceeds with his journey, the ratio of all true future answers that he will give (by predicting at least 1/10 or at least 1/x) to all future answers declines. There is a strong temptation to seek some formula which would take this fact into account, and, in order to get greater refinement, make the probability fall as he progresses. Any such procedure would lead to a gross fallacy. In dealing with probability it is essential to abide by the principle that a probability is a relation between premises and a conclusion. But as the traveller proceeds with his journey he gets no new information of any kind that is relevant to the estimate of this probability, and it would, therefore, be fallacious for him to alter his estimate. The traveller is assumed to be in complete ignorance in regard to the total length of the continuity. Consequently he is in complete ignorance as to what relation the length he has already travelled bears to this total length. Therefore, he cannot bring the length of travel already accomplished into any relation to the formula. Being totally nescient, as we assume, he is altogether lacking in evidence on which to base any guess in regard to the length of continuity on which he is travelling. In this respect he is in marked contrast with the normal condition of sophisticated man. The latter almost always, when he makes a journey on a continuity, has some kind of prior evidence in regard to its probable length; accordingly the sophisticated man does quite right to make his estimate of the probability of a continuation for at least 1/x fall as he proceeds. It is the fact that we are habituated to proceeding on this basis that makes it seem paradoxical to insist that there must be no change in the probability estimate as the journey goes forward; none the less that insistence must be maintained, if we are to avoid fallacy. Any reduction in the estimate of probability would imply a guess as to the length of the continuity in question. Some might be inclined to put forward the view that an arbitrary guess was as likely to err on the side of over-estimate as on the side of under-estimate; this would be an application of the Principle of Indifference in its most vicious and fallacious form. The adjustment of probabilities based on such a guess would, save by a mighty coincidence, lead to a continuing succession of errors. What we have to do in this case is to decide on our formula at the outset, and then to adhere to it ; we have to adhere to it because in the course of the journey we get no new relevant information. If we cannot decide upon a formula at the outset, we cannot decide upon one at all. The formula that we decide on is not itself derived from experience but is, in the language of Carnap, 'L-true'. The possibility of drafting such a formula depends on our initial decision to express the prediction in terms of an aliquot part of the length already travelled.

There is an analogous temptation to the one discussed in the foregoing paragraph. This is the temptation to argue that in the total array of answers as seen from every point of view less weight should be given to the earlier points of view, since the traveller knows that he has already proceeded some distance, though he does not know how great that distance is, in proportion to the whole length. Now there is undoubtedly an a-symmetry in the relation of the traveller to the line : at each point he has accomplished some part of the journey — he knows not what proportion — from the beginning onwards, but he has not covered any part of it from the end backwards. It is this a-symmetry that gives rise to the requirement that some proportion of all the answers in the array must be eliminated before an estimate of the probability is reached. Before the journey has started there is no a-symmetry ; the ratio of true to false answers, as viewed before the journey has begun, is given by the simple formula $x/x + 1$. As soon as the journey starts the a-symmetry arises ; the fact that there is this a-symmetry is known and thus constitutes a new piece of evidence, which must be taken into the reckoning at once, viz. from the beginning onwards.

The formula which provides for eliminating early answers by giving equal weight to each point of view requires that one half of all answers in the array be subtracted. This is clearly right. Before the journey starts, no answers must be subtracted ; during the journey half the answers must be subtracted ; when the journey is over, the problem is at an end. If in the formula one gave less weight to the earlier points of view from which the chain of answers is surveyed, this would require the subtraction of more than half the answers. This would give too much weight to the a-symmetry and count it twice over. Once the journey has begun, a new piece of evidence comes into the picture, namely the fact of a-symmetry. We must make full allowance for this immediately. As the journey proceeds, no further relevant evidence becomes available for the formula and therefore the formula must be retained unaltered. The formula requires us to exclude one-half of the total array of answers and this is clearly the right proportion to exclude in order to give full allowance for the a-symmetry.

There need be no doubt about the feasibility of constructing an 'L-true' formula at the outset of the journey. We can say in advance that both our formulae, the simple and the squared, will certainly be verified by *ex-post* counts made in the appropriate manner. I do not know if it is considered unworthy to present the sceptic with an argument based persuasively on a strong case. Consider a prediction of no more than one-millionth part. Does he seriously contend that it is impossible to state in advance of the journey that this prediction will be much more often true than false, even when allowance is made for true answers already given ? But what applies to the one-millionth part, applies with an appropriate reduction of force to bolder predictions also.

We must now proceed to the next, and crucial, stage in the argument. One-tenth may be regarded as a natural unit of measurement ; it is one that can be adopted by a man in a condition of total nescience. We have to make a beginning with such natural units. With these may be contrasted conventional units, such as yards, seconds, years. Our nescient traveller may already be acquiring some interest in conventional units. For instance, if the continuity is an instance of spatial progress, he may be interested in the number of steps taken, and he may call one step forward a yard. (Or he may measure time by his pulse.) He may accordingly be interested to make a prediction expressed in yards, *e.g.* that the continuity will proceed for at least one yard more. Our formula is essentially expressed in natural units, and has nothing to say about such conventional units. But it may give information indirectly. Suppose that the traveller has already proceeded for ten yards. One yard is equal to one-tenth of ten yards. We now revert to the axiom given at the end of

Chapter II. 'If it is the case that B is true if, and only if, A is true, then whatever probability pertains to A pertains to B also.' Applying this to the case before us, we can assert that the continuity will proceed for at least one yard more if, and only if, it proceeds for at least one-tenth more. It is certainly true that a yard is equal to one-tenth of ten yards ; whatever, therefore, is probable in relation to one-tenth of ten yards is probable in relation to one yard. Therefore the probability of the continuity proceeding for at least a yard is, in these circumstances, $100/121$ $\left(=\dfrac{10^2}{(10+1)^2}\right)$. If, on the other hand, the continuity has already proceeded for twenty yards, the probability of its proceeding one yard more is equal to the probability of its proceeding for one-twentieth of its length to date ; x is in this case 20 and the probability of one yard more is $400/441$ ($=109 \cdot 747/121$). Thus the probability of continuance for at least one yard has substantially risen. Similarly, if the journey has lasted for 100 yards, the probability of its proceeding for at least one yard more is greater than the probability of its so doing after ten yards or after twenty yards. From these relations we may infer an increasing probability of the journey lasting for at least one yard more as the journey proceeds. This is true also of any other conventional unit of measurement. It may be called the law of increasing probability of continuance. *This is the Principle of Experience.*

We may pause here to take breath. It may be well to re-phrase the formula in more popular terms. We might put it that if one is journeying over an expanse, but in total ignorance of whereabouts on it one is, one is unlikely to be on the extreme edge of it. This notion of 'extreme edge' must be expressed in natural units. The improbability is constant in relation to any given natural unit, whatever the size of the expanse ; whatever that size, one is equally unlikely to be within one-millionth part of the edge. The expression of this improbability in terms of conventional units will depend on the size of the expanse. If in blind man's buff one finds oneself on the drawing-room carpet, it is not unlikely that one is within a yard of the edge of it ; to be within a yard of its edge would not be to be on its extreme edge. But if one has got

F

lost in a journey on the Sahara Desert, one is not likely to
be within a yard from its edge, for to be so would be to be
on its extreme edge. So far our strict argument has related
to one continuity only. The popular interpretation just given
becomes more appropriate when we develop the argument to
consider the case of a class of continuities. None the less it
may help us to understand the trend of the argument if we
anticipate a little.

I call the direct use of the Principle of Experience for
making predictions 'simple induction'. This is not, of course,
to be confused with 'induction by simple enumeration'. On
the use of simple induction by sophisticated man I shall have
much to say. It is plainly brought into frequent use by primitive man and infants. One discriminates between those things
which are expected to continue and those which are not by
the length of time for which they have already continued.
After a little experience the general contour of the landscape,
the position of the seashore, etc., are expected to continue,
whereas the cloudscape of the sky is not. The infant expects
the four walls of his nursery and the position of the door,
windows and fireplace to remain the same, whereas people
or domestic animals come and go. These expectations are
solely based on the length of time for which the things in
question have already continued. This is a correct application
of simple induction, and gives the subject valid grounds for
expectation.

To return to the strict argument, the formula provided
assumes that the continuity in question comes to an end in
due course. It may be, however, that some continuities are
of infinite length. If this is the case, it makes predictions
based on simple induction valid in probability *a fortiori*. To
allow for the possibility that the continuity in question is of
infinite length, we should say that the probability of its continuing for at least one-tenth is *at least* $\frac{100}{121}$. The need for
the insertion of an 'at least' in a probability statement will
recur in many connexions ; the fact that it figures so little in
treatises on probability theory indicates that the theory has
been developed on lines not directly relevant to induction.

It is now time to expand the scope of the argument. So
far the class of premises having a common quality A that has

been considered is the class of all premises present to a traveller on one particular continuity.

This formula gives a correct proportion of true answers, if answers are given continuously throughout the continuity. But in many, although not all, cases, the queries to which the answers are rejoinders may be occasional and sporadic. If we group these queries on a particular continuity into a class, the formula will not necessarily, or even usually, give a correct proportion of true answers within that class. In order to cover these cases it is necessary to widen our class. We may consider all queries by an observer in relation to the continuance of all continuities as a single class. We may suppose a great number of such queries in all. It will be evident at once how we may apply the formulae to the larger class. But we can only do so if we introduce a postulate.

In the course of this volume postulates will be introduced from time to time. In all cases they will eventually be treated in one of two ways : either they will be shown to be in fact true or they will subsequently be shown to be unnecessary. It may seem vexatious to introduce a postulate, only with a view to withdrawing it later ; but a postulate may serve as a tool of thought, even in cases where in the last analysis it can be dispensed with. In the present instance it is hoped to show that the postulate can be justified ; discussion of this is deferred until later in this chapter.

The required postulate is that, if a man makes a great many enquiries concerning the continuance of continuities, these will be equi-proportionally dispersed among the sectors of the various continuities. Let each of the continuities in question be divided into the same number, n, of sectors, where n should be as great as possible ; these sectors may be called the 1st, 2nd, 3rd, etc., sectors of their own continuities. The required postulate is that the number of queries lying in the 1st sector of their own continuities shall be equal to the number of queries lying in the 2nd sector and equal to the number of queries lying in the 3rd sector, etc. It will be remembered that the squared formula depends on the assumption, which is also a necessary fact, true by definition, that the traveller spends an equal amount of time in each sector of one particular continuity. The postulate enables us to make a

similar assumption that there is equal probability of the enquirer being in the first, or in the second, or in the third, etc.,
sector of the continuity with which he is immediately concerned. Thus by this postulate it becomes possible to apply
the formula derived from a journey on one particular continuity to a larger class of cases, consisting of sporadic enquiries
on a large number of continuities.

It is to be observed that this is not a postulate about
nature ; it is concerned only with the distribution of enquiries
about nature.

When we are concerned with a string of continuous enquiries on one particular continuity and can derive a probability by relating an individual enquiry to the class of enquiries
on the same continuity, I call the inference in probability
'unconditional simple induction' ; no postulate is necessary.
In cases where enquiries are occasional and sporadic and we
need in consequence, in order to get a probability, to relate a
particular enquiry to a wider class, namely to the class of all
enquiries on a number of different continuities about their
continuance, I call the inference in probability 'conditional
simple induction' ; a postulate regarding the equi-proportional
dispersion of such enquiries is then needed. The common
'A' quality present in the total class of such enquiries, which
is the source of an entailment in probability, is simply 'I have
been travelling on a continuity'.

Before proceeding to the vital question of how the postulate
is to be justified, it may be well to say something about the
fields of enquiry in which simple induction plays a part. In
the life of sophisticated man it does not play a major rôle
explicitly. This may account for its neglect in logical theory.
It continues to play a most important part in the background,
but, because this is implicit, it does not attract attention to
itself. In the case of the myriads of continuities of every
day we are able to attach to each of the specific kinds of continuity with which we are confronted some hypothesis regarding the normal length of life of that kind of continuity. This,
as has already been indicated, entitles us to argue in a way
diametrically opposed to that of simple induction ; as the
continuity proceeds, it comes nearer to its normal length of
life or goes beyond it, and consequently the probability of

continuance declines. If one attends an academic lecture the probability of its continuance, whether in terms of natural units such as one-tenth of the time it has lasted already, or of conventional units such as five minutes, remains high and fairly constant — the chance that the lecturer may faint only rises very slightly — for about half an hour. Thereafter it begins to decline, since he may run short of materials ; after about three-quarters of an hour it declines rapidly and continues to do so until the end. This attachment of a normal length of life to each kind of continuity is itself the result of an inductive inference, but not of simple induction. The attribution of a normal length may be similar to the attribution of other characters as the usual properties of various classes of objects, or it may flow from our belief in some laws of nature. Such attributions spring from inductive processes of a different type, which will be considered later. I give four main categories of fields of operation of simple induction, without claiming to be exhaustive.

1. Simple induction has been required at the outset of all enquiry, whether by mankind or by each individual separately. It enables us to distinguish between durable and transient elements in our environment. It is the first step in the emergence from total nescience. We are able to discriminate by means of it, and at the outset by means of it alone, between those physical objects which may be expected to retain their character for the time being and those which are here now and gone the next moment or in a short time. Our need to do this before we can make further progress in any kind of investigation need not be elaborated.

It may be held that primitive man or the infant carries out this inductive process by instinct or hereditary mental reaction. It is not necessary to dispute this. Hume has enlarged at great length on this innate tendency. He may have been psychologically correct in regarding this tendency as essentially an unreasoning one, although it would be unwise to be dogmatic on this matter. But what Hume did not recognize was that this alleged innate disposition has a general tendency towards suggesting conclusions, which is, by and large, consilient with correct logical processes. Bradley referred in sarcastic terms to the rôle ascribed by contemporary inductive logicians to 'primitive credulity'. 'Sudden at this crisis and in pity of distress, there leaves the heaven with rapid wing, a Goddess — Primitive Credulity. Breathing in the ear of the bewildered infant she whispers "the thing which has happened once will happen once more. Sugar was sweet, and sugar will be sweet." And Primitive Credulity is accepted forthwith as the mistress of our lives.' The story proceeds to narrate the cruel disillusionment of the child and its recognition of the gross deceptiveness of the goddess. No doubt the unmodified application of primitive credulity would lead to many false results ; at most we only claim probability for its conclusions, and those have often to be modified by considerations springing from other forms of inductive argument. But in its general tendency primitive credulity is a trustworthy guide ; if early man did indeed depend on it in default of reason, that was fortunate ; he was thereby enabled to furnish himself with many correct conclusions which facilitated the subsequent emergence of a more fully conscious reasoning process. We have continued to rely to a great extent on simple induction.

2. Simple induction plays a primary part in the process by which we justify ourselves in giving credence to our memories. This will be fully expounded in a later chapter. It is clear that we cannot proceed far in any inductive process without the information provided in memory. Here again, if primitive man trusted his memory by innate disposition rather than by reason, this was a fortunate tendency, which we may now justify *ex post* on logical grounds ; without it the species could hardly have survived. Since we cannot make progress in inductive reasoning without being able to rely, in part at least, on the informativeness of memory, it occurred to me that a vindication of memory should be undertaken in an opening chapter in any Treatise on Induction. If one was guided by the temporal order of the evolution of knowledge, it would certainly be correct to do so. But the order required by logic is different. The vindication of memory involves the use of various logical methods ; accordingly these have to be expounded first. They can best be expounded by citing illustrations in which we have to draw on information provided by memory. Simple induction yielding significant results clearly

requires memory, since the length of continuities occurring within a specious present is too short to give us extrapolations of significant duration and probability. It is to be observed, however, that although we could not make much use of induction without the aid of informative memory, the validity of the inductive process itself is not dependent upon the informativeness of memory. A method for advancing knowledge might be quite valid, and yet in certain kinds of world quite unusable. The principles of induction are 'L-true' and do not, therefore, depend upon an empirical fact such as the informativeness of memory. If we had no memories to rely on, the principles of induction would still be correct, but, unhappily, largely useless. But it would be difficult to expound those principles without illustrations, and accordingly in these early chapters I assume that memory is informative. When the principles have been expounded, it will be possible to use them to show how the hypothesis that memory is informative can be established as highly probable.

3. It seems likely that simple induction is in constant current use, albeit implicitly and without drawing attention to itself, in conjunction with other inductive methods, both in matters of everyday life and even in scientific research. We may make recondite researches against a background of assumptions that certain accepted features of the environment, and indeed of our tools of research themselves, remain constant during the research. We do not have to re-examine everything that might be relevant at every stage. It seems probable that some of these background assumptions rest on simple induction only ; they merge into those referred to in the next paragraph.

4. I now come to the field for simple induction that is the most important from the present point of view which we have as sophisticated people. All statements about the future depend on simple induction, and on that only. It will in due course be seen that other forms of induction only justify inference from the known to the unknown within the range of possible observation ; but the future lies outside that range. For opinions about the future we have to depend directly on the Principle of Experience itself ; we argue that, things having been thus and thus for a shorter or longer time, they

are likely to continue to be so. It has been shown that this argument is a valid one. There are two consequences of this, one negative and one positive.

(1) It clips the wings of our presumption. In the nineteenth century there was some tendency for scientists to claim that they had discovered for certain the immutable and eternal laws of nature. Nothing of this sort can be allowed. In accordance with our analysis extremely high probability can be claimed for a continuance of such laws of nature for a moderate period ahead ; but if we essay a vast extrapolation forwards through countless ages, the probability of our being correct dwindles and wanes, and finally falls to a negligible quantity. Now scientists using inductive methods other than simple induction may be able to infer with exceedingly high probability that certain laws of nature have been operating within their range of observation ; in establishing their findings they may be able to bring into play, in accordance with probability theory, high factorial numbers and high powers of numbers, yielding supra-astronomical odds in favour of their laws. I shall use this word 'supra-astronomical' from time to time. I understand that modern scientists have calculated that our finite universe consists of a number of atoms of the order 10^{78}. Any odds greatly in excess of this number in favour of an alleged fact or law I shall call 'supra-astronomical' ; in such cases we may be deemed to have practical certainty. This may seem to be claiming too much on behalf of the scientists, in view of such revisions of theory as have recently occurred in relation to Newtonian physics. But the laws supported by such high odds should always, if properly stated, be subject to fine limits of tolerance, and the relativity correction for phenomena formerly within our range of observation presumably lies within these limits. Furthermore, it will be seen that there are never very high odds in favour of a law without exception ; but there may be exceedingly high odds in favour of a generalization allowing only exceptions so rare as to be negligible. Now high odds of this kind can never be claimed in favour of simple inductions, where we cannot bring high factorial numbers or high powers of numbers into play. Accordingly we can never have inference amounting to practical certainty concerning a substantial length of future time.

A sharp distinction must be drawn between the assurance we are entitled to feel in regard to laws governing phenomena which, although unobserved, are within our range of observations, and the assurance we are entitled to feel in regard to alleged laws operating in a more or less remote future.

We may, however, have quite high assurance, satisfactory enough for all practical purposes, in regard to the near future. If we are satisfied that certain laws have been operating for hundreds of millions of years, the formula of simple induction gives an exceedingly high probability that they will continue during our lifetime, and quite good probability that they will continue for a considerable period thereafter. Beyond that we cannot go. The question may be raised here how far into the past our knowledge extends. This can only be dealt with very cursorily here. I assume that we can trust human testimony and records. This trust itself depends upon a kind of inductive inference to be discussed later,[1] for which, in certain cases, very high probabilities may be established. A vital distinction must be drawn between opinions about the past that are merely the result of extrapolating backwards, and those due to 'traces of antiquity' present in our midst. Opinions about the past that are merely due to our supposing that because things have been such and such during the period of human observation they have probably been similar for an indefinite period backwards, only have the probability that pertains to simple inductions ; they are fully as dubious as similar opinions about the future.

'Traces of antiquity' are an altogether different matter. Here the case is that certain present facts, e.g. stellar orbits, agree with the hypothesis that certain simple laws have been operating for a very long time. It may be possible, in accordance with certain principles to be explained in a later chapter on simplicity, to establish an exceedingly high probability for such a hypothesis. We may then take the highly probable hypothesis of long duration as the premise of a simple induction extrapolating those laws into the future. We can assess a probability for future continuance by the ordinary multiplication theorem. The probability attaching to the hypothesis of the antiquity of the laws must be multiplied by the

[1] Cp. p. 85.

probability, by simple induction, of their continuance ; this may yield what for practical purposes we may regard as a very high probability for a continuance of the laws into such part of the future as is near enough to be interesting to us.

It may be observed that the early Christians have been unduly derided as simpletons for expecting a rapid 'end of the world'. They lacked information making it reasonable to suppose that the past of the universe they knew had been a very long one. Records were scanty, scientific archaeology and astronomy non-existent, and they only had the tenuous evidence provided by traditional history. The number of generations enumerated in the Gospel of St. Luke was only seventy-five. They had no reason, other than that provided by simple induction, for extrapolating the supposed existence of the universe backwards into an indefinite past ; simple induction would not have yielded any high probability for a long past. An early termination of the whole affair was, therefore, not inherently improbable. The 'traces of antiquity' that the scientists have since discovered have completely changed the situation for us now.

(2) If we surrender, as we must, the whole domain of the future to simple induction, that takes a vast load off the shoulders of other forms of induction. That load has indeed been greater than they could bear, and this may well account for the progress of inductive logic having been so much retarded. We have been asking sundry empirical methods of investigation to yield conclusions of a high probability in relation to ranges of time and space of infinite, or anyhow of indefinite, extent. The idea that our poor limited enquiries could give us information about a mighty region of unknown bounds should surely always have been very suspect. It will be indicated that there is no possibility whatever of obtaining any finite probability for a law purporting to obtain in an infinite population. We can get terrific probabilities, amounting to practical certainty about the characteristics of objects which, although not directly observed, are within our range of observation, albeit one extended by telescopes, by records, by 'traces of antiquity'. All forms of probability, other than those yielded by simple induction, are based on some such reasoning as the following : if such and such a law has not

been widely operating, it is a very curious thing that we should have come across so many examples of its operation and no contrary cases. This clearly only applies to our range of observation ; but the future is outside that range. If Newton's Laws of Motion were grossly wrong — excluding such errors within fine limits of tolerance as have been shown by the relativity correction — it is singularly curious that we have found no motions inconsistent with them through all this time and over so wide a range of observation. But suppose that Newton's Laws are destined to have a temporary reign only, and that the exceptions will be in the future ; then it is not curious at all that we have not come across them. It does not follow that we must adopt an attitude of complete scepticism toward the future, although much current logical doctrine implies that we really should ; to do so would grossly violate common sense. In this matter common sense is right ; simple induction gives us valid grounds for attaching high probability to predictions, but only if these are sufficiently circumspect.

When we have taken this great load of requirements off the forms of induction other than simple induction, it will appear that the task that is then left will be more manageable. Many of the traditional difficulties can be overcome. We shall, however, need a considerable reorientation of our thoughts.

It is now time to address ourselves to the postulate required for conditional simple induction. First it is expedient to explain and reject two ways in which the postulate might be defended.

1. Some might be inclined to claim boldly that the postulate is merely an application to the case in point of the Law of Large Numbers. We have already had illustrations of this in the case of dice, where it is claimed that a so-called 'unbiased' die will in the long run tend to show each of its facets an approximately equal number of times, and that, where there is bias owing to defects in manufacturing processes, the resultant biases will in the long run be equally distributed among the six facets. The case of the observation of continuities might seem to be similar ; it would accordingly be claimed that our occasional queries about the future lengths of continuities would have a so-called 'random' distribution over their respective lengths, and that consequently in the long run they would be equi-proportionately distributed over those

lengths. That is the postulate that we require ; but it is to be feared that the Law of Large Numbers is unacceptable as a logical foundation. We cannot regard this Law as a universal law of nature *a priori*. If we attribute an equi-proportionate distribution in various classes of case, we can properly do that only as a result of experience, and not prior to it. It is true that we have found this class of case to be rather widely disseminated, and we are accordingly favourably disposed, by a kind of reasoning that will be discussed later, to accept new candidates for entry into the class with a less intensive testing of their claims than would otherwise be necessary. This is a matter about which we may still hope to get greater understanding by a careful examination of the other known properties of the whole class of cases in which the Law of Large Numbers is found to operate. It would be premature and dangerous to include the case of occasional enquiries about continuities in the class at this stage. If further investigation of the characteristics of that class give us grounds for doing so, that will be all to the good. We cannot claim good grounds at present.

2. There is quite a different type of justification which is frequently adduced. It will appear in due course that this postulate is one of a class of similar postulates used in empirical reasoning. The following type of argument in favour of the whole class has been adopted. Empirical reasoning has yielded good results ; this success serves to validate any postulates that are required for it. This argument is unacceptable, because circular. Professor Braithwaite has, in a notable passage ,[1] made a heroic attempt to break this circularity. I remain unconvinced by his reasoning. The success of empirical methods is said to justify the use of the postulates implied by them, in the sense that if we continue to use those methods and thereby to imply those postulates, we shall continue to have success. This argument implies that our *experience* of success in empirical methods is a ground for expecting a continuation of success ; it implies, in fact, that *experience* is a good guide. We are here asked to use a certain principle of argument, namely that experience is a good guide, in order to justify a postulate that is required if that principle of argument is to be correct. In fine, the postulate is used in order to justify

[1] *Scientific Explanation*, pp. 274-92.

the postulate ; this is irretrievably circular. The point may perhaps be seen more clearly if put negatively. Let us suppose that empirical methods had in fact yielded no success. Would this tend to invalidate the postulate used in empirical methods ? Clearly not. It could only be argued from our negative results in using empirical methods to our being likely to continue to have negative results, if the postulate required for arguing from experience is correct. But if it is correct, we are not likely to continue to have negative results. (A finite number of negative results could always be attributed not to faultiness in the method, but to an improbable run of bad luck.) If the postulate is not correct, then the negative results that we have had give no pointer either way in regard to future success. Thus whether the results are negative or not could make no difference to the probability of success in future. Consequently whether the results are negative or not could have no bearing on the truth of the postulate.

The postulate for conditional simple induction, as presented so far, has been stated in what may be called its strong form : this is the postulate that in a large number of cases the occasional enquiries about the further continuance of various continuities will be equi-proportionately distributed over the sectors of all continuities taken together. One may also state the postulate in a weaker form, namely that occasional enquiries about the further continuance of continuities will not be discernibly biased towards the latter end of continuities. The strong postulate yields precise probability numbers for conditional simple inductions. If only the weak postulate obtains, it would be impossible to substantiate these precise numbers ; but if there was no discernible bias towards the latter end of continuities the method of simple induction would not be frustrated. Conditional simple induction would no longer yield precise probability numbers, but we could show that on average the values of the numbers obtainable on the strong postulate would not be substantially reduced. For conditional simple induction to be frustrated altogether there would have to be a strong and consistent bias towards the latter end of continuities. The degree and extensiveness of the probabilities that we can obtain by assuming the strong postulate to hold is a mirror-image of the amount of the bias that would be necessary to frustrate induction. I can only claim to justify the postulate in its weak form.

The range of application of conditional simple induction may be divided into two parts, namely (1) its application to date and (2) its application from now onwards.

Let us consider first its application in the former range. The justification for the postulate within this range is a very simple one ; it has been found in our experience to be true. We have not found, as a matter of plain fact, that no sooner do we notice some continuity than it presently comes to an end. This treatment of the postulate for conditional simple induction within the range defined is different from the treatment that it will be possible to accord to similar postulates that are required for other forms of induction. In the latter case no claim will be made to establish the postulates ; the eventual claim will be that they are unnecessary. The reason for this difference of treatment is as follows. In the case of experienced continuities the probability class has, subject to exceptions mentioned below, been subsequently explored in full ; the continuities have come to an end *ex post*. We can, therefore, look back on the situation as a whole ; we have in the final state what is called in traditional logic a complete enumeration. In those kinds of induction, on the contrary, where we are arguing from a sample to a larger population, we may never see, and usually never do see, the unobserved members of the population *ex post* : we never reach a complete enumeration of the class. Consequently we cannot say *ex post* whether the observed samples have been representative or not. But in the case of continuities we eventually see the whole class. The purpose of simple induction is to give us advance information before the continuity comes to an end ; when a number of continuities have done so, we can look back and see whether on the whole our sporadic enquiries have been discernibly biased. It is certain that we have not found so great a bias as to frustrate the purposes of induction.

We have not got a fully complete enumeration because a number of continuities are not yet ended. Their continuance into the present makes the general argument, derivable from continuities not having tended to end so soon after enquiry as to frustrate induction, hold *a fortiori*.

It may be argued that our knowledge now, making the retrospect we are able to make, is greater than the knowledge available when the postulate was first used in making conditional simple inductions. It may well be that some of the inductions made in early stages, although justified *ex post*, could not have been justified at the time that they were made ; and it may accordingly be said that this is a poor sort of justification. Here again we have an example of how fortunate man has been — but according to Darwin this was not altogether an accident — in his hereditary dispositions. He may have been inclined to place a greater reliance than was justified upon the postulate required for conditional simple induction ; thereby he had success. It is only in retrospect that we can see that the required postulate was true.

2. Next we have to take the question of the application of the postulate required for conditional simple induction from now onwards. This may be justified by *unconditional* simple induction. Our retrospect indicates that we have been travelling for many generations over vast ages in a universe in which the postulate required for conditional simple induction has held, anyhow in its weak form. By unconditional simple induction we are not likely to be on the extreme edge of such an experience. The reason why unconditional simple induction, rather than conditional simple induction, can be applied in this case is that the query whether the continuity in question, namely the continuance of the postulate required for conditional simple induction, would continue, has been continuously implicit from the first beginning of our reasoning powers. In all the particular predictions we have made, and we have been making them continuously, we have asserted as our major premise that experience is a good guide. We may not have rightly understood *why* it is a good guide ; that point has already been dealt with. But that we have relied on it continuously as a guide, and not merely sporadically, is evident. To hold experience to be a good guide is to affirm the postulate required for conditional simple induction, at least in its weak form. Thus we may regard our present belief that the weak postulate will continue to hold for the time being as a member of the class of cases arising on this one continuity, namely the class of beliefs, stretching throughout the whole period of our

predictive life, that experience is a good guide. If we always believe that we are not on the extreme edge of that class of cases, we shall be right much more often than we are wrong ; this is what we mean in saying that it is probably correct to trust experience ; that holds at present, as at other times.

It might be objected that, having summarily rejected the argument from experience in favour of experience, I have now reasserted it in a new form. This is not so. The argument rejected was the argument from the *success* of experience. The argument now presented has two arms : on the one side it relies on unconditional simple induction, which is 'L-true' and does not lean on experience ; on the other it relies, *not* on the success of experience, but on certain observed facts in experience, namely the lack of discernible bias in our en-quiries towards the latter end of continuities in cases where the continuities have subsequently come to an end. The difference between relying on the success of empirical methods and relying on certain observed facts will come out very strongly when we have to deal with the postulate *prima facie* required for sampling. If we could rely simply on the success of sampling methods in the past, we could accept the postulate required for sampling without more ado ; we shall reject that argument as circular. Nor shall we be able to dispose of the postulate required for sampling in the way that we have dis-posed of the postulate required for conditional simple induc-tion ; for, unlike continuities, the populations about which we make sampling inferences are not usually eventually pre-sented to us *in toto*.

It may be well at the close of this chapter to restate in popular words the essential nature of the principle of experience on which all science and all common-sense knowledge depend. If we are crossing an expanse, but know not what part of it we have reached, we are unlikely to be on its extreme edge ; when we say that this is 'unlikely' what we mean precisely is that if we always believe that we are on its extreme edge, we shall much more often be wrong than right ; and conversely.

CHAPTER IV

INVERSE PROBABILITY

WE saw that simple induction might be characterized in popular language by saying that if one is proceeding over an extension, but one has no clue as to which part of it one is on, then one is unlikely to be on its extreme edge. This can be brought into relation with our definition of probability by saying that if in those circumstances one believes that one is on the extreme edge, one will much more often be wrong than right, and conversely. This principle is the ground of all our varied expectations in regard to the future ; we rightly assume that for the time being the order of events will proceed on the lines that we have been used to heretofore.

It may be well at this point to give a similar popular characterization of other forms of induction. It is always dangerous to make a universal proposition, and I accordingly only make this one provisionally. It appears to me that all forms of induction, other than simple, have the following general pattern. If property Q is not in fact almost always conjoined with property P, is it not a very curious thing that out of all the thousands, perhaps hundreds of thousands, of times that P has been seen, it has always been seen to be conjoined with Q ? Or again, if a certain law does not generally hold in certain defined circumstances, is it not a very curious thing that out of all the thousands, perhaps hundreds of thousands, of cases in which those circumstances have been observed, there has never been a case when the law did not hold ? It is our next task to establish that the common-sense tendency to regard this evidence as favourable to the hypothesis that P is usually conjoined with Q or that the law in question usually holds in the circumstances specified is logically correct. If this is the essential nature of the inductive arguments to be considered, it is clear that the generalizations induced only hold for the range from which the observations have been drawn. If the exceptions to the conjunction or to the law all lie outside the range, it is not at all curious that they have not been observed. The whole of the future is clearly outside the range ; hence it is satisfactory that these forms of reasoning are not required to vouchsafe information about the future, and that our expectations in regard to the future are already looked after by the principle of simple induction. It will have been observed that the popular account was stated negatively. I believe that a great majority of all valid opinions in probability are essentially based on the improbability of their contradictories.

The first reaction of experts in probability theory might be that there is an element of truth in the popular views that have just been characterized, but that they cannot be proved correct or accepted, unless we postulate that there is some prior probability for the hypothesis that P is regularly conjoined with Q. The popular reaction to such a claim would be immediate and negative. What on earth has any such prior probability got to do with the case ? The ordinary man sees no reason whatever for dragging in an assumption about prior probability ; it appears to him to be altogether unconnected with the logical cogency of the experience. It is our task to show that the popular reaction in this sense is sound.

If this characterization of forms of induction other than simple induction is correct, these forms of induction consist in a process of sampling in the broadest sense of that term. We take our observations to be representative of a wider range of unobserved facts. In what follows the word 'sampling' will be used in this very broad sense ; it is to be distinguished from sampling in the narrower sense intended in technical 'sampling theory'. The last-mentioned theory is concerned with induction by simple enumeration in its purest form, but the theory of sampling in the broader sense may cover situations in which the proximate method of enquiry is somewhat different ; for instance it covers the case where an opinion carrying a very high degree of probability may be based on a single laboratory experiment. This is clearly far removed from the theory of sampling in the narrow sense, yet it rests indirectly, in a way that will later be described, on the general theory of sampling. Sampling in the narrow sense again

subdivides into two distinct classes. In some cases it is designed to ascertain and establish a statistical frequency in
nature. Sampling in the narrow sense, however, is by no
means always, and perhaps not even usually, directed to this
purpose; it is more often directed to test whether among
phenomena subject to various influences an alleged causal
factor is operating. I use the word 'cause' reluctantly and in
a special sense; it is a main contention of this volume that
our knowledge gained by induction does not and cannot entail
the view that there are any inner necessities in nature; by
the operation of a 'cause' in this context it is merely meant
that the form of sampling investigation in question is directed
to establish a generalization, viz. that, where a certain phenomenon P is present, Q is usually present also; this kind of
purpose of a sampling enquiry is to be sharply distinguished
from that of establishing a statistical frequency.

Returning to sampling in the wider sense, I propose to
give an example of opinions in probability that spring up at
an early stage in man's enquiry about the world around him;
these opinions are almost coeval with the earliest forms of
simple induction, they are rightly held to be of very high
probability, amounting to practical certainty, and they are the
necessary prerequisite for further investigation. I refer to the
opinions that the world around us consists of what we think
of as durable physical bodies. This group of opinions is
familiar enough; it may be summarized by such statements
as that, if we shut our eyes and open them again, we shall
find all as before; if we make bodily movements the phenomena presented to us will undergo certain perspectival changes
in accordance with a regular system of principles; if we walk
forward in one direction then turn through two right angles
and walk forward again, we shall find phenomena similar to
those just experienced appearing in the reverse order.

This group of opinions has been the subject of famous
philosophical controversy. I must touch on this, albeit very
briefly, in order to isolate the logical problem involved. The
philosophical problem comprises, and often confuses, two
quite distinct problems, which, on a broad interpretation, may
be associated respectively with the names of Berkeley and
Hume, and which may be called respectively the metaphysical

problem and the logical problem. We are not concerned with
the former, and need only characterize it at this stage, in order
to get it out of the way. By a free hand interpretation, and
without any claim to strict textual criticism, the Berkeley
position may be summarized as follows : if it is desired to
give a comprehensive description of the world, this may be
done by enumerating all the experiences that conscious beings
have and by a series of hypotheticals of the form that, if a
conscious being moves in a certain way or proceeds in a
certain direction, he will have such and such an experience.
It is held that this description of the material world is exhaustive
and that nothing more can be said. As against this, the realists
contend that we must suppose there to be permanently existing
bodies, which support and give grounds for the series of hypotheticals. The battle is then joined. The strongest argument
on the Berkeley side is fundamentally that of Occam, namely
that we should not postulate entities unnecessarily ; it is held
that these supposed physical bodies are unnecessary, because
everything could in principle be described by the aforementioned hypotheticals without reference to bodies, and, furthermore, it may be added — in conformity with modern tendencies
— that the statements purporting to refer to them are meaningless, since everything that can be said by way of description
of them is already contained, directly or indirectly, in the
hypotheticals. When we are asked to characterize them
further, we can point to no evidence, actual or possible, that
would support or go against the hypothesis that any further
characteristics exist. On the other side it appears intellectually
repulsive to suppose that the Universe turns itself on and
off, like an electric light, in accordance with the whims of
sundry people as they stroll about. This is what I call
the metaphysical problem and I shall say nothing more on it
here.

The logical problem is altogether different. The Berkeley
description in its barest form includes the hypothetical that if
I return to my study at any time, I shall have certain visual
and tactual experiences in accordance with the normal configuration of that study. This gives rise to a logical problem.
Why do we hold that that hypothetical is a true account of
the matter ? How do I know that if I retrace my steps, the

study will in fact show up in its usual form ? We exclude the possibility that it may have caught fire, etc. Why is there a presumption that, even in the absence of such external influences, it will be there at all ? The answer given is that this accords with experience, that, whenever I have retraced my steps, it has always been there. But what about those lapses of time when I did not revisit it ? How do I know that, had I revisited it at certain times when I did not revisit it, I should not have found it altogether absent ? This is the problem with which Hume was mainly concerned. It is quite independent of the interpretation given to the belief that my study is there all the time : it does not matter for this purpose whether that belief means merely that, if I went back to it at any time whatever I should have certain sensations, or that there are certain physical bodies that are there all the time. The choice between these two interpretations is irrelevant to the logical problem, which is simply the question what reasons there are for supposing the belief in the continued existence of the room to be correct, whichever way we interpret it. If I returned to my room one day and found nothing where the room usually is, I should certainly not be content to regard this as a merely metaphysical matter. Hume considered this question and concluded that there are in fact no rational grounds for this belief, but that it merely arises from a natural tendency of the mind, which likes to run along in uniform grooves and to fill up any gaps by positing — without logical warrant — the continuing existence of similar objects.

In fact we have here an instance of induction by sample. If my study really lapses from existence from time to time, what a very curious thing it is that I should never have struck it at one of those times. Similar arguments apply to all the familiar objects around us. In the normal course of our coming and going, we get a very large sample of the objects in the near neighbourhood, and by an ordinary induction of the sampling kind — the logic of which has still to be explained — we can get odds of supra-astronomical magnitude in favour of the opinion that the study and similar physical objects are almost always there. We cannot get very high odds in favour of the view that they are absolutely always there ; the odds against a single lapse for the minimum discernible time are no more than the ratio of the time spent in the study to the time not spent in the study. We may later reinforce our opinion that the room is always there by wider evidence drawn from a still larger sample in favour of such a principle as the conservation of energy. Direct sampling yields odds amounting to practical certainty that the room and similar physical objects are there almost all the time, subject only to exceptions that are so very rare as to be negligible.

Supra-astronomical odds can only be obtained in favour of objects within a near environment. For this purpose it is important to establish an 'origin' from which observations radiate outwards. On several occasions in his *Treatise on Probability* Keynes, rejecting the Uniformity of Nature as an obscure or useless principle, affirms that the only element of truth that he can find in it is the view that variety of position in time and space can be taken to be irrelevant in an inductive argument. This strikes me as diametrically opposed to the truth. A fixed spatio-temporal origin gives an indispensable starting-point for a valid sampling process ; it gives meaning to the notion of range of observations. Man's sociological habit of having at least a temporarily fixed habitat was probably of the utmost value in enabling him to acquire well-founded views about the stability of his environment. A being that wandered aimlessly and discontinuously on an uncharted course through space would have much greater difficulty in taking the first steps towards establishing by a sampling process the stability of physical objects.

It is true that in certain defined classes of cases, for instance those investigated by physicists and chemists, we may eventually come to acquire the opinion that certain types of concomitance of characters or certain types of law are independent of time and space throughout the wide universe of our most extended observations ; but these opinions are the result of experience and observation, and not the other way round. To retain the principle of the irrelevance of spatio-temporal position as something rescued from a supposed first principle of the Uniformity of Nature would be to imply that this irrelevance is a necessary presupposition of induction ; on the contrary, where such irrelevance is to be assumed, that can only be as the result of induction. In some matters, such as the pigmentation of animals or human veracity, the assumption of spatio-temporal irrelevance may easily lead to error.

In regard to the durability of physical bodies we can in due course enlarge the range of our opinion by relying on the testimony of others. The credibility of such testimony can only be established gradually and is itself an inference of sampling induction. Here again we eventually accumulate a very large sample and can establish high odds in favour. Some might hold that human testimony is often disappointing; but we may proceed in this sampling by a discrimination between the subject matters of testimony; we may find great unreliability on such subjects as sex; but for testimony on such subjects as whether a place called London is there all the time or not, we find by sampling — that is by putting reports to the test of verification from time to time — a considerable degree of reliability. And so we may comprise within our range of observation those matters on which we have reports and records.

We must now approach the task of examining this sampling process. The characteristic example is of this form. On the hypothesis that my room is almost always there — whether in the sense of Berkeley or the realists matters not — it is quite probable that I shall always find it there when I direct my steps in the way defined, the definition in question relating to what is meant by 'there'. On the hypothesis that my room is often not there, in the sense that I should not find it on tracing my steps to it, it is highly improbable — supra-astronomically improbable if my visits are fairly frequent — that I shall always find it there. I do always find it there. It is desired to infer that the hypothesis that it is almost always there is more probable than the hypothesis that it is quite often not there. Can this desire be met? What is logically implied in agreeing to this conclusion?

Let us reconsider this in relation to the concomitance of the properties P and Q. On a hypothesis that P is almost always conjoined with Q, it is probable that every P observed will be accompanied by Q. On the hypothesis that P is not almost always conjoined with Q it will by direct probability theory, that is by deduction, be improbable — perhaps very improbable, this depending upon the size of the sample — that every P observed will be conjoined with Q. Every P observed is found to be conjoined with Q. It is desired to infer that the hypothesis that P is almost always conjoined with Q is more probable than the hypothesis that P is not so frequently conjoined with Q. It is to be noted that in each of the first two premises we have a hypothesis giving rise to a probability. The third premise consists of an observation. We wish to argue from the observation to the superior probability of one hypothesis as against the other, which may be simply its contradictory. The premises are probabilities that are entailed by or contained in hypotheses together with a bare fact. By what logical process can we proceed to set up a probability for one or other of the hypotheses ? This is certainly what we seek to do. It is my contention that this essential situation occurs in all processes of induction other than simple induction. I would coin a phrase for this key step in the argument, if it is not presumptuous in so well worn a subject, and call it 're-versing the consequents'. It is this essential step that now has to be examined with the utmost rigour.

The situation points to the use of an argument in inverse probability of the general type that springs from the Bayes formulation ; but that formulation requires the assumption of prior probabilities for the hypotheses under consideration and in the general case these are not available for us. Consequently this type of approach must be rejected as a method of rescuing us from initial nescience, and an alternative must be found.

The following argument contains three stages. The first stage will consist in the definition of a postulate. The second stage will consist in a precise analysis of what is involved in 'reversing the consequents'. The third stage will consist in showing that the postulate is unnecessary.

1. I propose to construct what I shall call a 'sample line'. The construction is specifically designed for the argument in hand, has rather special features, and must accordingly be followed carefully. To make the argument clear it will be helpful to use concrete numbers. Let a sample line be constructed to illustrate the hypothesis that in a total population of P's 95 per cent have Q. It is desirable to give warning at the outset that, although the sample line is constructed on the basis of the hypothesis that 95 per cent of P's have Q, it is designed to point to the conclusion that *more than* 95 per cent

of P's have Q. Incidentally this type of argument has no
direct relation to an argument seeking to establish a statistical
frequency. All samples *of a given size* that exist in a population
in which 95 per cent of the P's have Q are to be assigned a
certain space upon the sample line. This line is to accommo-
date what Professor Braithwaite has called an 'omni-selectional
hyper-class'.[1] The samples are to be sorted out into kinds as
follows : every sample in which all the P's have Q is of one kind,
every sample in which all the P's except one have Q is of
another kind, etc. The space to be assigned to each *kind* of
sample is to be proportional to the number of samples of that
kind. Thus a kind of sample of a certain size, the number of
whose constituent samples consists of one-thousandth part of
the number of all the samples of that size in the population,
is to have one-thousandth part of the line.

Now this allocation of space on the line cannot be determined unless we know, not only the size of the sample, but
also the size of the total population. In certain cases of
sampling, the size of the total population may be guessed within
sufficiently near limits. In the case of the existence of my study
it is known definitely ; the total 'population' there is simply
the whole duration of time within which my various visits
have occurred. There are cases, however, where we have not
such information and we may not be content with a mere
guess. The proportions of space on the line to be assigned
to each kind of sample tend to become stable in the limit, as
the population increases toward infinity ; let us assume an
infinite population. This assumption may be regarded as the
most conservative possible assumption, in the sense that it is
the one most unfavourable to the view which it is desired to
establish, namely that more than 95 per cent of P's probably
have Q. It is thus the safest assumption. But it must be
noted that making this assumption does *not* imply that any
argument can be developed by sampling in regard to the
probable composition of a population of infinite size. The
tendency towards stability at the limit in the proportions of
the line to be assigned to the various kinds of samples has no
doubt been responsible for the notion that it is possible to
obtain by sampling a probability for a certain composition of

[1] In the terminology of Professor D. Williams, a 'hyper-population'.

an infinite population. This is a fallacy. The reason why it is not legitimate to argue from the stability of ratios in the limit to the probability of the composition of an infinite population is that the argument from sampling only applies to what lies within the range of observation, and an infinite population cannot lie within the range of observation.

The sample line is constructed to throw light on the opinion that *more* than 95 per cent of P's have Q. If we obtain a satisfactory result we can proceed to construct a sample line for all samples on the hypothesis that 99 per cent of P's have Q, in order to throw a light on the hypothesis that *more* than 99 per cent of P's have Q. We can then construct a 99.9 per cent line and so on. Note that we are concerned here with establishing a generalization asserting a regular con- comitance, not with establishing a statistical frequency. The words 'more than', which are inserted in each case, are tell- tale in this respect. They are a reflexion of the words 'at least' referred to in an earlier passage as likely to recur wherever probability theory is used to aid induction.

Samples are to be placed on the line in the following order. Those least helpful to the hypothesis that more than 95 per cent of P's have Q are to be placed on the extreme left. Here will come the group of samples in which no P's have Q. Next to this group will be the group of samples in which only one P has Q. And so on towards the right. On the extreme right- hand will be the samples in which all P's have Q.

Draw a line containing all kinds of samples of 540 members each drawn from an infinite population. On this line there will be approximately a billion samples (in the English sense of billion, viz. twelve os) in which at least one P lacks Q for every sample in which all P's have Q. Consequently the whole group of samples in which all P's have Q will occupy about one billionth part of the whole line at the extreme right-hand end.[1]

---

[1] The probability that in a sample of 540, drawn from an infinite popu- lation, in which 95 per cent of the P's have Q, all the P's will have Q, namely the number of samples in which all P's have Q as a fraction of all samples of 540, can be found by the formula, $^{n}C_p \times \left(\dfrac{95}{100}\right)^{p} \times \left(\dfrac{5}{100}\right)^{n-p}$, where n is the number of items in the sample (540) and p is the number of items in the sample having Q (also 540 in this case). Since $n = p$ this reduces to $\left(\dfrac{95}{100}\right)^{540} = \dfrac{1}{1,080,000,000,000}$.

Sample Line

(Sample : 540.   Population : infinite)

Sample line drawn on hypothesis that 95 per cent of P's have Q. To each *kind* of sample is assigned a length on the line proportional to the number of its members. The kinds are arranged from left to right in ascending order of the number of their members having Q ; thus the group on the extreme left consists of samples in which no P has Q ; in the next group of samples one P in each sample has Q, etc.

The thick section represents all samples in which all P's have Q.   It constitutes $\dfrac{1}{1,080,000,000,000}$th part (approx.) of the whole line.

It is now possible to define the postulate required for induction by sampling ; it may be called a postulate of 'fair' sampling. Note, however, that this does not mean that it is postulated that any given sample is fair. If we postulated that our samples were fair, we should obtain certainty about an unobserved empirical fact by an inductive process ; for we could attribute the frequency of Q in our sample to the population as a whole. The postulate is not that any given sample is fair, but that on a long run of experience our sample of samples is fair. The postulate is that, taking the class of all the samples that we consider for their evidential value, *these will be equally distributed among the sectors* of the sample lines as drawn. This is clearly analogous to our postulate for conditional simple induction, namely that in an experience of many continuities the occasions of interrogation concerning their further continuance are equiproportionately dispersed over the sectors of the continuities.[1] But the sampling postulate, unlike that for simple induction, will not later be vindicated, but will be withdrawn as being unnecessary. In a population in which 95 per cent of P's have Q there are a billion samples of 540 in which at least one P lacks Q for

[1] Sectors, as before, mean equal parts, which may be made as small as we please.

every one sample of 540 in which all P's have Q ; consequently, on the postulate that our sample of samples is fair, if we are confronted with many populations in which 95 per cent of P's have Q, we shall only come across a sample of 540 in which all P's have Q once for every billion times that we come across a sample of 540 in which at least one P lacks Q.

I propose to use the word 'deceptive' in this argument. It will be used by definition in relation to a specified hypothesis, and it will apply only to a group or groups of samples ranging from a certain point on the line to the extreme right-hand end. A sample will be said to be a billionfold deceptive in relation to the hypothesis on which a sample line has been drawn, if the group on the extreme right, or any other group along with other groups to the right of it, only occupies one-billionth part of the sample line. Thus a sample of 540 in which all P's have Q would be a billionfold deceptive in relation to the hypothesis that in the whole population only 95 per cent of P's have Q. The meaning of calling it deceptive is that, if it is true that in the population only 95 per cent of P's have Q, there are a billion samples in which at least one P lacks Q for every one sample in which no P lacks Q. Samples in which not more than one P lacks Q are more frequent, in fact about 28 times as frequent, as the samples in which no P lacks Q. Such samples would accordingly be about 35 thousand millionfold deceptive in relation to the hypothesis that only 95 per cent of P's have Q in the total population. In reckoning the deceptiveness of the sample in which one P lacks Q, one should reckon in all the samples to the right of it on the line — in this case the samples in which no P lacks Q. This gives a further indication that no direct use of the argument we are considering can be made for establishing a statistical frequency.

2. We are now approaching the innermost core of the problem of induction, namely the crucial step of 'reversing the consequents'. So far we have established by means of a postulate that we shall in a long range of experience only come across a billionfold deceptive sample once for every billion times that we come across less deceptive samples of that size. If on a certain hypothesis a certain sample before us is a

billionfold deceptive, we are confronted with something which, starting with that hypothesis, we should pronounce in advance to be very improbable. We then seek release, so to say, from this improbability by rejecting the hypothesis, *i.e.* the hypothesis that 95 per cent of P's have Q, and by substituting for it some other hypothesis, such as that 99.99 per cent of P's have Q, according to which what has happened would be less improbable. We want to transfer the improbability of what has happened on the assumption of a certain hypothesis on to the hypothesis itself, and to say that some other hypothesis, on which what has happened would be less improbable, is more probable. Are we entitled to do this ?

I now supply a new definition. I call a sample a billionfold 'suggestive' of frequent concomitance, if it would be a billionfold deceptive in relation to a hypothesis specifying a definite frequency of concomitance. Thus in our example the sample of 540 in which all P's have Q would be a billionfold suggestive of the frequent concomitance of P with Q, since on the hypothesis that no more than 95 per cent of P's have Q it is a billionfold deceptive, and one can only find escape from the improbability that its deceptiveness connotes by accepting a hypothesis that more than 95 per cent of P's have Q. It is to be observed that all samples that are a billionfold deceptive are also a billionfold suggestive ; but not conversely. There may be many suggestive samples which are not deceptive at all ; the sample of 540 P's all having Q is a billionfold deceptive if the hypothesis that in the whole population only 95 per cent of P's have Q is true. But it may not be true. It may be the case that in the total population all the P's have Q. In that case the billionfold suggestive sample is not deceptive at all. If a sample line were drawn in relation to a hypothesis which happened to be a true one, namely that in the total population all the P's have Q, the samples in which all P's have Q would occupy the whole extent of the sample line.

Now when we examine samples it is quite clear on the face of them whether they are suggestive or not ; to discover their degree of suggestiveness in relation to various hypotheses one draws various sample lines that are determined by those hypotheses. One may draw a sample line for the hypothesis that 95 per cent of P's have Q, or that 99.9 per cent of P's have

Q, etc. ; in relation to those hypotheses the samples in which
all P's have Q have defined degrees of deceptiveness ; their
degrees of deceptiveness are also their degrees of suggestiveness in relation to those hypotheses ; thus a sample which is
a billionfold deceptive in relation to the hypothesis that only
95 per cent of P's have Q is a billionfold suggestive in the
sense of suggesting that more than 95 per cent of P's have
Q ; all the same it may not be the case that more than 95 per
cent of P's have Q. When we look on a sample we can see
on the face of it what its degree of suggestiveness is, but what
we cannot tell is whether it is deceptive or non-deceptive. It
might easily happen in an irregular universe that all samples
suggestive in a certain degree were also deceptive in that
degree in relation to hypotheses of concomitance of more than
a certain amount ; for instance it might be the case in our
universe that no second quality Q was ever conjoined with
any first quality P as often as 95 times per 100 in any population whatever. We might, nevertheless, have samples of
540 in which all the P's had Q ; all these samples would be a
billionfold suggestive of more than 95 per cent of P's having
Q, but they would also be a billionfold deceptive, since in fact
in no case in the universe supposed do more than 95 per
cent of P's have Q. Thus in such a universe all samples that
were suggestive in relation to that hypothesis would be deceptive also. How do we know that our own universe is not
like that ? Our dilemma in induction is that while we can be
perfectly certain that a given sample has a given degree of
suggestiveness in relation to each hypothesis regarding concomitance, we cannot know whether it is deceptive or not. Its
suggestiveness appears on its face ; its deceptiveness is hidden.
This might seem to constitute an impasse.

Luckily there is something that we do know on the basis
of our postulate. We know the rate at which samples of
various degrees of deceptiveness occur among all samples
examined. We know that there are a billion less deceptive
samples for every one that is a billionfold deceptive. Our
postulate states that we shall come across billionfold deceptive
samples at the rate at which they occur, viz. not more than one
per billion times that we come across a less deceptive sample.
Now there is another piece of knowledge that we should in

principle be able to bring into relation to this piece of knowledge. We should be able to ascertain the rate at which billionfold suggestive samples are in fact occurring to us. Let us
suppose a range of investigation in which samples that are a
billionfold suggestive are occurring at the rate of one per 1000
samples. If this is so, there are odds of a 1000 million to one
in favour of any given billionfold suggestive sample being non-
deceptive. This means that there are a 1000 million to one
odds in favour of the hypothesis suggested by the billionfold
suggestive sample being true. Thus, subject to the postulate
and with the aid of a sample, we have established with certainty
odds of 1000 million to one in favour of a hypothesis. This
means that it is quite certain that if we believe a hypothesis
supported by evidence of this kind we shall be right 1000
million times for every once that we are wrong. This strikes
me as a satisfactory conclusion. We cannot get certainty, but
where the sample is large, as in the case of familiar objects,
we may achieve supra-astronomical odds.

We may revert to the definition of probability. What, in
the case of reversing the consequents, is the nature of character
A that is required in any argument in probability? The
character A justifying a conclusion in probability of the type
just described is present only when there is a combination of
two premises of the following type. (1) There must be a
sample suggestive of hypothesis H in the sense of being improbable on the hypothesis not-H. ('H' in all that follows
stands for any hypothesis suggested by a sample under consideration.) (2) This sample must belong to a class of samples
all having the same degree of suggestiveness, that are occurring
with a given frequency in our experiences. Express this frequency as 1 per x samples. If this frequency is less than the
frequency of the sample within its own hyper-population of
samples on the hypothesis not-H, then the occurrence of this
sample has *no* evidential value at all in favour of the hypothesis H — however improbable its occurrence may be on the
hypothesis not-H. If, on the other hand, the frequency of
occurrence of such samples is greater than the probability of
each sample on the hypothesis not-H, we can infer by the
sampling postulate what proportion of these suggestive samples
are non-deceptive. The rate of occurrence of deceptive samples

among samples of equal degree of suggestiveness is equal to the theoretical value of the rate of occurrence of samples of a given degree of deceptiveness divided by the actual rate of occurrence of suggestive samples of that degree of sug gestiveness. If d is the degree of deceptiveness ($\frac{1}{d}$ = probability of sample on hypothesis not-H = rate of occurrence of samples of this degree of deceptiveness among all samples of same size), and samples of this degree of suggestiveness are occurring at the rate of 1 per x samples, the rate of occurrence of deceptive samples among those suggestive samples is equal to $\frac{x}{d}$. The probability of hypothesis H is in these circumstances equal to $\left(1 - \frac{x}{d}\right)$. Where this expression is equal to o *or less*, the sample has no evidential value for hypothesis H, however improbable it may be on hypothesis not-H.

A precise number is available by deduction for the improbability of the sample on the hypothesis of not-H ; but it will rarely be possible to supply a precise number for x, which, in relation to 'reversing the consequents', may be called the 'deflator'. At best it may be possible to supply some rough order of magnitude for x. Mathematical intuition may come into play. When the odds against the occurrence of the sample on the hypothesis of not-H are very high, *e.g.* supra-astronomical or of the order of a billion to one, we do not have to bother with the deflator. The conclusion may be regarded in any case as a 'practical certainty'. Many findings in the hard sciences are of this character, and many of the findings of common sense also, such as the continued subsistence of my study during my absences — whether that be defined in a Berkleian or a realist manner. In most cases there will be considerable vagueness about the correct value for the deflator, and it is this indeterminateness that imports imprecision into many arguments in probability and is responsible for our inability to provide a precise probability number for the final conclusion. If the difficulty were only one of counting the number of items in our sample, that could be overcome by taking sufficient trouble. But to compute the rate at which suggestive samples are occurring in our broad run of experience is a much more complex matter and would involve a kind of counting that is beyond our powers. In relation to many matters of common sense this difficulty is insuperable and we have to be content with vague estimates, or indeed guesses. In scientific work methods may be devised for overcoming the difficulty.

It is to be observed that by the technique of the sample line and with the aid of the sampling postulate, which is presently to be withdrawn, we have established a probability in favour of a hypothesis, which may in favourable circumstances amount to practical certainty, *without assuming any prior probability for that hypothesis*. We have obtained complete release from the Bayes-type formulation of the inverse probability principle and rendered otiose the painstaking work of Carnap in seeking a suitable method for distributing equal initial prior probabilities among possible configurations of the universe.

Once again it is needful to draw breath. It cannot be denied that the doctrine here presented involves a formidable paradox. One of the premises required for any argument in probability that involves 'reversing the consequents' is the rate of occurrence of suggestive samples in a broad field of observation. The particular inductive argument for which knowledge of this rate is required is normally related to a particular hypothesis, let us call it H. It is here put forward that an essential premise required for giving rational credence to H is the concurrent rate of occurrence of suggestive samples ; but these other suggestive samples have, in the ordinary sense of words, nothing whatever to do with H. Thus this doctrine seems to violate a principle of logic, which might perhaps be thought to be the most fundamental principle of all : namely that evidence that taken by itself would have no bearing on the probability of H, is irrelevant to H. How can the success or non-success of quite different investigations, the suggestiveness or non-suggestiveness of samples related to hypotheses that have no connexion with H, have any bearing on the probability of H ? Yet it is vital, if we are to understand induction, that we should accept this paradox.

I must endeavour to be persuasive. Consider a scientist of remarkable persistence and longevity, and, one might add, ineptitude, who makes a billion laboratory experiments, all of negative results.

> Gaily bedight
> A gallant knight
> In sunshine and in shadow,
> Had journeyed long,
> Singing a song,
> In search of Eldorado.
>
> But he grew old —
> This knight so bold —
> And o'er his heart a shadow
> Fell as he found
> No spot of ground
> That looked like Eldorado.

At long last, having made an experiment bearing upon a proposed law of nature of the first importance, he gets a result which would be a billionfold deceptive, if the law were not true. His heart rejoices. He deems that he has found his Eldorado.

Alas, it is not so. One must adjure the good knight to examine the gold dust in his hand more carefully, and he will see that it is but common sand glistening in the sunshine. He has done a billion experiments, and it is only likely that one of these should show results that are a billion-fold deceptive. That they are a billionfold suggestive has, in these circumstances, no tendency to corroborate his hypothesis. In fine his long record of failure is relevant to the evidential value of his observations on the occasion of supposed success. The truth of this springs out clearly in the extreme case I have taken. If it is true in this case, it must be true in weaker cases also and throughout ; it is in fact a general principle that the evidential value of observations for the hypothesis that they are supposed to support depends upon the frequency with which observations of a suggestive kind are occurring within a range of experience.

If we survey the course of science since the Renaissance, we are struck by the frequency, by comparison with earlier periods, with which successful hypotheses have occurred to the minds of researchers ; the success of the corroboration in each separate case has been reinforced by the general frequency of successful corroborations. Successful corroborations may be compared with trees in a forest that protect one another ; plant one of these same trees in an exposed desert and it would not survive.

The fact that one of the premises required to give probability to a particular hypothesis is the rate of occurrence of favourable observations in general, and that, unless we are careful, the value of this rate may be a very dubious matter, points to the need for what might be called laboratory work or, where a laboratory is inappropriate, for a systematic approach to investigations, in which failures as well as successes may be duly noted, and in which the number of samples coming up for consideration may be circumscribed and defined. It is difficult for the man in the street to specify how many samples come before his notice.

In this connexion it is important to observe the danger of suggestive samples ; it must be remembered that what we know about samples of a given degree of deceptiveness on the basis of our postulate is the rate at which they occur among *all* samples ; we know nothing *a priori* about the rate at which they occur among suggestive samples. In an irregular universe the rate at which deceptive samples occur among suggestive samples may be much higher than the rate at which they occur among all samples ; it is only the latter rate that is provided by the fair sampling postulate ; consequently there will be great danger if what initially provokes a line of thought is the occurrence of a suggestive sample. The man-in-the-street is peculiarly a prey to this danger. Our universe is regular in some aspects, irregular in others. Scientists have succeeded in concentrating their attention on characteristics of it among which there is a wide prevalence of regularity, but the superficial manifestations of the universe with which the man-in-the-street is largely concerned have much irregularity. If, in this world of irregularity, he allows his train of thought to be actuated by a suggestive sample he is in danger, for an abnormally high proportion of suggestive samples, as compared with samples generally, may be deceptive.

This warning may seem out of line with the general tenor of this work, which is to claim that simple enumeration lies at the base of all inductive inference. Does not a suggestive sample make a fine beginning for a process of simple enumeration ? The answer must be in the negative. A line of thought initiated by a suggestive sample is amply vindicated when the sample gives supra-astronomical odds, prior to deflation, in favour of a generalization ; in such cases no value that could reasonably be given to the deflator would serve to reduce the probability below 'practical certainty'. We clearly do not pass in review a supra-astronomical or even an astronomical number of samples. But where the odds are lower, the danger is that the deflator may seriously reduce the probability. It is not self-contradictory to claim that simple enumeration is the basis of all induction and yet that induction will only gather momentum when enough prior knowledge has been gained to provide starting-points for fresh enquiries other than those directly suggested by simple enumeration. Where the line of thought is initiated by a suggestive sample it will be needful in estimating the correct 'deflator' not merely to take other samples that have been looked at for their evidential value, but other samples that *might equally well have been looked at*. A schoolmaster may notice that the top boy in each of his classes has red hair ; he may work out that there are considerable odds against this coincidence unless there is a fairly frequent association of cleverness and red hair in the population as a whole ; but any probability that he may get in this way will be greatly reduced by the deflator that it is appropriate to apply. This may in fact be the first time that he has given consideration to such a correlation ; but we have to take into account, in order to estimate the deflator, the various correlations he might have considered, *e.g.* that of all the other colours of hair with cleverness, that of all the different colours of eyes, that of the shape of the head, of height, size of feet, size of wrists, chest measurements, etc., and he might have sought to correlate each of all of these qualities not only with cleverness, but with athletic prowess, with neat hand-writing, with punctuality. In fine one must consider all the various correlations that he might have made of the same general kind as the one he has made and use this number to deflate the probability that he gets from his sample ; if his hypothesis is at all complex we may have to introduce factorial numbers, which are usually so helpful in establishing probability by sampling, into the deflator, where they will work against him. This applies notably to people who embark on such foolish enterprises as showing by cryptograms that Bacon wrote the plays of Shakespeare.

There has been much argument about whether one secures higher probability in favour of a hypothesis if one frames the hypothesis *before* securing observations tending to corroborate it. There has been a feeling that there is safety in having the hypothesis before one first. On the other side logicians have been up in arms, pointing out that the order of time is irrelevant, that given observations have the same evidential value in relation to a hypothesis whether they are made after or before the occurrence of the hypothesis to the investigator's mind. Up to a point this is true. But the opposite point of view, which has also been felt to have something in it, derives support from the doctrine of the deflator. If the observations come first, they may have been selected, out of a much larger number of samples available for investigation, by reason of the fact that they were suggestive; if the hypothesis is made first, that is a safeguard against the observations being selected for consideration merely because they are suggestive. If the observations attracted attention because they were suggestive, then a higher deflator has to be applied to the probability of the hypothesis which they support than would be the case if the train of thought was the other way round. Keynes gives an example (page 305) with reference to Dr. Playfair's hypothesis about the specific gravities of allotropic forms of elements; Dr. Playfair's attention was attracted by the fact that the specific gravities of three such forms of carbon were varying roots of the number 12, and was disposed to generalize to other elements. Keynes holds that such an argument starting simply by one's attention being attracted by such a concomitance is weak, and rightly so; but he gives the wrong reason, namely that the hypothesis in question has no prior probability. The real reason is that if a suggestive sample comes up for consideration merely because it catches the eye, a large deflator has to be applied to the probability which it suggests. The method of hypothesis, however, has no unique prerogative in safeguarding the investigator from the danger of suggestive samples. A predetermined plan for a series of investigations, *e.g.* the systematic investigation of the properties of certain compounds, may be quite free of any preconceived hypothesis, and yet be an equally good safeguard against the dangers of suggestive samples. If in the course of such a predetermined investigation certain concomitances or laws show up in the samples examined, that will be most welcome ; it will only be necessary to apply a small deflator, for the predetermined plan safeguards us against the danger that we have been attracted to a suggestive sample out of a much larger range of candidates for examination ; the total number of samples that need be taken into account in assessing the deflator in this case is simply the sum total of observations occurring within this particular investigation.

A further word may be said about the paradox involved in holding that the evidential value of a specific piece of evidence for a specific hypothesis depends on the rate of occurrence of pieces of evidence that have no specific bearing on the hypothesis at all, but merely a logical structure similar to the piece of evidence before us. Concentrated attention should serve to dispel the sense of paradox. For the very notion of probability contains a reference to matters other than those before us. It has been argued that it satisfies the general notion of what people mean by probability to define 'X_n is probable' as meaning that 'it does not often happen *both* to have evidence of the kind that is before us *and* for the conclusion to which it points not to be the case, and X_n is the conclusion to which the evidence before us points'.

This definition explicitly refers to evidence other than that before us, but of the same general kind, *i.e.* of the same logical structure. Consequently it should not seem strange that, in order to assess the evidential value of the evidence before us, we should have to refer to the occurrence of other bits of evidence of the same logical character, but relating to quite different hypotheses, viz. to hypotheses of different material character.

Consider the following sequence of premises :

1. It seldom happens both that one gets evidence of the logical character A_p and that what it points to is not the case.
2. I seldom get evidence of the logical character A_p.
3. I have now got a piece of evidence of the logical character A_p.

Nothing follows.

But, if we substitute for 2 above an alternative premise 2* 'I often get evidence of the logical character A_p,', from 1 and 2* together one can infer (4) that out of the times when I get evidence of logical character A_p, that to which it points is seldom not the case. Then, taking 3 and 4 together, I may infer that what the evidence before me points to is probable.

In fine, since the very word probable has a reference to a group of logically similar occasions, it should not seem surprising that its applicability in any particular case requires a reference to an actual group of such occasions (viz. those of the surrounding experience).

Before proceeding to the next and final phase of the argument, we may compare the doctrine set out in this phase with certain other views. It is when confronted with the need for reversing the consequents that traditional logic has resorted to an inverse probability principle of some kind, which, however modified and refined, stems originally from Bayes's formulation. This requires a knowledge of prior probabilities. No such knowledge is required by the doctrine that I have advanced, but we do require to know the rate at which samples of a certain general kind are appearing within a field of experience. This knowledge has work to perform in enabling us to reach a conclusion. In the Bayes-type formulation, the knowledge of prior probability has work to do. It is not to be supposed that logicians have had any relish for an assumption of initial prior probability; the apparent need for it occasioned Keynes, for example, much anxiety, and in the end he was incompletely satisfied with the arguments that he had furnished in its favour. But logicians have clearly seen that the improbability of a phenomenon X on the hypothesis not-H, and the occurrence of X, are not sufficient alone to establish the improbability of not-H; hence the prior probability of H had reluctantly to be introduced. Knowledge of the rate of occurrence of a certain kind of sample does the work that is done in the other approach by the assumption of prior probability, and accordingly makes that assumption unnecessary.

It is not to be denied that this alternative approach has its own characteristic disadvantage; it imports an element of vagueness into arguments of probability, because the rate of occurrence of kinds of samples is difficult to assess, and probably almost always impossible to assess with precision. Moreover, it introduces into a given argument considerations which *prima facie* appear irrelevant. Under the Bayes-type approach, by contrast, the argument is self-contained ; there is no reference to the extraneous question of the rate of occurrence of similar samples. The trouble about that approach is simply that the assumption of initial prior probability is unacceptable ; accordingly it will not serve in the early stages of the accumulation of knowledge. If the approach that I recommend imports an element of vagueness into the argument, that will not condemn it for the judicious mind ; rather it should commend it as realistic. There *is* an element of vagueness in many of our arguments in probability. Vagueness must not be confused with lack of validity. A movement of thought may be correct, even although its terms cannot be defined with exactitude ; the notion that probability consists essentially in a frequency is not inconsistent with the number for that frequency being determinable only by such terms as 'large', or 'very large'.

It is to be observed that the Bayes-type argument in inverse probability would require, *in addition* to some such assumption as the Principle of Indifference, a sampling postulate. The sampling postulate that I have formulated will be shown to be unnecessary in the third phase of this argument, and it could similarly be shown to be unnecessary for arguments of the Bayes type. In this respect there is nothing to choose between the alternative approaches. The point is mentioned here, however, because it is important to see clearly the fundamental difference between the Principle of Indifference on the one hand and the sampling postulate on the other ; there is some danger of confusion here. The Principle of Indifference makes an assumption about nature ; it lays down that when there are a certain number of exhaustive alternatives, and we are in total ignorance as to which is the case, we are entitled to assign equal probability to each. If one defines probability by frequency, this implies that nature manifests each alternative an equal number of times. By contrast, the sampling postulate has nothing to do with the composition of nature, but is concerned only with our investigation of nature. It makes the assumption that the relative frequencies of our observations bear a relation to the relative frequencies of different kinds of observables ; this requirement entails no assumption regarding the composition of nature itself.

One further point must be made. The rate of occurrence of samples of a given degree of suggestiveness in our experience is an awkward concept, because the rate is difficult to establish with numerical precision. To some, especially those who crave after tidiness, it may even seem a repellent concept. In consequence of this repulsion, some might be driven forward on a renewed search for reasons for positing initial prior probabilities, in order to avoid having to use this 'rate' as an essential premise in inductive arguments of a sampling kind. Such an attitude must be unequivocally condemned. Even if we could accept, as I hold that we cannot, the existence of initial prior probabilities, that would not justify us in dispensing with the concept of rate of occurrence of suggestive samples. For, whether we like it or not, the rate of occurrence of such samples does affect the cogency of each in establishing the conclusion to which it points. We can only ignore this fact and endeavour to spew it forth at our peril. We cannot ignore an element that affects the validity of argument without risking fallacies resulting from giving equal weight to arguments of varying validity.

The earlier drafts of this chapter were composed before my researches led me to acquire Professor Donald Williams's volume entitled *The Ground of Induction*. I will say at once that I am in cordial agreement with its general tenor, and notably with the principle set out on pages 93-104. I accept what he says there as an important contribution to the general theory of induction, and I would venture to say that in these few pages more is to be found of relevance to the central problems of logic than in many treatises of greater elaboration and technical apparatus. It may be useful to compare Professor Williams's position with my own.

First, it must be observed that his approach, no less than mine, requires a sampling postulate. He implicitly assumes that this is acceptable, and in a later passage makes merry play with those who could impugn it by affirming that their scepticism implies that there is a naughty demon at work con-

stantly rearranging phenomena with a view to upsetting our
inductions. I do not think that such a type of slightly rhetorical
argument suffices to confound the sceptics, and I hope that
what I shall say in the third phase of this argument, when the
sampling postulate will be withdrawn, will be deemed to deal
with them more decisively.

Professor Williams approaches induction by sampling on
a wider front than I have done. We have seen that an argument in probability consists in referring the case in hand to a
wider class of cases. In this chapter I have been concerned
with samples in which all the P's have Q and have sought to
relate those samples to the class of samples of the same size
in which all P's have Q, in order to frame an argument in
probability that in each case a high proportion of the unobserved P's also have Q. The type of induction that Professor
Williams recommends would cover this case and also arguments in probability in favour of statistical frequencies in
nature. The class to which he relates a given sample in order
to establish a probability is the class of all samples of the same
size, whatever their composition. He bases himself on the
fact that there are more samples resembling their populations
with a given degree of closeness than there are samples not so
resembling their populations. The proportion of samples
resembling their populations becomes progressively greater as
the size of the sample is increased. Consequently if, when
confronted with a large sample, one believes the population to
resemble it (within defined limits), one will much more often
be right than wrong. In other words, one will probably (or
very probably) be right. This is a perfectly valid justification
of an inference in probability. I submit that Professor Williams
is here stating an important part of the general theory of
induction.

In this general argument Professor Williams does not
refer to any particular kind of sample; consequently there
need be no reference to the rate at which any particular kind of
sample is occurring. The reference to a seemingly extraneous
matter, namely the value of this rate, which was essential in
my argument, is unnecessary for his. The weakness in Professor Williams's approach is that, by basing himself so widely,
he does not get very strong probability, unless the sample is

exceedingly large. The reason for this is that some types of population have a much wider dispersion of samples than others. Professor Williams is very happy because, with a sample of 2500, which is after all a rather large one, he can reach a probability of at least ·6826 that the proportion of P's having Q in the population is within 1 per cent of the proportion in the sample. This is not a notably high probability. No doubt with a very much larger sample he could get a much higher probability. This may be relevant in a number of cases. In contrast, however, to Professor Williams's probability of approximately 2 : 1 in favour of the composition of the population being within 1 per cent of that of any sample of that size, my method, by concentrating on a special kind of sample, viz. in which all P's have Q, yields (before deflation), with so large a sample as 2500, odds of 56,000,000,000 : 1 in favour of the number of P's having Q in the total population being within 1 per cent of 100 per cent. Even after deflation the odds will still be very high indeed in favour of the composition of the population being within 1 per cent of that of the sample. Indeed, in this kind of case, we may be said to have that 'practical certainty' which is so common a feature of everyday life.

The large discrepancy between my result and that of Professor Williams is accounted for by the fact that there is a greater dispersion of samples in most of the range than in the immediate neighbourhood of 'all P's have Q' and 'no P's have Q'; the frequency curve has a sharp declivity when it approaches all or none, as shown in the binomial expansion. For example, we may take Professor Williams's choice of a sample of 2500. In a population the composition of which, in regard to the presence or absence of a certain attribute, is 50 : 50, there are about twice as many samples showing 50 : 50 as there are samples showing 51 : 49 ; and in a population the composition of which is 51 : 49 there are about twice as many samples showing 51 : 49 as there are showing 50 : 50. 100 per cent has the same distance from 99 per cent in percentage points as 51 per cent has from 50 per cent ; on other scales 100 per cent might be judged nearer to 99 per cent than 51 per cent is to 50 per cent. Yet among samples of the same size, namely of 2500, drawn from a population in which 99 per cent of P's have Q, there will be 65 thousand million samples

in which exactly 99 per cent of P's have Q for every one sample
in which 100 per cent of P's have Q. This is a fact of cardinal
importance ; it should be made to do work in the inductive
process. Some highbrows may regard it as a mere banausic
detail of arithmetic ; I venture to submit, on the contrary,
that it should occupy a central position in any treatise on the
first principles of logic. By Professor Williams's approach,
any sample before us is related to all the samples that exist of
the same size ; his argument is that, since we know that a
certain proportion of all samples of a given size have a composition which has a certain given proximity to the composition of the population from which they are drawn, we can
assign that given degree of proximity to any sample before
us with the probability indicated by that proportion of all
samples that are within that given proximity to the populations
from which they are drawn. Since his probability is found
by reference to the class of all samples, he has no need to worry
about the particular kind of sample, viz. whether it is one
suggesting that 50 per cent, 70 per cent or 100 per cent of the
P's have Q. I, on the other hand, have taken as the basis of
my argument a sample in which all the P's have Q, and the
argument is assisted by the fact of its being a sample of that
kind and not of some other kind, such as 50 per cent of the
P's have Q. I am able, in consequence, to reach a far more
interesting probability in favour of the composition of the
sample being very near the composition of the population.
But I have to pay a price for this advantage ; namely, I have
to include, within the premises of the argument, a reference
to the rate at which this kind of sample is occurring within
the general experience. And this means introducing some
element of vagueness, because there may be vagueness in
assessing the value of the 'deflator' which it is appropriate to
apply. Where the probability before deflation, of hypothesis H
(based on the improbability of the phenomenon on hypothesis
not-H), is very great — and this applies in many cases of
common sense and science — the vagueness of the value of the
deflator is of little importance. In other cases it may be more
damaging. None the less it will often be worth while to take
advantage of the special features of the 'all P's have Q' or 'no
P's have Q' type of sample, that are due to the character of

the binomial expansion, rather than use Professor Williams's more general criterion. Despite these criticisms of Professor Williams's approach, I hold it to be a perfectly correct one, and an important constituent part of the whole theory of inductive logic.

Scientists in recent centuries have succeeded in probing beneath the heterogeneous character of observable phenomena, into a region where nature shows much greater uniformity. This has enabled them to take more frequent advantage than is possible for those only observing the familiar phenomena of common life, of the sharp declivity of the frequency curve of samples in the proximity of 'all P's have Q' or 'no P's have Q'. This accounts for the greater certainty with which scientists feel they can announce many of their findings by comparison with the doubt and perplexity that beset so many of the affairs of ordinary life. The superficial phenomena also have their own frequencies ; but as these often have middling values as between 0 and 100, there is much less opportunity of making observables yield the secret of what those frequencies are with any high degree of probability. It is true that in its most recent developments physics appears to be passing away from the world of uniformities to that of statistical frequencies. This is a relatively novel departure in a field in which there is a great prevalence of uniformities established by inductions of kinds still to be discussed, and in which high prior probabilities are available for new hypotheses. So long as the logician is not able to give a correct account of why, when I return to my study, I have reason for believing that it will be there, it can hardly hope to have success in analysing the most recent arguments of physics. Is it too much to hope that this leeway will be made up rapidly ? I have the suspicion that this may be important. Hitherto the logic of the sciences has been largely implicit ; the scientists have not been able to give an account of it that would satisfy strict logicians, yet none the less they have been confident of the validity of their various thought processes and that not merely because, as pessimistic logicians aver, they have had pragmatic success. But it is possible that physicists are approaching a position in which a correct logic would be of service to them in their own problems.

From the time of Aristotle onwards, logicians have concen-

trated much of their attention on the premise that all P's have
Q. In his brilliant and fascinating volume entitled *Introduction
to Logical Theory* — these epithets cannot unhappily be taken
to apply to his chapter on inductive reasoning and probability
— Mr. Strawson calls attention to the fact that logicians have
been more concerned with 'all' than 'most' and adds that
'logicians like to present a tidy system of interconnected rules'.[1]
There may be an element of truth in this ; but, if so, it is, at
least in certain connexions, an unfortunate propensity. In
any subject, in logic above all, its principles should conform, in
regard to tidiness and untidiness, to the nature of the subject-
matter and the stage of development of the study.

We have seen that the premises for further argument that
induction vouchsafes are seldom of the kind 'absolutely all
P's have Q', these only being obtainable by complete enumeration, or otherwise on a very large sample, and with low probability, for a finite population. On the other hand, induction
often vouchsafes 'all P's have Q save for exceptions that are so
rare as to be negligible' with very high probability indeed, to
which may be added the further fact that it is not impossible
that 'all P's have Q'. In such a situation it would not be at all
an unworthy tidying-up operation to posit as a premise for
further argument that 'all P's have Q'. So far we may have
sympathy with the quest for tidiness.

The main reason why logicians from early days have shown
special interest in 'all P's have Q', as against other proportions
of P, is that nature has been found to be fairly fertile in uniformities. If our universe had been found to operate mainly
and in most of its parts on Mendelian lines, so that 'half the
P's have Q' was a situation of predominant importance, it is
quite likely that logicians would have begun their exercises
in a different way. For 'all', 'some' and 'no' they might
have substituted 'more than half', 'exactly half', 'less than
half' and 'no'. While the traditional categorization has three
'constants' (two precise and one vague), this categorization has
four 'constants' (two precise and two vague) ; but it is to be
observed that this categorization has greater precision in that
its vague constants are less vague : 'more than half' is less
vague than 'some'. Under this categorization 'all' disappears,

[1] P. 49.

as it might well if 'all' was in fact a highly exceptional and freak phenomenon. The main reason why the traditional categorization has been preferred is, no doubt, that it conforms best to a predominant pattern in the universe in which we happen to live.

But there is a second reason hardly less important : that inherent in the declivity of the frequency curves of samples in the neighbourhood of none and all. Let us suppose that our actual universe was about equally favourable in its composition to 'all P's have Q' and 'half the P's have Q'. At first blush one might suppose that logicians would in those circumstances hesitate between the two kinds of categorization just classified. But that is not so. For in such a universe we should be able to establish the cases where all P's have Q with far higher probability than we could the cases where half the P's have Q ; in fine we should often have knowledge (practical certainty) about the all-P cases, while remaining very much in doubt about the half-the-P cases. This would be a perfectly good reason for logicians setting out with the 'all, some, no' categorization. This is a consideration that should always find mention in treatises on logic, even in treatises on deductive logic only. Before embarking the student upon a prolonged consideration of the 'all P's have Q' case, it would be right and proper for the logician to set out good reasons for giving large attention to this type of case. Among those reasons the sharp declivity of the frequency curve of samples that I have already mentioned should have a high place.

While I have no doubt that the two reasons stated have in fact been the real reasons why logicians have given so much attention to 'all P's have Q', the quest for a tidy system may also have been among the reasons. There is danger in laying stress on the quest for tidiness. If, as I believe, the central themes of logic essentially involve untidiness — at least until we have developed far beyond our present phase in the task of developing them — an undue emphasis on tidiness may divert the attention of logicians away from the central themes and cause them to concentrate upon those trivialities where tidiness can be more easily achieved.

Finally, it is to be observed that the summit of success obtainable in the foregoing type of reasoning is achieved when we establish a very high probability for some such hypothesis as that more than 99 per cent of P's have Q or more than 99·999999 per cent of P's have Q. We can never establish more than a low probability for absolutely all the P's having Q ; the probability that we can establish in favour of the hypothesis that absolutely all the P's have Q, supposing that all the P's in our sample have Q, is simply the ratio of the size of the sample to the size of the total population. This seems to jar badly with such common-sense beliefs as that my study is there absolutely all the time, and not simply that it is there so nearly all the time as to make no practical difference, and with the views of scientists who present their findings as absolutely universal laws.

This limitation must, however, be accepted. The words 'more than' do something to soften the jar. Here recurs the point, more than once dwelt on, that the probabilities usually established by induction are, or entail, not absolute but minimum probabilities. The ascription of a certain probability, let us call it p, to the view that more than 99·999999 per cent of P's have Q does not entail assigning any positive probability to the view that ·000001 per cent of P's lack Q. In regard to this small fraction of the P's our cognitive relation is one of total nescience. If in our sample no P lacks Q, there is no evidence at all for the view that any P in the total population lacks Q ; we can set up no probability, however low, for the view that there is a P that lacks Q.

In this respect it is to be noted that our method is superior to the Bayes-type inverse principle. By our principle, so long as the sample is wholly favourable to all P's having Q, there is no probability, however low, for the view that one P lacks Q. Under the Bayes-type principle there will always be some probability after a finite sample that one or more P's lack Q. For, if we start with the hypothesis that all P's have Q the Bayes-type formula requires that there be some prior probability for the hypothesis that not all P's have Q. If this is an *initial* prior probability, *i.e.* if we start with no prior specific evidence whatever, the prior probability that not all P's have Q will be very high indeed. This prior probability may be greatly reduced by a large sample in which all P's have Q, but it can never be eliminated altogether. But this is absurd. If there is no specific evidence, whether before or after our enquiry, in favour of the hypothesis that some P's lack Q, there is no sense in concluding that there is some probability, however low, that some P's lack Q.

The fact that we cannot find high probability in favour of those uniformities for which the human mind so craves, even if only for the sake of tidiness, need not cast us down too much. These absolute uniformities, if they exist, can never impinge on our consciousness unless we have a complete enumeration, in which case we shall have certainty. We are interested in the uniformities that are exhibited in particular observables, and for these we can have high probabilities without the mind making absolute uniformity the middle term of the argument. Thus if there is 99·999999 per cent probability that at least 99·999999 per cent of the P's have Q, we can obtain by multiplication the probability of any particular P having Q. It is 0·99999999 × at least 0·99999999, which is equal to at least 0·9999999800000001. We note that the words 'at least' must be prefixed to the desired probability in favour of the particular P having Q and that there is no probability that it lacks Q, i.e. no evidence in favour of its lacking Q.

There is a classic passage in Mill about a dye mixer who argued from particulars to particulars ;[1] the question has been raised whether this logically involves the truth, not apprehended by the dye mixer, of some hypothesis of universal uniformity. It appears that the argument from concomitance in one set of particulars to concomitance in another set of particulars establishes a far higher probability for its conclusion than could be established for a generalization positing absolute uniformity of concomitance. On the other hand, it is always possible to find an hypothesis asserting a certain (high) frequency (p) for the concomitance of Q in the whole population of P's which has higher probability than the hypothesis asserting that same probability (p) for the concomitance of Q in any particular case. Thus both sides in this historic argument have some right on their side.

3. I must now revert to the need for dispensing with the sampling postulate. By the use of this postulate it has been possible to establish with high probability the existence of

[1] *Logic*, Bk. II, ch. 3, section 3.

much stability and much uniformity in our universe. We have to confess the fact that all this apparent stability and all this apparent uniformity may be due to a bias in the sample of samples that has constituted our evidence. It may be noted that the degrees of probability and the amount of uniformity constitute a mirror image of the amount of systematic bias there would have had to be in our sample of samples if the universe is not in fact as we suppose it to be, but quite irregular.

Now someone may quickly interject that we can surely dismiss the idea that there has been all that bias. On the hypothesis that the seeming regularity has been due to bias, we should be holding that the apparent continuance of my study has been a happy coincidence, that if I had happened to go where I supposed I should find it on certain days when I did not go there, or at certain hours when I did not go there, I should have just found it not there. And similarly with all the other familiar objects of our world. And it may be that when scientists have weighed and measured elements and found uniformity, this again has been a happy coincidence, that if they had chosen other samples or weighed and measured the samples they did choose at other times, they would have found quite different specific gravities, etc. The objector will say that all this is inconceivable, that there just cannot have been that amount of bias in our observations. If the universe is in fact irregular, it would mean that thousands, nay millions, of times, we should have lit upon the extreme billionth or trillionth right-hand part of the sample lines. To suppose any such thing is just too improbable and incredible.

This is certainly a natural reaction, and I do not wish to express lack of sympathy for it. But we have to remember that we have on our track the deductive logicians with their superior airs. They will not hesitate to point out that this bias, which is said to be so incredible, is not impossible. Nothing can be adduced that entails its contradictory. The keen aversion to admitting the possibility of such a bias may be merely a psychological trait. So long as we have no cogent reason for rejecting its possibility, we are bound as logicians to entertain it.

Furthermore, quite apart from our unwillingness to expose ourselves to the criticism of the deductive logicians, there is another decisive reason against admitting that this colossal bias is inherently 'improbable'. We could only do so by abandoning that definition of probability on which the whole of our justification of induction has been built. Probability was defined as a relation between premises and conclusion; only by an insistence on this have we been able to rebut criticisms and expose fallacies. But in the case in point, namely the alleged improbability of *all* our experience being so strongly biased, there are no premises; consequently the word 'improbable' is inapplicable. Premises must constitute a part of our experience; there are no premises relative to the possible bias of our experience as a whole; this would mean bringing in some considerations from outside all experience, but that is impossible. Consequently if we adhere to our definition as I contend that we must, there is no meaning in saying that it is improbable that all our experience can have had this bias.[1]

Since a bias cannot be declared improbable, the only available alternative is to show that the postulate of un-bias is unnecessary. Happily it is not very difficult to do so.

By way of preliminary, we may revert to the old gambit by which it is sought to justify inductive methods, namely that reasonings based on those methods have had success in the past. This type of argument has already been shown to be circular, but it may be useful to dwell on it. What is the precise nature of the successes that are alleged? The answer to this is usually that these methods have enabled us to make predictions which have been fulfilled. Something has already been allowed in favour of the special value of a successful prediction, namely as one among other methods for safeguarding us against the dangers of suggestive samples.[2] We are not concerned with that here. It may be said in this wider connexion that there is no special logical merit in a successful prediction. If we have a sample of 540 in which all the P's are Q, we may predict that the 541st P will have Q; and if it indeed proves to have Q, we shall then have a sample of 541. That is somewhat better evidence in favour of members of

---

[1] The probability that, after all, evidence against bias may be found *inside experience* is discussed in Chap. IX, pp. 232-236.

[2] See p. 99 above.

the unobserved population of P's having Q, since a sample of 541 is somewhat better than a sample of 540, just as a sample of 540 is somewhat better than one of 539. That is all that we gain by the success of our prediction. A successful prediction is psychologically impressive and may thus make us lean more strongly to a given belief. But all that is really impressive in this connexion is the large size of the sample of 541. When we stand back and survey that sample, it is clear that its evidential value is quite independent of whether we decided to adopt a belief that almost all P's have Q after our sample had reached 200, or 300, or 400, etc. It is, in fine, the size of the sample in its final form that counts, and not the number of predictions that we may or may not have made in the course of its accumulation. If in fact P is not usually conjoined with Q, and our sample of 540 was grossly biased, the appearance of the 541st sample also having Q merely shows that the bias is being consistently maintained. The existence of so great a bias may be surprising; that is the very point that is now under consideration. The success of predictions during the course of the accumulation of the samples brings no further light to bear on their logical significance.

Let us now suppose that during the range of human experience to date neither the postulate in its strong and strict form, nor any weaker version of it, has been true, so that induction has been totally frustrated. This means that throughout the range in question there has been a terrifically strong, widely pervasive and persistent bias in our observations, and that nature, instead of having that regularity and uniformity which we normally attribute to it, has outside our direct experience been quite irregular; we suppose that the apparent regularity has been due to the bias of observations. Now we may make a supposition, the consequence of which is interesting. Let us suppose that this bias will continue for a time into the future; we assume that its various features are preserved, and in particular that consistency which made predictions successful in the past. If this does indeed happen, if, that is, the bias is sustained, we shall find that our observations in the forward stretch of time correspond with expectations. The bias will itself make everything proceed in identically the same way as that in which it would have proceeded if nature

had had that regularity which we should have been justified
in attributing to it, had our past observations been unbiased,
and which we have in fact attributed to it. We should observe
no change in the shape of things. We should not in the near
future be able to detect the bias of the past, just as the success
of past predictions (on this supposition) prevented our discerning a bias in observations of the still remoter past. In
fine, we might claim — if only we knew what was going on —
that although induction had not revealed the true characteristics of nature to us, it had enabled us to make successful
predictions with just as great an efficiency as if it had revealed
the true characteristics of nature. This might make us inclined
to give a favourable estimate of the usefulness of induction.
This argument, however, depends on the supposition, which
might at first be thought gratuitous, that the bias will continue. Suppose that the bias stops dead now. Then we shall
certainly be in trouble ; everything will go awry ; all our predictions will be falsified, and we shall find ourselves confronted
with complete chaos.

But now it is needful to ask another question. Let us
adhere strictly to the supposition that nature is in fact irregular and that all the seeming regularity is due to the persistence through great ages of a strong, pervasive and consistent
bias in our observations. The further question we have to
ask, and we must ask it in all seriousness, is — is this bias
likely to come to a dead stop now ? By the principle of unconditional simple induction such a dead stop would be extremely
improbable. I use improbable in the strict sense. If we have
been travelling over a vast range of experience pervaded by a
bias of this character we are not likely now to be on the
extreme edge of that experience. By unconditional simple
induction, all is likely to go forward with the seeming regularity
to which we have become accustomed. In other words, it
matters not whether the seeming regularity has been due to
a real regularity or due to bias ; either way, by unconditional
simple induction, observables are likely to present themselves
to us with their accustomed regularity. Considered as an
instrument of prediction and for assigning probability to
specified arrangements of observables, induction will have
proved a valid instrument, whether nature is really regular or

not ; that is, whether our great sample of samples in the past has been biased or not.

A further point of the first importance must be observed in this connexion. Let us now reverse the supposition and suppose that nature has been regular to the full extent that would be indicated by induction if the postulate in its full and strict sense (equi-proportional distribution of samples along the sample lines) has been correct. What warrant have we for supposing that this regularity, which we now take to be real, will continue into the future ? None whatever, save that vouchsafed by the principle of unconditional simple induction. And so we come to this. When we consider how things will be and what our powers of prediction are, our justification for beliefs is precisely the same, and is of precisely the same strength, whether, on the one hand, nature has in fact been regular and our sample of samples unbiased, or on the other hand nature has in fact been irregular and our sample of samples systematically biased. In either case our power of prediction rests, and rests only, on the principle of unconditional simple induction, that is on the principle of experience. That principle is no more powerful in making us suppose that a regular order of nature will continue to be regular into future time than it is in making us suppose that a strong, pervasive and consistent bias will continue strong, pervasive and consistent into future time.

We may consider other suppositions. For instance, it might be that our sample of samples has been somewhat systematically biased though not so biased as to frustrate induction altogether, and that nature has had some regularity, albeit not so much regularity as we have been inclined to suppose. What, then, will happen in the near future ? Precisely the same. By unconditional simple induction the weak bias is likely to continue ; by unconditional simple induction the weak regularity in nature is likely to continue ; the product of these effects will be to present us with a future experience that will be identical with that which we should have if nature had been as regular as we have supposed it, or if nature had been altogether irregular and the seeming regularity solely due to a strong systematic bias in observations. And so we may ring the changes. However we combine regularity of nature with bias in our sample of samples, the result for the future always remains the same. *Therefore the postulate that our sample of samples has been unbiased can be dispensed with.*

It should be noticed that the principle of experience gives a more secure basis for inductive conclusions than its rival principle, which was favoured in the nineteenth century, the assumption of universal causation. At first sight it might appear that, if there are inner necessities in the succession of phenomena, and if we believe that we have gained an insight into those necessities, for instance that our inductions justify belief with a certain degree of probability that certain inner necessities do exist, we should be in a stronger position as regards the future ; if there is an inner necessity, nature must continue to operate in accordance with it. To the extent that we have found out that necessity, we shall be in a strong position for prediction. The foregoing arguments lead to the conclusion that the opposite is the case. For if it is inner necessity on which we rely for our beliefs regarding the future, we have no defence against the possibility that our various opinions about inner necessities are based on a biased sample of samples. If, on the other hand, we base ourselves on the principle of experience, we are in a better position. Our beliefs about the future no longer repose upon the assumption of inner necessities in nature, but on the simpler assumption that things having been such and such is a good reason for believing that they will continue to be such and such for the time being (unconditional simple induction) ; this basis for our beliefs in regard to the future frees us from dependence on the assumption that our sample of samples has been fair. Our beliefs have equal logical validity whether the sample of samples was fair or not, because the principle of experience justifies a valid belief in the continued operation of any systematic bias that there may have been. We have no corresponding safeguard if we make the assumption of an inner necessity in nature the major premise of our inductive reasoning.

It may be wondered why we have been at great pains to define a fair sampling postulate, if that postulate was presently to be withdrawn. A fair sampling postulate served a definite purpose as a tool of thought ; it is a case of climbing up on a ladder and then casting it aside. The fair sampling postulate is a tool which enables us to reach the following important disjunction. Our experience has been such that either nature within our range of observation has had a considerable degree of regularity, or our sample of samples within that range of observation has had a considerable degree of consistent bias. Our experience is inconsistent with a denial of the disjunction. The definition of a fair sampling postulate has enabled us to see that clearly. On the basis of this disjunction we can move forward securely in reaching valid beliefs. It is to be noted that this disjunction does not only serve us in good stead in relation to beliefs about the future ; it also serves us in relation to new beliefs that we may come to hold in future about the past. If our sample of samples has been unbiased and nature has been regular, then new inferences in relation to the past are clearly justified ; but if our sample of samples has been biased and we expect a continuation of that bias, then that continuation will apply to evidence relating to the past no less than that relating to the future, and will continue to justify new inferences about the past in the sense that any such new inferences made are likely to be corroborated thereafter.

In the following chapters the sampling postulate, or some analogue of that postulate, will continue to be used as a tool of thought. In every case there will be similar grounds for holding that the postulate can be dispensed with. It will not be necessary to repeat the argument in every case. All these postulates can be dispensed with, but we have already had one that has not been dispensed with, but has been taken to be true, namely the postulate required for conditional simple induction. The reason for this difference is that in the cases of sampling inferences of all the various kinds, we do not usually attain to knowledge of the composition of the entire population, so that the question remains open in each case whether the sample was fair or not, and so it remains open also for the whole class of cases, namely our lifelong experience, or the whole of human experience. But in the class of continuities a large number of continuities have in fact come to an end, so that we can see in retrospect whether the continuity postulate was justified or not. We may not be able to affirm that it was justified in its strong form, but we can at least see that it was justified to a sufficient extent not to frustrate induction.

Finally there is one form of induction that requires no postulate, namely unconditional simple induction. This consists simply in the direct application to phenomena of the principle of experience itself. It was justified by an argument illustrated in the square diagram on page 56. The argument assumed equal probability for the traveller being in any sector of his journey ; this is analogous to the postulate in the case of sampling that there is equal probability of a given sample belonging to each sector of the sampling line. Between the two cases there is this huge difference. The assumption of the equal distribution of samples, out of a large sample of samples, on the sampling line, is a mere assumption and can never be proved. The assumption of equal probability for the traveller being in any sector of his journey is not a mere assumption, but a belief that is known to be true ; we can say for certain that the traveller is an equal amount of time in each sector of his journey. In fine, the principle of experience is known for certain to be true. This knowledge underpins all other forms of inductive argument.

CHAPTER V

NATURAL KINDS

THE greatest care has been taken, in justifying induction, to make no presupposition about the character of the universe. This rule will be adhered to rigidly throughout. It may be helpful, however, in order to focus thought, to consider a possibility in regard to the universe, namely that it is what might be called totally irregular. I hasten to add that this view has nothing to recommend it ; it is a bare possibility with not a vestige of probability in its favour. The name chosen may be inappropriate ; there are surprising difficulties in the concept of total irregularity.

The concept, however, that I wish to use as a tool of thought may be defined precisely. The condition is that, when a particle or an event is present, there are equal probabilities of any other out of all possible particles or events being adjacent to it. This seems to be what is presupposed when the Principle of Indifference is recommended. To make this easier to consider, we may take the case of a coloured minimum sensibile and assume that there are a hundred available shades of colour. This would give fairly wide limits of tolerance to the definition of a particular 'shade' of colour. We should then say that the probability of the next adjacent minimum sensibile — working systematically in one direction or other — being of any one given shade of colour was one in a hundred.

The assignment of such a probability presupposes a quite definite arrangement, namely that, in the universe, or in that part of it under investigation, the numbers of times that each colour appears in adjacency to any one given colour, are in fact equal — or approximately equal. We have no reason to suppose that this is in fact the case, and that is why the Principle of Indifference has to be rejected altogether as a working tool. The reason why I suggest giving this definition of a state of total irregularity is that it is applying an assumption that we often use in cases where it is said that no law holds. In the cast of dice, and in a host of similar cases, we say that the fact that no particular law holds, *i.e.* that the exposure of one or other facet is subject to total irregularity, makes us expect that on a large number of throws each facet will be exhibited a roughly equal number of times. I have explained already that this cannot be derived from first principles, and must be taken to be a belief based on the experience of certain types of events. The notion that any inference in probability can flow from a so-called 'equal dispersion of ignorance' I regard as totally unwarranted.

We are considering accordingly the possibility that events in the universe occur like the exposures of the facets of an 'unbiased' die. It may be a little odd to call this 'total irregularity' since this tendency to equality among various possible combinations would seem to be rather a notable kind of regularity. But what is the alternative ? If B is juxtaposed with A a greater number of times than some of the other alternatives, this constitutes a tendency for B to be juxtaposed with A and in its turn seems to be a kind of regularity. One might be inclined to argue that the notion of total irregularity is self-contradictory. One either has the remarkable regularity of an approximately equal number of juxtapositions or the regularity constituted by the tendency of one kind of juxtaposition to be favoured. One might attempt a complicated kind of definition of total irregularity — although it seems odd that such a concept requires a complicated definition — such as that all tendencies are very weak and that they vary strongly from place to place and time to time. Such a universe would make induction somewhat difficult. It is to be noted, however, that the variation from place to place or from time to time would not be altogether frustrating to induction, since induction necessarily requires an 'origin', as has already been shown, and what is of immediate relevance to induction is the tendency around the 'origin' in place and time. This tendency must have a certain expansion in place or time, or it could not be described as a tendency at all and we should be back with the alternative of roughly equal distribution, which we call total irregularity. Owing to the difficulties inherent in the word 'irregular', I shall in what follows refer to the universe

characterized on the principles that govern the fall of so-called
unbiased dice as Heracleitean.

There is, however, a great difficulty in conceiving such a
universe. What holds in regard to the juxtaposition of one
or other colours with A holds also of its juxtaposition with
AB, with ABC, etc. Unless we are dealing with a very vast
universe, far greater than that contemplated by the physicists,
the Law of Large Numbers very soon ceases to operate. A
row of forty minimum sensibilia presumably does not occupy
more than two or three inches. Taking the finite universe of
the physicists, we find that, even supposing that a single atom
could generate a minimum sensibile, which it clearly cannot,
there would be no room for even one of all possible sequences
of forty in the whole universe. Thus, even if one had full
access to all the vastitudes of space, one would not expect to
find a strip of two or three inches of a given uniform colour
more than once — and this is allowing very broad limits of
tolerance in the definition of 'uniformity of colour'. How
then can we apply our Law of Large Numbers ? It might be
urged that one must allow a larger universe. It is asking for
much, in the interests of an *a priori* theory, to require as a
presupposition of inference a universe immensely greater than
that very great universe that is within the range of observation
of the physicists.

One thing is quite certain. The first conclusion that an
infant can reach when he first opens his eyes is that his part
of the universe is *not* Heracleitean. No tears need be shed
on that score. There is no initial probability, no, not the
lowest conceivable, in favour of a Heracleitean universe. In
other words, the very first thing we know is that we are located
in a region in which it would not merely be unwarrantable,
but sharply violate truth, to apply the Principle of Indifference.

What is clear at the outset is that our part of the universe
is one of repetitions. Incidentally it is also one of continuities.
It might be claimed that in the chapter on continuities one
stage in the argument was missed. If the universe was in fact
Heracleitean, the argument there set out would be incorrect.
In a Heracleitean universe there would always be a great
improbability that a continuity would continue at all, a vast
improbability that it would continue for more than three or

four minimum sensibilia. It did not seem that there was any need to dispose of this objection to our argument for the continuance of a continuity, since the hypothesis of a Heracleitean universe, having nothing to commend it and no prior probability whatever in its favour, does not have to be disposed of any more than any other fancy hypothesis. Having observed a continuity we can proceed straight to an argument derived from the logic of continuities.

We have next to consider the logic of argument in relation to repetitions. For this purpose a fundamental concept is that of a 'natural boundary'. A given region may have a certain uniformity — similarity of texture, pattern or symmetry — that marks it out from a heterogeneous background. I would give as an example a cat. The boundary of a cat is fairly clearly marked. It might be objected that a 'natural boundary' hardly seems to be a logical concept. Are we justified in singling out such a feature within our particular experience, which might not occur at all in another kind of universe ? In order to develop a system of logic, it is necessary, as in other disciplines, to work from the relatively particular to the more general. We must study the working of logical principles in various concrete cases ; it may be our hope that we shall be able eventually to advance to those remote abstractions where such a concept as 'natural boundary' plays no part. It might be claimed, of course, that we have to-day in current treatises a logic of such remote abstractions. My counter-claim would be that so far such abstraction has only been achieved by ignoring the main subject-matter of logic. We have to start at the beginning again ; if we incorporate in the subject of our study the actual processes of thought we shall have a long journey to make before we reach again that region of remote abstraction now dwelt in by the formal logicians.

It is desirable to consider a cat in relation to the hypothesis of a Heracleitean universe. A cat is in and by itself not a very Heracleitean object, as its internal structure contains so much repetition and symmetry. We may for the sake of this argument waive that point, and suppose a cat no more internally regular than any other region of space. Even so, on the Heracleitean hypothesis, cats would be extremely rare ; it would be very unusual indeed for a region of space to be filled in that

particular way. But this should not cause logical surprise.
For every other way of filling a region of space of that size
would be equally rare. It is a fundamental principle of logic
that the occurrence of an event that is extremely rare on
hypothesis H is not evidence against that hypothesis, if every
alternative possibility on hypothesis H is equally rare. The
appearance of the cat — still waiving the special characteristics
of its internal structure — would not by itself cast doubt on
the hypothesis, if such were entertained, that the universe is
Heracleitean.

One may take an analogy from the game of bridge. We
assume — from experience — that the selection of cards constituted by a 'hand' dealt from a well-shuffled pack is lawless.
When a bridge player takes up a hand, he may be thrilled to
know that the particular hand he has occurs only once in every
635 thousand million hands (approximately) that are dealt at
the bridge table. Indeed it is not strongly improbable — on
a very rough calculation — that the hand he takes up has
never been taken up before by any bridge player since the
laws of bridge were first drawn up at the Portland Club. But
since this would also be true, whatever hand he took up, the
rarity of this particular hand does not point to the pack not
having been properly shuffled.

But now suppose that a second cat appears upon the
horizon. This is an altogether different matter. Let the
bridge player's second hand in the rubber be precisely the same
as his first hand ; that would rightly surprise him. Of all the
times he plays bridge, he will only get the particular combination of the precise hand he holds first being followed by the
precise hand he holds second once in every $(635,000,000,000)^2$
times. This again gives no cause for logical surprise, for whatever hand he picks up the second time, the combination of the
two will be equally rare. But if the second hand is the same
as the first, that is a kind of rarity, assuming the pack to be
well-shuffled, that is not present on the other alternatives.
Applying a sampling postulate to well-shuffled packs we can
say that for every once that he picks up the same hand there
will be 635 thousand million times that he picks up a different
hand. This rare quality of sameness would not be present if
he picked up any other possible hand, and is therefore not

only a rarity, but a kind of rarity that tends to discredit the hypothesis that the pack has been well shuffled.   Similarly the second cat discredits the hypothesis, if anyone had been inclined to hold it, that the environment is altogether Heracleitean in character.

The question before us now is what principle of argument we may use when confronted by a repetition of this character. It is the natural boundary of the cat that gives us logical leverage.   Let us suppose that on the occurrence of the first cat, twenty-six characteristics are noted, and that these characteristics are *equally readily observable* ; we rule out, for example, dissection.   Let us suppose that in the case of the second cat only thirteen of the characteristics are observed ; part of the cat may be hidden by a door or the observer may not yet have had time to observe the cat from various points of view in three dimensions.   The natural boundaries of the cat constitute a pattern and the twenty-six characteristics of the first cat may be identified by their location within this pattern. When the thirteen features of the second cat have been observed, on the Heracleitean hypothesis there are astronomical odds against the hitherto unobserved features of the second cat being similar to the locationally correspondent features of the first.   And there are some odds against any one of the unobserved features being similar.   In fact no one would argue in this way in regard to the unobserved half of the second cat. We proceed in a different manner, and justifiably.   We say that if in fact the second cat has only thirteen features similar, within certain limits of tolerance, to those of the first cat, it is an odd coincidence that we should have observed those thirteen features and not any of the dissimilar features.

This argument, which is valid, has a familiar flavour.   It needs for its support a sampling postulate.   This postulate is similar to that required for arguments regarding the concomitance of P with Q.   Like that postulate, it serves as a tool of thought and can subsequently be withdrawn.   In the argument in relation to the concomitance of P and Q we were concerned with a population (all the P's in existence), a sample (all the P's observed), and a hypothesis, such as that 95 per cent of P's in the whole population have Q.   Regarding this case as analogous to the other, the 'population' (corresponding to

all P's in existence) is simply all locations defined by the
natural boundary at which the features were observed in the
first cat. The sample consists of the features observed in
the second cat. We then frame some hypothesis such as that
of the twenty-six locations occupied by the observed features of
the first cat only thirteen in the second cat will be similar to
those in the first. On the basis of this hypothesis, a sample
line can be drawn on the same principles as before. At the
left-hand end will be placed the samples of thirteen least favourable to the view that all the features of the second cat, observed
and unobserved, are similar to those of the first cat ; as we
move along the sample line we proceed to samples more favourable to the view that all the features of the second cat are
similar to those of the first cat. At the extreme right-hand
end of the sample line will be the samples most favourable to
the view that all the features of the second cat are similar to
those of the first cat. These will be the samples in which all
the features are similar. The sample line in the case in point,
viz. one drawn on the hypothesis that only thirteen features
in the second cat are similar to those in the first contains
10,400,600 samples.[1] Of these only one has all the thirteen
features similar ; and that is the one I have observed. Thus
what has been observed is highly improbable on the assumption
that only thirteen features of the second cat are similar to
those of the first. Some 'deflation' has then to be applied to
the improbability of the second cat having only thirteen similar
features on the lines explained in the last chapter. There are
extremely high odds against the observation unless many of
the unobserved features of the second cat are similar to those
of the first cat. There are even odds for and against it if only
one is dissimilar, since on that hypothesis there are as many
samples of thirteen lacking as having one dissimilar feature.

We may note the tremendous contrast between the argument we should use if proceeding from the Heracleitean hypothesis and the argument actually used. On the Heracleitean
hypothesis there are, despite the observed similarities, terrific
odds against there being similarities between most of the
unobserved features, and substantial odds against there being
similarity in even one of the unobserved features ; by the

[1] Viz. $^{26}C_{13}$.

argument before us, the position is entirely reversed ; there are very high odds against not finding any further similarities and substantial odds in favour of most of the other features being similar. The argument from the Heracleitean hypothesis would be fallacious because there is no reason to hold the Heracleitean hypothesis. It must not be thought that the argument on the sampling principle presupposes any prior probability in favour of repetition. We can develop that argument, not because we make any prior supposition about repetition, but because the repetition is actually there in the case of the thirteen observed features. No presupposition as regards the composition of nature is required, but only the sampling postulate. What gives leverage to the argument in this case is the existence of a natural boundary, providing a specific location for each of the various observed features in the first cat. This natural boundary provides the necessary premise for this type of argument by analogy.

It appears from the above that the argument by analogy has the fundamental characteristics of a sampling argument.

The question may be raised whether a similar argument can be applied to features not yet observed in either instance of the repetition. If these features can be specified by their occupation of a certain position within the pattern, a similar mode of inference can clearly be applied. In this case we take the 'population' to be all positions within the pattern. There are, however, in addition, properties of the objects, or, as we may call them, the structures, in question, besides those of the appearance of their parts, notably there are behavioural properties, namely changes with the passage of time or modes of reaction to changes in the environment away from its state on the occasion of the initial observations. While we are not, in empirical studies, concerned with an infinite number of things, there is an indefinitely large class of possible changes of environment in relation to which behavioural reactions might be considered. It would then be appropriate, when applying a sampling argument to our observations, to evaluate probabilities on the basis of an infinite population. High probabilities could then only be obtained if the sample was large ; that means in this case that the number of features observed to be similar in the two structures was large. It would be possible,

K

however, to get high probability on the basis of a smaller sample — sample again refers to the number of observed features, not to the number of observed structures — if we could specify a natural group of situations, behavioural reaction to which could be considered as a natural class — on lines similar to those on which we established the appearances of the various positions within the natural boundary as a limited group of the features to be examined.

The foregoing argument has been developed on the basis of our finding in at least two instances a significant degree of repetition within natural boundaries. The argument proceeds to establish probability for further repetition within those boundaries. This seems to give the typical logical foundation for the inference known as argument by analogy. It is possible that too much importance has been attached to analogy in some treatments of empirical logic. Fundamentally argument by analogy is a special application of the general principle of sampling, or argument by simple enumeration.

In approaching our exposition of the foregoing argument, we observed that the repetition on which it was based would be extremely improbable on the Heracleitean hypothesis. This characteristic must be examined. An objector might ask why the Heracleitean hypothesis should be dragged in, when it has been emphasized that the hypothesis has nothing whatever to recommend it *a priori*, and that the slightest tincture of experience shows conclusively that it is untrue in our part of the universe. It may, however, serve a useful purpose, namely in providing a criterion for measuring what may be called the 'strength' of repetitions.

This strength may be taken to be proportionate to the degree of the improbability of the repetition occurring on the Heracleitean hypothesis. In the organic world repetitions acquire strength owing to the multiplicity and complexity of the features of the structures that are repeated. As against this it often happens that the similarity of the correspondent features has rather generous limits of tolerance. The improbability, on the Heracleitean hypothesis of A having B next to it more than once out of several times depends on the number of available alternatives to B, and this in turn depends on the limits of tolerance allowed in the specification of B, when an instance B_2 is allowed to be 'similar' to another instance B_1. The wider the limits of tolerance allowed, the less improbable is the repetition, on the Heracleitean hypothesis, and consequently the 'weaker' the repetition.

In the inorganic world the observed features of repeating structures may be fewer; this weakens the analogy; but as against the loss of strength in the repetitions in this respect has to be set the great gain in strength through similarities having much finer limits of tolerance. Such properties as specific gravity, elasticity, melting-point, may be measured by suitable instruments with four-figure accuracy and be found identical. This means that if B is the value, say, of specific gravity in the first instance of a repetition, there are ten thousand alternative possibilities for B in the second instance. If two structures have at the outset no more than three similar features, but each of these can be shown to be identical with four-figure accuracy, there are a billion to one odds against this repetition on the Heracleitean hypothesis, and thus the repetition may be said to have a billionfold 'strength'.

Where structures consist of repetitions that are strongly improbable on the Heracleitean hypothesis, we may say, using a term of traditional logic, that they belong to a 'natural kind'.

This is an appropriate point at which to consider the problem of definition. I am not here concerned with the distinction already discussed, and to be discussed more hereafter, between 'ostensive' definitions, where the meaning of a symbol is specified by direct pointing, and definitions in which the predicate or predicates have already been defined. All definitions must be derived ultimately from ostensive definitions. The fact that these are sometimes not supplied for the basic terms in systems of symbolic logic is one of the grounds of uneasiness in regard to the logical significance of those systems.[1]

The present problem is concerned with the choice of complexes that we select for naming. In the course of experience

---

[1] Ostensive definitions and definitions closely derived from them are supplied in Chapter VII for some of the basic terms — truth, belief, etc. — an understanding of the meaning of which is taken for granted in the current pages.

a vast variety of complexes come before us, and if we sought
to name them all we should require more names than the
alphabet supplies and myriads of years in which to accomplish
the naming process.

In definition we normally confine ourselves to strong repetitions, although very rarely an extremely interesting sole complex
is given a (proper) name like annus mirabilis or Black Friday.[1]
Continuities (*e.g.* people, cities) are sometimes given names,
also proper.   First it must be laid down that we are free
to define things as we like ;   definitions cannot be true or
false.   In many cases, however, although by no means in all,
there is conjoined with the definition a hope, or perhaps we
should call it a belief in the implicit hypothesis, that the thing
defined can be shown *by experience* to be the seat of stronger
repetition than is contained in the definition itself.   When a
definition only specifies one property, we may restate the
implicit hypothesis as being that the thing defined is a natural
kind.   Since, if we were reckless, there could be a vast proliferation of definitions, and since we do not wish to be unduly
cluttered up, it is expedient to confine our definitions to cases
of strong repetition.

The expedience of a definition in cases where this is conjoined with the implicit hypothesis that the thing defined will
be shown *by experience* to be the seat of a stronger repetition
than that specified in the definition, can only be tested by experience.   Thus experience leads to the revision of definitions.
This fact has been blown out into undue prominence — if I
am correctly guided by the amount of effort Professor von
Wright devotes to his able refutation — by the 'convention-
alist' school of logicians.   According to this doctrine, all
generalizations are of a definitory character and the sole rôle of
experience is to lead to a revision of definitions.   Experience
has a more important task ; it gives guidance as to the truth
of generalizations.

No precise rules can be supplied for the framing of definitions.   We want so to proceed as to identify the seat of the
greatest possible strength of repetition beyond that specified

---

[1] Are these examples of 'logically proper names', of which Professor
A. J. Ayer says that 'they are not to be found in any actual language that is
known to me' (*Philosophical Essays*, p. 12) ?   Or do such names have to
refer to atomic or indivisible events ?

in the definition itself. We also have some regard to the frequency of occurrence of the thing defined. The desire for economy also plays some rôle, although this is not the main consideration. Thus if we believe that when there is AB, there is almost always ABCD, we may confine our definition to AB for the sake of economy. This is a matter of convenience ; we cannot accept Aristotle's fundamental distinction between the 'essence', which should be specified in the definition, and properties invariably conjoined with it. We may often leave normally concomitant properties out of the definition merely by way of economy, there being no difference in principle between those included and those excluded.

If, as a result of our experience, we include yellow in the definition of cat, we shall later find that we have limited the frequency of occurrence, excluding all the non-yellow cats without, by the inclusion of this property, gaining enough in the way of strength, viz. only the property yellow, to justify the limitation. The members of the class of all cats contain, I believe, as much strength of repetition, save for the one property of yellow, as the members of the class of yellow cats. It would be deemed that what we lose here by limiting the extension of reference, we do not gain by the increase in the strength of repetition within the field of reference. On the other side we must not make our definition so wide as to include as well as many instances of strong repetition, many other instances where the repetition is no greater than that contained in the definition itself. Thus we might take the relative sizes of the various features of the cat with very generous limits of tolerance. This might include cats, which are the seats of strong repetition, but also include logs, stones, etc. This would frustrate the purpose of our definition. In definition we may compromise between extension and intension ; the prime object is to specify seats of very strong degrees of repetition ; but if by sacrificing a little of the strength of repetition, one can include a much larger class of objects, it may be expedient to do so. In a very notable class of cases, we supply two simultaneous definitions, namely those of genus and species.

General experience sharpens our aim in seeking an expedient definition. This general experience brings to light the fact that in our universe we do not get a continuous grading of objects, with a narrow group having strong repetition, a very slightly wider group having perceptibly less repetition, and so on till the widest group has no repetition. On the contrary, we find very often that a certain group has strong repetition, while any larger group containing this one but more extensive than it has comparatively little repetition. This general experience spurs us on to think that some definitions are very much more expedient than others, namely those which specify as nearly as may be the precise group where the repetition is strong. In a universe not having this characteristic, the problem of expedient definition would be much less important.

This is a suitable point at which to refer to a notable and celebrated article by Professor Broad on induction.[1] Of the many works that I have read it seems to approach nearest, except for that by Professor Williams, to the doctrines of this volume — in two respects. He has a good account of natural kinds and of their improbability on what I have called an Heracleitean hypothesis, and he has an excellent passage (pp. 28-29) on the 'high unprobability' of our being on the edge of a great expanse having very peculiar characteristics within a wider universe. But he seems to have been inhibited by some deep-seated defeatism — which may perhaps be attributed to the intellectual atmosphere of Cambridge in the early twentieth century — from bringing together and developing his just observations as a vindication of induction. His article is written in the context of an alleged need to presuppose that nature has certain general features in order for induction to be valid. I detect a confusion here between what is needed if induction is to have scope and what is needed if induction is to have validity. If our part of the universe were not characterized by the features to which he draws attention, notably the presence of natural kinds, there might indeed be little opportunity for inductive methods ; it would not follow that the principles underlying those methods were invalid ; indeed it is not possible for such principles to depend on the existence of particular facts. Professor Broad seems also to suppose,

---

[1] 'The Relation between Induction and Probability', *Mind*, 1920, pp. 10-45.

nineteenth-century-wise, that one has to establish some modified form of universal causation as a prior postulate necessary
for the validity of induction, not recognizing that his own
arguments dispense with such a need. These arguments are
related both to the inductions of common sense and to those
of science, and it is not always clear whether the need for a
prior postulate applies to both spheres or to the latter only.
It is not to derogate from the high importance of this article
if one is driven to agree to some extent with its author in holding that it is 'confused and confusing' (p. 42).

A similar defeatism dogs the steps of Bertrand Russell and
in my judgement detracts from his wide-sweeping and penetrating work on *Human Knowledge, Its Scope and Limits*.[1] In
the same vein — and Keynes also belongs to this school of
thought — he thinks that the validity of induction presupposes
certain characteristics in nature. Without criticizing, or necessarily agreeing in detail with, the *content* of the postulates that
he claims induction to presuppose, as stated in his summary in
a concluding chapter,[2] I venture to suggest that most of these
can be established for our world, at least in a suitably modified
form, by an inductive process that does not presuppose them.
One significant and tell-tale point may be noted. In a passage
in which he is recommending these prior postulates, alleged
to be required for the validity of induction, to our sympathetic
consideration on grounds which presumably do not, and in
that context must not, themselves entail the validity of induction, he discusses an all-important relation between structural
similarity and 'causal lines'. He builds up a terrific improbability (p. 485), for the falsity of a certain relation — namely
that the numerous identical copies of a book originated in the
mind of a common author of them. What is the point of
this ? To throw dust in our eyes ? We can safely assume
that Russell's intellectual integrity is far too high for him
consciously to use an argument which he knows to be fallacious,
merely in order to secure a psychological acquiescence in a
doctrine he is recommending. If induction is invalid in the
absence of the postulate, how can it help him to build up, by
induction, a terrific probability in favour of the postulate ? It

[1] Published 1948. George Allen & Unwin.
[2] Bk. VI, chap. ix.

is to be feared that we must turn against Russell the argument
he brings so often against professed solipsists and must point
out that he cannot help reasoning as an inductivist *before* he
has established the postulates that he deems necessary for
induction, and even — worse and worse — when he purports
to be arguing philosophically.

It was stated at the outset of the discussion of definitions
that there is often a hope, or implicit hypothesis, that the
definition will be *found by experience* to specify a class, members of which will be the seats of strong repetition, and non-
members of which will not exemplify much repetition of this
particular kind. When this is not found to be the case, it
cannot be said that the definition was incorrect, for we are
free to define as we like, but only that the conjoined hypothesis
was incorrect. And it may follow that the definition was inex-
pedient. In many cases of definition there is no such conjoined
hypothesis. We may take as an example the definition of one
million. It is true that the classes within the class specified
by one million have many common properties that are not
contained in the definition of the class of classes of one million.
Thus the definition may be said to specify seats of repetitions
that are much stronger than the repetition specified by the
definition itself. But this further repetition is not, and is not
expected to be, ascertainable *by experience*, and for this reason
we are bound by definition to exclude the class of classes
constituted by one million from those said to belong to a single
'natural kind'. All the common properties in the class specified
by one million are *entailed by* the definition of one million.
We could of course, if we chose, conjoin to the definition of
one million the hypothesis that one million is a natural kind,
and that if we examine some of the classes comprised within
the class we are likely to find many common properties not
entailed by the definition. We might, for example, examine
a number of classes of one million each, to find if their numbers
tended predominantly to be pink, light, hard, etc. We should
soon find ourselves doomed to failure, and infer that the hypothesis that we had sought to conjoin to the definition of one
million, namely that what was specified was a natural kind, was
wrong. We do not in fact entertain any such hope, or make

any such hypothesis, when we define a million. This fact serves to mark the distinction between mathematical concepts and general empirical concepts.

The exclusion of mathematical concepts from the class of natural kinds follows from defining natural kinds by reference to the Heracleitean hypothesis. The natural kind is more marked the greater the 'strength' of the repetition, and this strength is measured by the improbability of the repetition if the Heracleitean hypothesis were true. If, after the observation of certain similarities within natural boundaries, further similarities are observed, these further similarities increase the strength of the repetition because and to the extent that the total repetition, including the added similarities, is more improbable on the Heracleitean hypothesis than the original repetition (definition). But if the further similarities are entailed by the original similarities, their presence does nothing to increase the strength of the repetition. If AB entails ABC, a repetition of ABC cannot be more improbable on the Heracleitean (or any other) hypothesis than a repetition of AB. Consequently the addition of C does nothing to increase the strength of the repetition. This distinction is fundamental, because it is the ground of division between the empirical sciences on the one hand and the purely deductive systems on the other.

I propose to make some observations about physical concepts. These are to be distinguished from the kinds of empirical concepts hitherto discussed by way of illustration, in that they cannot be directly defined in terms of observables. I refer to such concepts as mass and electron. This subject has recently been given a masterly and powerful treatment by Professor R. Braithwaite.[1]

It has been hoped that, although these physical entities are not directly observable, they might be defined indirectly in terms of observables. Professor Braithwaite advances the view that this hope cannot be realized and that the physical entities can have no definitions in the ordinary sense at all ; rather they are to be implicitly defined by the part they play in a whole deductive system. I believe that what I have to

[1] *Scientific Explanation*, chap. iii.

say is not in conflict with Professor Braithwaite's essential thought on this matter.

I suggest that in the case of a physical entity, whether the definition be indirectly in terms of observables, or, in the manner of Professor Braithwaite, implicitly in terms of the parts played in a deductive system, there is a conjoined hypothesis that the entities in question are natural kinds. This means that when the entity in question repeats, there will simultaneously be repetition of greater strength than that specified in the definition or entailed by the definition, whether indirect or implicit. This serves to distinguish the entities of physics from those of mathematics. And it is by virtue of this distinction that we hope to be able to extend our knowledge of the properties of the physical concepts by observation and experiment. In this respect the entities of physics resemble those of common observation. We believe that a given entity of physics is the seat of more repetition than is specified in or entailed by the definition. Whereas among more superficial phenomena the complex defined may contain sufficient features to justify a probability, by the analogy argument, that more repetition will be found within its natural boundaries than is specified in the definition, this will not necessarily be so in the case of a definition in physics. It may be asked why, in this case, we should make the hypothesis that the entities defined are the seats of stronger repetition. In making hypotheses, as in making definitions, we are as free as air and can do what we like ; but the hypotheses, unlike the definitions, may subsequently be proved to be incorrect. It is the genius of the scientist, often and rightly applauded, that enables him to make hypotheses concerning the existence of strong natural kinds hidden from observation, that are often proved correct.

Professor Whitehead once wrote as follows : 'It has been popular to define force as the product of mass and acceleration. The difficulty to be faced with this definition is that the familiar equation of elementary dynamics, namely $mf = P$ now becomes $mf = mf$. It is not easy to understand how an important science can issue from such premises. . . . Again we should be in equal danger of reducing dynamical equations to such identities as $P/f = P/f$.'[1]

---

[1] *The Principles of Natural Knowledge*, p. 19.

We may be rescued from this dilemma if we say that there are two elements in the alleged definition, namely (1) the definition itself, and (2) the hypothesis that force has further properties which can be revealed by experiment and which are not logically entailed by its being *mf*. Since the definition of P as *mf* does not constitute P as a natural kind, we may re-word the hypothesis by saying that force will prove to be a natural kind.

The observations supporting the theory of relativity suggest that a correction is required to the old definition of force. A more complicated definition is brought forward containing a reference to the velocity of light. This does not imply that the old definition was wrong. We are perfectly entitled to frame the general concept *mf* and call it what we like. Yet it is felt that the new facts require a correction in the old definition. What was wrong ? Not the definition itself, for a definition cannot be wrong. What was wrong was the hypothesis that the entity specified by the old definition was the seat of more repetition than that contained in or entailed by the definition itself. Experience has proved that to be wrong. If we stick to the old definition we shall find — save in cases (relatively low velocities) where the limits of tolerance are broad enough to give identical results from the two definitions — that the entity *mf* has no properties other than those logically entailed by its being *mf*. The other empirical properties supposed to pertain to force will not pertain to *mf*. And so if we want to train our thought upon something which has empirical properties that can be fruitfully investigated, we must drop the old definition and adopt the new one in accordance with relativity theory. It cannot be said that the old definition was incorrect, but only that it has proved inconvenient ; what was incorrect was the conjunction, $P \equiv (def)mf$ and P is a natural kind.

Traditional logic comprises the distinction between genus and species. The treatment accorded to it in the old books was of very great dullness ; it was presented as part of systems of classification, and not shown to have any close connexion with the vital process of inference. In fact it is of quite central importance in induction. It has been seen that two simultaneous definitions can be accorded to a given repetition, one inclusive of a larger number of instances but containing less strength of repetition per instance, the generic definition, and one containing a smaller number of instances and a higher strength of repetition per instance, the specific definition. In the genus, wider limits of tolerance may be accorded to the similar features ; or the number of similar features may be smaller than in the species.

We may find that a certain type of feature is observed to be present throughout a genus, but only within wide limits of tolerance, while within each species separately there is similarity in regard to this feature from member to member of each species within very narrow limits of tolerance. For instance, it may be possible to establish specific gravities and melting-points of chemical elements within very narrow limits ; the similarities within the genius as a whole consist simply in there being some specific gravity and some melting-point. The existence of fine limits of tolerance for the similarities in each species may be regarded as a property of the genus itself. This property is established for the genus in the ordinary way — by sampling. We may be able to hold with very high probability that this property belongs to all members of the genus with exceptions so rare as to be negligible. The belief that certain kinds of feature are invariant within fine limits of tolerance from member to member of each species is often based on a vast sample ; this sample may contain literally millions of instances showing no exception to the rule that the type of feature in question is invariant within the species. In such a case we should have supra-astronomical odds in favour of there being almost no exceptions to the rule that within the genus those features are invariant from member to member of each species. It is when these conditions are present that the single crucial laboratory experiment, which has become so famous in logical discussion, is possible. It may be desired to establish the reaction of some new-found chemical element that has not yet been tested. One experiment may suffice for this purpose, although it is deemed expedient to repeat the experiment as a check upon the accuracy of observation and to ensure that it is conducted in proper conditions. There is no need to quarrel with the scientists who assure us that the further experiments are not required nor intended to get a wider sample of cases of the reaction of the element in question, but merely to make quite sure that the experiment has been properly performed. The additional experiments are in fact supplementary tests of the observer, not of the thing observed. To the older logicians, this seemed to point to an assumption of universal causation. More recently it has been cited to cast doubt on the basic worth of induction by simple enumeration and to support ably formulated proposals for supplanting induction by a so-called hypothetico-deductive method. All this is a mistake.

In fact the inference in question, namely from the instance shown in a single experiment to the generalization that the element always reacts in this way, derives its extremely high probability from a very vast sample indeed. It rests fairly and squarely on simple enumeration. The vast sample consists in all those cases where, in respect of this type of feature, the various species of the genus (chemical elements in the case in point) show invariance from member to member. This property in the genus having been established by an enormous enumeration, one can argue with confidence in a particular case that if the feature is found specified in a certain way in one member of a species, it will be similarly specified within fine limits of tolerance in other members.

An instance of this kind of thing is to be found in the relativity observations carried out in 1919. Light belongs to that small *élite* of physical entities whose features are found to be invariant within very fine limits of tolerance indeed. When the light rays were observed to bend, no one argued that those particular light rays bent, but that others might not. No one held that it would be necessary to get a number of observations on different occasions to make sure that other light rays behaved similarly to those and thus gradually build up a moderate probability that all light rays would behave in a similar manner in the neighbourhood of mass. It may be argued in the style of Keynes that theoretical arguments based on other facts gave a prior probability in favour of the hypothesis that light rays do so bend. This was no doubt a supporting consideration. But it would not give nearly enough support if the generalization in regard to light rays had no more inductive evidence in its favour than would be afforded by one instance of the conjunction of P with Q. The evidence for the invariance of properties of this type rests upon such a vast enumeration that one can assume with enormously high probability that there is invariance in the case of a newly established property of the general type under consideration, even on the basis of one instance.

The foregoing conclusion is related to matters discussed in the first chapter.[1] An argument from simple enumeration, that is a sampling argument including the process of 'reversing the consequents', is one that belongs to the *first* stage in the acquisition of knowledge by induction. It does not presuppose the uniformity of nature in any form whatever, nor initial prior probabilities of any kind. We may define a natural kind within our own experience by specifying features that make the repetition 'strong' by the measuring rod of the Heracleitean hypothesis. We may then find that in a large sample a further characteristic is invariably conjoined with the characteristics specified, and establish high probability, still by an argument from simple enumeration, for the almost invariable concomitance of that characteristic.

We may then begin to move on to the second stage of induction with the aid of the genus-species relation. We may define some genus by reference to common characteristics of its members. We may find by a large sample that members of the genus normally have some further common characteristic, *e.g.* that they melt at some point of heat. The similarity of the characteristic from member to member of the genus may have large limits of tolerance, *e.g.* by no special degree of heat being specified. Within the genus we may find that we can define a number of species carrying the characteristics of the genus, and that at least some types of characteristic have much finer limits of tolerance from member to member of the species, *e.g.* specific melting-points. Again using a large sample, we may ascribe a high probability to the genus having the following characteristic, let us call it U : namely, that the particular members of its various species resemble each other within each species in respect of certain kinds of properties within very

---

[1] Cp. pp. 11-12.

fine limits of tolerance. This being a characteristic of the
genus, we have, when we come to a hitherto unexamined
species of that genus, a high prior probability that in regard
to certain properties its members will show similarity within
fine limits of tolerance. We can then establish what those
properties are in detail with high probability by a small sample
or even, subject to errors of observation, by one case.

The movement of thought which assigns the characteristic
U to the given genus belongs to the second stage of induction
and requires no assumption of the general uniformity of nature
nor of any prior probability. The attribution of U to the
genus is by virtue of simple enumeration. When we have
firmly established U with high probability as a property of
the genus, we can move forward into the third stage. We
then find that we begin our investigations on the basis of a
high prior probability in favour of certain types of uniformity
and reach high probabilities in favour of certain uniform
characteristics with the aid of quite small samples. The
'harder' sciences have long since been operating mainly in
the third stage. What is presupposed as a (high) prior probability in those sciences is not any general uniformity of nature,
a presupposition difficult to define and inherently unwarrantable, but the general prevalence of uniformity in respect of
certain types of natural kinds and certain types of property,
this general prevalence having long since been established at
an early stage in the development of the sciences in question
by the method of simple enumeration using a very vast sample.

It is relevant at this point to touch upon a problem that
has been a matter of famous philosophical controversy, namely
the existence of other selves, *i.e.* of sentience in other living
bodies. Brief reference has been made [1] to the problem —
sometimes, but wrongly, thought to be analogous — of the
existence of independent material bodies. In regard to the latter
we saw that there was a twofold problem, namely the logical
problem of whether we were justified in filling up the gaps
when we are not observing bodies by hypotheticals of the type
that 'If I made appropriate physical movements I should
observe such-and-such', and the metaphysical problem of

[1] Chapter IV.

whether there really are continually existing things in themselves or entities correlated with the observer's actual or
hypothetical sense data. At first sight it might be thought
that the question whether there really are such entities is a
similar one to the question whether there really are sentient
beings residing within the other bodies that present themselves to our sensible experience. In fact these questions are
of a totally different character in two respects.

First, when we ask whether certain material entities supposed to be correlated with our sensible experiences do or do
not really exist, we are asking whether things exist about
whose character we can specify nothing whatever — nothing,
that is, additional to what is specified in the hypotheticals with
which they are supposed to be correlated. In fact we are
asking whether certain things, we know not what they are,
exist or do not exist ; this does not appear to be meaningful.
The case of other sentient beings is altogether different. When
I wonder whether the figure sitting opposite to me on yonder
sofa is really another conscious being, I am wondering whether
sensations are occurring roughly similar to those which I believe I would have were I sitting on yonder sofa. We know
fairly precisely the kinds of qualities we mean to assert the
existence of, when we attribute to other selves emotions,
cognitive experiences, hopes, etc. In this regard the alleged
other selves or persons are not in the least like the alleged
things in themselves of the material world.

Secondly, it would make no difference to any experience
we have had or will have, so far anyhow as we can judge at
present, whether these material things-in-themselves exist or
not. It seems that nothing in experience could afford evidence
in favour of or against these things-in-themselves. I must
not put the matter too dogmatically. It may be that our
thinking will take a new turn that we cannot now foresee,
which will alter the possibilities of the case and our attitude
towards it. I have safeguarded myself with the words 'so far
anyhow as we can judge at present', and there the matter may
rest. I would suggest, on the contrary, that in the case of
other selves evidence may be found, and further strengthened,
in favour of — or possibly against — their actual existence.

It has to be admitted that the development of modern

science has overthrown or greatly weakened the evidence on which mankind has traditionally relied, and on which most people probably still rely, for believing in the existence of other conscious beings. The enquiring mind is continually on the look-out for hidden, as well as open, continuities, similarities and regularities in the phenomena of nature, and this look-out has had much success. Human and animal bodies seem to display considerable irregularity of behaviour, by comparison with other physical objects. By making the hypothesis that other human bodies contain conscious minds, like our own, which store impressions and desire objectives, we can reduce these irregularities to order. This must not be regarded simply as a tidying-up operation, a manifestation of the desire to find regularity where there may be none. There is strong probability in favour of the hypothesis. If the behaviour of human bodies was lawless there would be a terrific improbability against their behaving so much in conformity with what conscious experience and desires would direct, if only those existed. We should favour the hypothesis of consciousness to escape from this terrific improbability, so long as there is no alternative hypothesis to provide means of escape from it.

Unfortunately science has provided an alternative hypothesis by its account of the human brain. We are informed that the brain is well stocked with electricity and has a thousand million valves. When we consider what our poor little electronic machines can do, we may well hold that the existence of the brain by itself removes the improbabilities that would exist if we had to assume bodily behaviour to be unrelated to past experience or present need. Therefore we do not have to drag in the hypothesis of consciousness.

We are accordingly driven to a different type of evidence. In the world of living bodies we find great differences, as between different properties, as regards invariance from one specimen to another. A member of a species that normally has five fingers may lack one or develop a sixth. But there are some characteristics which we do not find missing in some specimens, or present in a few specimens and absent in the remainder. I refer to such characteristics as the circulatory, respiratory, digestive and nervous systems. In a species, at least

L

one member of which contains one or other of these characteristics, we do not find viable members lacking it. I should
be hard put to it to define the nature of the characteristics
thus found within our experience to be universally present, if
present at all, in living species. One might perhaps say that
they pervade or have relations with most of the separate parts
of the organic structure. On this kind of definition consciousness is certainly a characteristic which should be present in
all or none of the members ; it has relations with almost all
parts of the organism.

It is to be stressed that for the existence of this characteristic only one member of the human species — or of all animal
species for that matter — can be examined, namely oneself.
On the other hand, the sample which is evidence for the rule
that certain types of characteristic are present in all or none
of the individuals of a species is very vast indeed. Either our
sample is a very biased one or the exceptions to the rule must
be very rare indeed. It is always wiser to assume that one is
not a rare exception. If, on occasions when there is no evidence
one way or another, one assumes that one is not a rare exception, one will more often be right than wrong. This means
that consciousness in other living bodies is highly probable.

One may look at the matter in another way. We have
seen that scientists are often content with one crucial experiment. In the case of the bending light rays they had to be
content with one for the time being, and they were satisfied
with that. This contentment depends on their believing on
the basis of a very wide sample that certain types of property
are invariant as between different members of a species. If
one light ray behaves in a certain way in certain circumstances
the others can be relied on to do the same. In testing living
bodies for consciousness there can only be one crucial experiment and that is with our own body. Is the sample, on which
we depend for evidence that certain types of pervasive characteristics are present in all viable members of a species or none,
sufficient to give us confidence in this case ? I suggest that
it is. And in relation to the question whether the proposition
that our living bodies are conscious is meaningful, the fact that
still wider evidence about the pervasive characteristics of living
bodies would be relevant to the truth of the proposition indi-

cates, by the criteria of logical positivism, that the question is meaningful.

We may have that same kind of confidence in the real existence of other sentient beings on the strength of one instance, namely that of our own sentient existence, that scientists have that other light rays also will be observed to bend in the neighbourhood of mass.

There is one final difficulty in this connexion, however, to which it is needful to draw attention, namely the bearing of the withdrawal of the fair sampling postulate upon the case for the existence of other sentient beings. This must be deferred for a fuller discussion in Chapter IX.

CHAPTER VI

SIMPLICITY

In the foregoing chapters we have dealt in turn with certain categories of existents : namely continuities, simple concomitances, repetitions of complex structures. In each case we have developed arguments which have implied denying the truth of the Heracleitean hypothesis, anyhow in application to our range of observations and to the existents in question. In each case the inductive argument outlined has been framed in relation to the type of existent in question ; the mode of argument has been appropriate to the type ; the most fundamental argument of all, namely the direct use of the principle of experience, is appropriate for dealing with continuities as such. Those who make the consideration of symbols their starting-point in logical studies may be surprised at finding such *ad hoc* and particular concepts as continuity and repetition playing a part in an analysis of the most fundamental logical principles. In each case, leverage for argument was derived from the special characteristics of the concept. It may be claimed that this is a sign that the principles set forth do not belong to the highest level of abstraction. That may be so. It does not follow that the principles are incorrect. In logic, as in other studies, we cannot hope to find the most abstract principles ready made by some innate precognition. We have to climb to the highest level of abstraction by the humdrum method of getting an understanding of the true principles operating at a lower level. I cannot forbear repeating my suspicion that the over-ambitious and over-hasty attempt to formulate logical principles at the most abstract level has diverted the minds of logicians from the fundamental problems of their subject.

It is to be emphasized that the existents which have played their part in the foregoing arguments, namely the continuities, etc., are by no means like the entities of physics in being intellectual constructs, or — if Professor Braithwaite will not allow us to regard physical entities as intellectual constructs — in having implicit definitions only. All these existents are given in experience, and their definitions are ostensive. There is no doubt about their existence. We can point directly to them. In the case of existents which can be defined ostensively, namely by direct pointing, it is not only unnecessary but also fallacious to attempt a definition in terms of other entities or concepts. It would be quite wrong, for instance, to attempt to derive these concepts from those aboriginal concepts with which symbolic logicians are concerned, themselves apparently rising fully formed from a truth table like Venus from the waves.

In this chapter we shall be concerned with another fundamental concept with characteristics giving leverage for its own type of inductive inference, namely Law. This relates to successions of events. We say that a law is operating when the succession can be described in a quantitative formula of the general type of $x = f(t)$ or $x = f(t, y)$.

The hypothesis that a certain law holds has two aspects. (1) If only certain events among those in a more extensive chain of events are observed, the law, if correct, enables us to fill in the gaps in the unobserved parts of the process as a whole. (2) If we are convinced that a law is operating throughout a certain process, we may make the hypothesis that the same law operates in other cases also, where similar properties are present. To take the second point first, our right to hold the hypothesis that the law usually operates wherever similar properties are present, depends in the first stage of inductive enquiry on ordinary sampling methods. At a later stage great assistance is often obtained from the genus-species relation discussed in the last chapter, namely when throughout a genus certain types of behavioural property, expressible in 'laws', are observed to be invariant within fine limits of tolerance from member to member of its various species. This enables us to proceed with a high prior probability from the alleged operation of a newly discovered law of this type in the case of one member of a species of that genus to its operation in the case of other members of the species also. What applies to the uniformity of properties from member to member of a species applies to laws also, and this aspect need not be further considered in this chapter.

We must revert to the first mentioned aspect of this case. The hypothesis that a law operates involves usually, though not necessarily always, filling in gaps. We do not normally observe the whole process from start to finish, but take certain observations within a total process from which we wish to infer that the law is operating throughout the process. We seek to fit a formula to the observations that we have. This is Mill's Method of Concomitant Variations. It has a prime importance in induction, only less than that of the Method of Simple Enumeration. It ranks far above the Methods of Agreement and Difference, which are little more than methodological precepts akin to the instruction to use clean instruments in an experiment.

It is well known that many basic laws of science are of great simplicity. The hypothesis of a law is only considered worth entertaining if it is fairly simple in relation to the number of observations it covers. And it is a cardinal maxim of science to prefer a simple law to a complex law when both fit the facts. Why is this ?

In what follows I am greatly indebted to Professor Harold Jeffreys for having given strong emphasis to the basic importance of this preference for a simple as against a complex law in all scientific enquiry, and for the example of a choice between alternative laws.[1] But I am not indebted to him for his own explanation of this preference. His account provoked my thought and was thus the proximate cause of the solution which I am about to offer. It also provoked another train of reflexion, namely, that the whole theory of probability requires revision from the beginning onwards. That Professor Jeffreys did not see the solution of this problem to which his own account of it so clearly points I attribute to the fact that writers on probability theory, including one as distinguished as Professor Jeffreys himself, are bogged down by formulations of the Bayes-Laplace type, which made a false start.

That preference should be given to a simple law is a point of agreement between us. Professor Jeffreys holds that any simple law has higher prior probability than a complex law

[1] Harold Jeffreys, *Scientific Inference*, pp. 36-51.

which is in accord with the same facts. I suggest, on the contrary, that the preference rightly given to the simple law is not a first principle at all, but is clearly deducible from more fundamental principles of induction or inverse probability, as I shall presently explain.

I object to Professor Jeffreys' position on two grounds :

1. The assumption that a simple law has superior prior probability as such is quite unwarrantable. We have no logical right whatever to assume, prior to investigation, that the universe is constructed on simple lines. On the contrary, its basic laws and structures may be extremely complex. Simplicity may have an aesthetic appeal ; simple laws may appeal to us on utilitarian grounds ; but all this has nothing to do with logic.

2. Prior to investigation or previous empirical evidence, no laws have any probability whatever. Accordingly simple laws cannot as such have greater prior probability than complex laws.

In both *Scientific Inference* and *The Theory of Probability* Professor Jeffreys affirms that the simple law is preferred because it is deemed more likely to give correct prediction.[1] That is certainly a good reason for preferring it. But it does not seem to occur to Professor Jeffreys that it is his duty as an exponent of the theory of the subject to consider *why* it is deemed more likely to give correct prediction. He is content with his own dogmatic assertion of superior prior probability. In the later volume he becomes quite petulant with logicians who are sceptical about prior probability. Scientists and the human race generally, he claims, have done very well by an *a priori* preference for simplicity. It is for logicians to fall into line. But I would suggest to Professor Jeffreys that, if a logician can find no good reason for the preference, there is an alternative open to him other than endorsing a bogus prior probability : he can remain silent, pending more fruitful ideas. And I would further suggest to Professor Jeffreys that the scientists, whose successes we all applaud, do not in fact establish their conclusions by inserting values in their equations for initial prior probabilities. The prior probability story is a rigmarole expounded by probability theorists for one another.

[1] *Scientific Inference*, p. 38 ; *Theory of Probability*, p. 4. Reichenbach (*Experience and Prediction*, § 42) stresses the predictive value of simplicity ; his treatment has interest, but is vitiated by his sceptical background.

The true explanation of this problem has the merit of beautiful simplicity. Professor Jeffreys — my gratitude for whose exposition I have already expressed — takes the case of six observations of a solid of revolution rolling down an inclined plane and finds that they obey the very simple law $5x = t^2$, where x is the distance in centimetres travelled from the beginning and t the time in seconds from the beginning. He observes that an indefinite number of more complex formulae could also be devised to fit these same observations.

Once again we may obtain logical leverage by considering the Heracleitean hypothesis. This might be used in relation to the case in point in one of two ways. We might suppose a great many observations of a great many solids : the hypothesis of lawlessness would lead us to expect that all values of x (within certain limits, presently to be discussed) would be represented a roughly equal number of times for every value of t. Alternatively we might suppose one motion proceeding for a great duration and observations taken continuously ; we might further make the proviso that the solid did not move upwards ; let x' stand for the distance travelled between t_r and $t_r + 1$; then in a very large number of observations, on the hypothesis of lawlessness, all values of x' would be represented a roughly equal number of times. It is clear that if the hypothesis of lawlessness were true, we should expect a vast number of patterns to be shown as we proceeded with repeated sets of observations, or as we extended one set of observations for an indefinitely great duration.

The set of six observations only, that we actually have, in which $5x = t^2$, does not render the hypothesis of lawlessness impossible. If the relation between time and distance in this kind of case were indeed lawless, we should actually get six observations conforming to $5x = t^2$, but only very rarely. Can we on the strength of this at once proceed to 'reverse the consequents' ? Can we argue that, since (i) on the hypothesis of lawlessness observations will very rarely accord with the formula $5x = t^2$, and since (ii) our particular set of observations, which is the only one we have, does accord with that formula, the hypothesis is improbable ? The matter is not so easy. The rarity of the set of observations we have is not enough to discredit the hypothesis. For if the hypothesis is true, and it

could be, any other set of particular observations would be
equally rare. The hypothesis is possible; if it is true, the
particular set of observations we get *must* be very rare; therefore the mere fact that we have got a very rare set of observations does not tend to discredit the hypothesis.[1]

So far we have tried to get leverage for argument from the
proposition that our collection of observations is one that
would very rarely occur on the hypothesis of lawlessness, but
we have found no leverage there, since on the hypothesis of
lawlessness, which is a possible hypothesis, we *must* get a very
rare set of observations. Can we say anything more about
these observations? We assuredly can. We can say that the
events observed *obey a simple law*. This is a property that
they have over and above that of being a particular set of six
numbers within certain limits. And it is a property which
would not be possessed by the vast majority of sets of observations which we should get on the hypothesis of lawlessness.
This consequently endows our observations with a kind of
rarity, on the hypothesis of lawlessness, which is different from
that rarity which pertains to them as being merely a particular
set of six numbers.

There is another property we can ascribe to them. These
observations also *obey a more complex law*. Professor Jeffreys
has interesting things to say in both his volumes about methods
of grading laws by their degree of complexity; I will return
to this question. Let us suppose that the next most simple
law that the six observations conform to is one of the rth
degree of complexity.

We may agree that the fact that a particular set of observations constituted like ours would occur very rarely on the
hypothesis of lawlessness does not tend to discredit the hypothesis, because on it a set constituted in any other way would
be equally rare. By like reasoning the fact that our set is
subject to a law of the rth degree of complexity does not have
a strong force tending to discredit the hypothesis of lawlessness
because many sets would on that hypothesis be found subject
to some law or other of the rth degree of complexity. It is
true that sets obeying the *particular* complex law exemplified
by the set before us may be very rare on the hypothesis of

[1] Cp. p. 124 *supra*.

lawlessness ; but that is no more a reason for rejecting the hypothesis of lawlessness than the fact that the *particular* numbers in the observation occur very rarely. In the latter case we are saved from having to reject lawlessness by the fact that the particular numbers in any observed set would be equally rare, though different from those in the set before us ; in the former case we are saved from having to reject lawlessness by the fact that many of the other sets, although not obeying the particular complex law that the set before us obeys, would obey some law or other of equal complexity-ranking. But in the case of the simple law not only would the overwhelming majority of other sets not obey the simple law that the set before us obeys, but they would not obey any simple law whatever. That requires us to look more favourably upon the hypothesis that a simple law is in fact operating.

May I return to the analogy of a hand at bridge ? When you pick up a hand at bridge you are contemplating an arrangement of cards of most extreme rarity. It is not very improbable that such a hand has never been picked up before by any of the millions of people who have played bridge. But you do not then turn to the dealer and say, 'Are you sure that you shuffled this pack ?' The reason is that whatever hand you picked up would comprise an equally rare arrangement. But suppose that having arranged the hand you were struck with the following facts. In one of the suits the cards are three away from each other, *e.g.* 2, 5, 8, etc., in two of the suits they are four away from each other, and the remaining suit consists of two adjacent court cards. Now it is true that hands to which such a formula would apply occur exceedingly rarely at the bridge table. Would you, having this in mind and the fact that the pack had previously been used for a game of patience which might have sorted the cards into some systematic order, be disposed to ask the dealer if he was sure that the pack had been shuffled ? The answer is in the negative. Although it might be extremely uncommon to get a hand to which this formula applied, it would by no means be so uncommon to find some formula or other of no greater complexity than this formula to apply to a hand dealt. In your hand the spacing of the cards in one suit is different from that in the other two ; without increasing the complexity of the formula one could have the cards in one or other of the suits spaced at intervals of two, five, six, etc. away from each other ; and the peculiarity of the cards in the fourth suit is of an altogether different kind from that in the other three. With these degrees of freedom it should be possible to describe a good many hands by a formula of no greater complexity than the one just used, and consequently the matter does not call for comment. But let the hand consist of thirteen clubs. There are only three other hands out of all possible hands at bridge complying with a formula of that degree of simplicity and, having regard to the previous game of patience, one would require a very clear memory indeed that the pack had been shuffled.

Part of one's time is spent in seeking for relations where there are none. Within that time sets of six observations will quite often be met with that obey complex laws. But only very rarely will one be met with obeying a law of extreme simplicity, and by very rarely I mean only once in every few hundred million sets examined. Consequently we have a far better reason for rejecting the hypothesis of lawlessness when confronted with a set of observations obeying a simple law than we have when confronted with one obeying a complex law. And when a set obeys both we prefer the simple law. We may even, as Professor Jeffreys observes, prefer a simple law which almost fits the facts, but not quite, to a complex law that fits them exactly, attributing the inexactitude in the former case to some error of observation or to the presence of some undetected disturbing influence. The reason is that the improbability of getting observations *nearly* approximating to *some* simple law, if no law is operating, is much greater than the improbability of getting observations *exactly* approximating to *some* complex law if no law is operating.

This vindication of the logic of preferring the simple law does not depend at all on any assumption of prior probability.

In estimating the probability of a simple law two magnitudes are involved. First, there is the improbability of getting a certain type of sets of observations if a law is not operating and, secondly, there is the deflating factor which has to be introduced whenever we 'reverse the consequents'. When the observations indicate a very simple law, the odds under the first head are very great and the deflating factor may safely be neglected. (But, as I suggested earlier, if a research worker conducted experiments for a billion years in a laboratory with null results and then got a set of observations suggesting a very simple law, the deflating factor might be of the same order of magnitude as the odds in its favour ; happily we need not worry our heads with such a case.)

But we still have to consider the first part of the calculation. We have observations favouring the hypothesis of a certain law and what we have to calculate are the odds against getting such observations if the hypothesis of lawlessness is true. First, we must calculate the number of differently constituted sets of observations that can be made if the hypothesis of lawlessness is correct. This will depend on the number in each set and increase strongly as that number is increased. It will also depend on the outside limits within which we postulate that the values of the observations must lie ; I shall deal with this point presently. Secondly, we must evaluate, if we can, what on the hypothesis of lawlessness is the number of differently constituted sets of observations within the limits allowed, all of which obey *some law of equal simplicity-ranking* to the law embodied in the observations we have. The ratio of the former number minus the latter to the latter give the odds against getting a set embodying a law of equal simplicity-ranking to the one observed if the hypothesis of lawlessness is true. But we have got such a set of observations. We then 'reverse the consequents'. The odds as stated above, having been deflated somewhat to allow for the process of reversing the consequents, express the probability that the simple law in question is true.

It is to be noted that the second number in the crucial ratio defined in the last paragraph is the number of differently constituted sets of observations obtainable on the assumption of lawlessness that would obey any law whatever of equal simplicity-ranking with the law to which our observations actually conform ; it is *not* the number of differently constituted sets of observations — presumably only one — that would obey the law in question. In the case of a very simple law this distinction may make no great difference, because either way the odds will be very favourable. But in the case of complex laws the distinction makes a large difference and greatly weakens the evidential value of observations which comply with a complex law. It may be very rare indeed among lawless phenomena to get observations obeying the particular complex law exemplified by those before us ; but that is little more significant than the fact that it is very rare indeed to get the particular set of numbers that are embodied in the observations before us. Rarity which consists merely in things being the particular things they are is not significant as pointing to law, because such rarity is omnipresent in a lawless universe. To find significance in favour of law, one has to consider the *general character* of the rare objects ; the general character of a set of observations that obey a particular law of the rth degree of complexity-ranking is that they obey a law of the rth degree of complexity-ranking ; but, unless r is substantially smaller than the number of observations before us, observations of that *general character* would not be very rare in a lawless universe ; therefore their presence would not be strongly evidential in favour of law. But the sets of observations having the general character of obeying any law of high simplicity-ranking are exceedingly rare, and, therefore, their frequent recurrence would be high evidential value in favour of the presence of laws.

A set of observations conforming to a law has a cogency in establishing the truth of that law that is in inverse ratio to the number of sets of observations which would occur in the absence of any law and conform to ANY LAW OF EQUAL SIMPLICITY-RANKING *with that to which the observed set conforms.* I submit that this proposition is a first principle of induction. I do not recall having seen it set out in any treatise. The preference for a simple law over a complex law, where either would fit the observations, follows as a corollary, for in a lawless universe there are more sets of observations conforming to one or other of all the laws of the $r + 1$th degree of complexity than there are conforming to one or other of all the laws of the rth degree of complexity.

It follows that Professor Jeffreys has been pursuing a most important line of thought in attempting to grade laws according to their complexity. My quarrel with him relates only to his objective, namely that of getting a criterion for assigning

prior probabilities. In *Scientific Inference* he suggested that
the criterion for grading a formula should be 'the sum of the
order, the degree and the absolute values of the co-efficients',
the last-mentioned being reduced to whole numbers.[1] In the
Theory of Probability he says that the criterion should be the
'number of adjustable parameters'.[2] In such matters I must
speak with the utmost diffidence, as befits a layman. I venture
the judgement that the *latter* criterion strikes me as correct.

Adoption of this criterion enables us to reduce the basic
principle involved to great simplicity. Any set of six observations whatever will comply with some formula or other having
six adjustable parameters. Consequently the compliance of
the six observations before us with a complex law expressible
in a formula with six adjustable parameters has no evidential
value whatever in favour of that law. Only a relatively small,
but still substantial, proportion of all possible sets of six observations will comply with some formula or other having five
adjustable parameters. The proportion of observations out of
all possible that comply with some formula or other of given
complexity ranking decreases strongly as the number of adjustable parameters is reduced, until we get the extreme rarity of
observations complying with a formula with only one adjustable parameter. This is the true basis of the preference for
simplicity. We prefer the simple hypothesis on account of
the extreme rarity of sets of observations that would on the
hypothesis of lawlessness comply with any formula whatever
of equal simplicity ranking. And of course this rarity increases
strongly as the number of observations in the set increases.

We assess in the first instance the probability of observing
sets of magnitudes on the hypothesis of lawlessness by using
the postulate that our sample of samples is fair ; as before it
can be shown that inferences justified by assuming that postulate to be true are equally well justified by the principle of
experience or simple induction if that postulate is in fact false.
It is to be noted also that argument in favour of a simple law
requires a 'reversal of consequents' as explained in Chapter IV,
and the final probability is weakened in accordance with the
principles involved in that 'reversal'.

We must now face the question, which I postponed, of

[1] Pp. 45-6.   [2] Pp. 100-1.

what ought to be regarded as the maximum possible range of
variation in x (or x'), on the assumption that no law is operating.
I have the idea — but this is where the wings of my logical
aspiration are clipped by scientific ignorance — that available
methods of measurement may often set limits to the range of
values of x. We are dealing with empirical knowledge, not
pure mathematics, and therefore only interested in the values
of a magnitude that can be precisely ascertained by a measuring
instrument. I am aware that science is acquainted with very
large numbers, but I believe that the instruments that measure
hundreds of millions of units do not usually give accuracy to
the nearest ten, or even to the nearest thousand, units. It is the
number of accurate digits in the numbers recorded that matters
to us, not whether those digits relate to billions, millions or
millionth parts of conventional units of measurement.

However, if this recipe for imposing limits fails, I have
another suggestion. We could adopt the postulate that the
utmost range of x in a lawless universe is fixed by the outside
values of x actually observed. This may be imposing a restriction on x for which we have scanty evidence. But it is
not logically objectionable because it tends to *weaken* the force
of evidence in favour of laws. If narrow limits are imposed
on variations of x in a lawless universe, this strongly reduces
the number of all possible differently constituted sets of observations of x in such a universe ; the smaller this number,
the less evidential value has a set of observations embodying
a law in favour of that law. In fine, we should be adopting what
is called in economics a 'conservative' estimate — that is one
which, if it errs, understates the value of something that we
want to have a high value. My proposed postulate in regard
to x carries conservatism as far as it is possible to go ; for,
whether a law is operating or not, the actual range of the
values of x cannot be smaller than the range of its observed
values.

Let us return to the other term of the fundamental ratio,
namely the number of all differently constituted sets of observations that would comply with all formulae of the rth
degree of complexity-ranking. We need to estimate this. So
stated, the requirement seems plain. But it may be — I do
not know — that it is beyond the power of mathematicians to

meet it. Or do I underrate their powers and their actual achievements in this field ?

In everyday life and, I have no doubt, in a large part of science, in cases where evidential value seems strong, there is no need to make precise evaluations ; what is basically mathematical intuition, whether explicitly recognized as such or not, suffices to carry us to the conclusion. But where the favourable odds are not so large, intuition hesitates ; in everyday life we have to be content with uncertainties, and often with erroneous judgements.

The various branches of science, on the other hand, have, I am well aware, developed subtle mathematical techniques for estimating 'significance'. I am not competent to judge the value of many of these. Whether the scientists who use these techniques explicitly concern themselves with the logic that justifies them, I am not sure. It is by no means always necessary to them to do so, nor discreditable to them, if they do not. My doubts are raised by the fact that writers with wide and deep knowledge of the mathematical aspects of modern science in its various branches do not always deal satisfactorily with the fundamental logical aspects.

It is only with these that I have been concerned. I claim to have established that the preference for simplicity can be justified without any reference to prior probabilities. The preference for simplicity is not based on a prior probability of simplicity ; it is a logical corollary of the basic principle of inverse probability.

CHAPTER VII

TRUTH, BELIEF AND KNOWLEDGE

In the foregoing chapters the meanings of certain cognitive expressions have been taken for granted. It is perhaps in accord with the spirit of empiricism to begin with rough materials, the general character of which is perceived, and proceed to refined concepts and hypotheses. Furthermore, the definition of a concept can be better understood if we already have illustrations of its application.

It is not possible, however, to proceed to a vindication of memory without more precise definitions of the principal ideas belonging to the field of epistemology. The definitions to be provided are in agreement with, and indeed flow from, the basic tenets of empiricism. The philosophy of empiricism has fallen out of fashion in recent years, although lip service is often paid to it, sometimes by those whose general views do not entitle them to do so. Accordingly the definitions that follow may seem strange to some, and out of accord with current modes of thought. They are bound to be so, because current modes of thought are out of accord with empiricism.

In my view, and I suggest that any genuine empiricist is bound to hold such a view, logic is concerned with how a sentient being, when confronted with certain data (similarities in experience, etc.), may *safely* proceed to opinions about other matters. I do not conceive that logic is specifically concerned with the analysis of symbolic systems, although symbols may aid the logician, just as they aid the physicist.

In the spirit of Hume, I hold that concepts in the field of epistemology are by no means exempt from the rule that they must be defined either (*a*) ostensively, or (*b*) in terms of others that have been defined ostensively. There may of course be any number of links in the chain of definitions; but the starting-point must always be an ostensive definition. Any system of logic that does not so start is faulty in principle and the total structure that may be built up, however elegant and subtle and far-reaching, is thereby discredited.

The reader may feel an under-current of objection to what follows, owing to a sense that such ideas as truth and knowledge have a wider range of application than that accorded to them in the text. That need not be denied ; but that wider range is beyond the scope of the present work. What is affirmed is that, in order to understand their application in the wider range, it is necessary first to isolate occasions that make ostensive definitions possible.

One may think of an ostensive definition in terms of physical pointing. But this has no special property entitling it to monopoly. Pointing is itself symbolic. One usually looks in the direction indicated by extrapolating the line from the armpit to the finger point in the direction of the finger point ; but one might have a convention that one should look in exactly the opposite direction.[1] In some cases the 'pointing' may have to be accomplished by the use of common words, cunningly devised to direct attention to the right things. There is no hard-and-fast rule for communication ; one seizes upon any method that one hopes will achieve the correct result. In communing with oneself, no symbolism is required, one just looks at the relevant thing. This seizing upon any material that may be handy is analogous to that use of ordinary English words that one finds in the opening chapters of treatises on symbolic logic of the highest brow.

In the process of identifying basic cognitive concepts, the existence of a specious present appears to be quite essential. It is essential not only for the task of indicating basic concepts to others, but to that of identifying them oneself. It does not seem that any progress at all could have been made in knowledge without it.

Our present awareness is not confined to a geometrical point of time, but has some temporal extension. This is well established. The most familiar illustrations are concerned with sound sequences. The sight of motion is another case in point. If our awareness were confined to a geometrical point, we should look out upon a completely stationary universe. Some might argue that a succession of static views could produce the illusion of motion, like the cinematograph which so much impressed the mind of Henri Bergson. This

---

[1] Cp. L. Wittgenstein, *Philosophical Investigations*, p. 75.

will hardly do, for, if awareness at each point were insulated, it is difficult to see how the illusion could arise. Furthermore there must be some doubt as to the meaning of unextended moments of awareness, for our awareness through successive presents often continues uninterruptedly over a finite temporal duration. Could a succession of geometrical points do so ? Or should we have to assume blind patches between them ? If we observe motion very carefully, *e.g.* a bird in flight, our awareness seems to have a temporal centre of gravity which moves along with the bird. This centre may be regarded as the absolute present. But our present awareness plainly extends on either side of it.

A specious present may comprise 'impressions' — sensible experience of various kinds including internal sensations — and mental thoughts or imaginings. Following Hume, I take the ultimate elements of which our imaginings are compounded to be the 'faint' images of impressions ; to these must be added symbols, which will be discussed presently.[1] Let it be understood that whenever I speak of an 'imaginative' structure hereafter, this may consist, either in whole or in part, of symbols. I am informed that there are many who have little capacity for visual or other imaginary. Their thinking must presumably be constituted almost entirely of groups of symbols. Their case must be catered for, and in all that follows 'group of symbols' may be substituted for imaginative structure without detriment to the argument. While each ingredient in a structure of images must resemble an item of sensible experience, we find ourselves able to arrange the ingredients in a pattern which may not correspond to any sensible experience.

The specious present has two ends, not precisely demarcated, the disappearing end and the other ; I call the former the backward and the other the forward end ; this defines 'backward' and 'forward' in this context. It may serve also to define temporal 'before' and 'after' within the limits of the specious present.

We may, if we choose, imagine a structure temporarily adjacent to the forward end of our specious present. For instance, if we are watching a bird in flight, we may within

[1] See below, pp. 170-2.

this specious present imagine a forward course for it on an extension of its present arc, the image being attached in our imagination to the forward end of the specious present. We may also, in a more humdrum way, imagine the continued stationariness of stationary objects around us.

Presently the specious present catches up on us and we may have a sensible impression of a bird actually flying along the arc as previously imagined. The image and the subsequent sensible event can easily lie in the same specious present. One specious present passes continuously into another. For exposition I will select two overlapping specious presents. I also artificially divide each specious present into two parts. In the first part of the first specious present there is the sensible impression of the bird in flight; in the second part of it there is an impression plus an imagined extrapolation of the flight forwards over a continuation of its present arc. The first part of the second specious present is the same as the second part of the first; in the second part of the second specious present there is the sensible vision of the bird flying over the arc imagined in the first part. It may be convenient to give this in the form of a diagram:

1st Specious present

	A	B
Sensible	Impression of bird in flight	Impression of bird in flight
Imaginative		Imagined extrapolation of bird's flight

2nd Specious present
B here stands for identical experience shown by B above

	B	C
Sensible	Impression of bird in flight	Impression of bird's flight on arc as imagined in B
Imaginative	Imagined extrapolation of bird's flight	

The structure of the lower part of B is identical with that of the upper part of C, the former being a faint replica of the latter.

In this case we have within one specious present (the second shown) an example of an imaginative structure being a copy of a sensible structure. The imaginative structure and the sensible structure are mutually related as replicas of one another. Being a copy of a sensible structure may be regarded as an attribute of the imaginative structure.

In a single specious present there may be many instances of such a copy relation. You may think that driving a car in a busy street, where we have of necessity to make numerous imaginative extrapolations forward and hope for dear life that the subsequent sensible experiences will correspond, is inappropriate to illustrate the mental history of primitive nescient man. But there is no reason to think of him as crouching eternally in an empty cave. Furthermore the extrapolation in imagination of the continued stationariness of stationary objects — prognosis of the stability of which is very important for the preservation of life — itself gives very numerous examples within one specious present of the copy relation between an imagined structure and a subsequent sensible structure.

Similarities are noticed in experience. If we see many red objects, we notice their similarity in all being red. If we see many particular copy relations, we notice their similarity in being copy relations. If we see many particular copy relations in all of which the two terms are sensible experience and imaginative experience, we notice the similarity as between these particular copy relations in that each has two terms of that type. The two terms consist of an imaginative (or symbolic) counterpart and a sensible counterpart. To an imaginative counterpart having this kind of relation to a sensible counterpart we give the general name true.[1]

In this ostensive definition of 'true' we have chosen a

---

[1] Where symbols are used throughout the imaginative process, the structures would be said to be true, if the lively counterparts corresponded with the meanings previously assigned to the symbols (see below, p. 170). But while many sophisticated people may make little use of images, it is doubtful if images could have been dispensed with altogether in the initial stages of piecing together an idea of the world in which we live.

particular location for the sensible replica, namely one adjacent
to the forward end of the specious present. As the scope of
our imagination grows, we acquire the power of imagining a
wider range of locations and of imaginatively filling them in
as we like. These various locations must have some specified
relation to an origin, either our present here and now or some
other origin defined by reference to our present here and now.
I suggest that even in the widest extension of the application
of the idea of truth, this limitation, that is the need for reference to a determined location, must be recognized.

The notion of truth so far given is confined to particular
truths of fact. There are other types of truth such as those
pertaining to disjunctions, hypotheticals or beliefs of general
import ; it is convenient to defer our brief consideration of
these until we shall have defined the nature of belief.

But before we proceed to that task, there is more to be
said about particular truths. The resemblance detected between the image and its counterpart may be more or less close.
This fact seems to be in contrast with the hard and fast distinction normally made between true and false. In certain
cases where the resemblance is not complete, we can subdivide the image into those parts where the resemblance is
complete and those in which it is not, and we can say that the
image is true in some respects, namely in the former respects,
but not in others. This does not completely solve the problem.
Even in the approved parts of the image, the relation of resemblance may not be absolute. This may be due to the fact that
the image is less sharply defined than its sensible replica ; the
image may be constructed out of coarser materials. We do
not say that it is 'not true' unless it could be corrected without
being made more precise. Unfortunately it is not always
obvious whether it could be so corrected. We may look at a
cubist portrait and complain that it is not sufficiently like the
sitter. The rejoinder might then be made, that, given the
cubist style and its limitations, it would be impossible to get
a closer resemblance. But how do we know ? Perhaps a
more skilled painter, desiring to achieve a likeness, could in
fact, within the limitations of that particular style, get a closer
likeness. Thus some question would remain whether the
image could be said to be true or not.

Even if it could be clearly established that the image could be corrected towards closer resemblance, we are not always inclined to say that it is false. We might judge that the image of the bird's flight was so near what actually happened as to be regarded as a correct prediction. If someone upon entering a town expressed the belief that it contained a million residents, and if reference to the census showed a population of a million and ten residents, we should be impressed with the truth rather than the falsity of the initial belief. In order to introduce precision into the distinction between truth and falsity, one might define allowed limits of tolerance in advance. This definition rests upon an arbitrary decision. In defining limits of tolerance, one draws an artificial boundary line within the realm of possible degrees of resemblance, with the images inside the boundary to be reckoned true, and those outside false. In fact we make an artificial dichotomy. In some cases, such as those instanced above, the location of this boundary line is quite arbitrary. It may be claimed that in other cases the nature of the subject provides a natural boundary line. This need not be denied. But it will often be found that the precision suggested by the nature of things is not so great as seems at first sight. It might be said that if I knock at the door of the house and believe my friend to be at home, either he is or he is not; my belief will be either true or false. But suppose that he turns out to be in the garden. It might be said that we had been initially careless in defining the limits of tolerance and that the garden ought to be have been included. But supposing that he had gone across the road to post a letter, and was absent only for two minutes; this is very different from, for instance, being abroad on a continental travel.

Some might be inclined to reject the doctrine of limits of tolerance and require absolute precision in the resemblance. There would still remain the difficulty, noted above, due to the roughness of the materials and the ambiguity, which cannot be overcome, about whether a more precise image could have been constructed with those materials. The replacement of images by symbols does not materially affect this point, since our stock of symbols is also limited. Whether we adhere to precise resemblance, or subscribe to the doctrine of limits of tolerance, our proceeding is arbitrary in a high degree. We are concerned to define a property the essential nature of which is resemblance ; this is a resemblance occurring in a certain class of cases, namely the resemblance between an imaginative structure of specified imaginative location, and a sensible structure. It is of the essence of the resemblance that it should be of greater or less degree. If we decide to insist upon precise resemblance — even that being subject to the ambiguity about what the materials used are capable of — we decide arbitrarily to ignore degrees of closeness of resemblance in cases when the resemblance is not exact. We may decide to ignore them, but we cannot thereby do away with their existence ; the images having more or less resemblance, have more or less of that quality which we are seeking to define ; yet in our definition we are ignoring that more or less. If we define limits of tolerance, we decide to ignore both the more and the less inside the defined limits and also the more and less outside the defined limits. All this is quite arbitrary. I am not saying that it is not justified.

In the foregoing chapters the concepts of true and false have been used. But it will have been noticed that in many points in the argument there was reference to limits of tolerance. This reference, and the complication which it introduces into our arguments, is the price that has to be paid for the simplification gained by the 'true and false' dichotomy. In the various kinds of inductive argument considered, the specification of limits of tolerance, both as regards premises and conclusion, can make a tremendous difference to the degree of probability with which the argument can endow the conclusion. The weakness and artificiality of the true and false dichotomy must be recognized at every point in the development of the principles of logic ; and a specific reference to limits of tolerance is required at many points.

Truth has been defined ostensively. It is a special kind of copy relation in which the resemblance can be more or less close. It must not be inferred from the presence of 'more or less' that we have here a relativist doctrine of truth. Relativist doctrines of truth imply that the truth quality cannot be defined without reference to some outside matters ; on the contrary, it is here claimed that the truth character is inherent in the pair of phenomena and can be defined without further reference. It is a doctrine of absolute truth. It is still further removed from the obnoxious doctrine of pragmatism.

Falsity does not appear as a separate quality ; its apparent separateness and contrast is generated by drawing an arbitrary boundary line among the gradations of possible resemblance. There is one quality — a specific kind of resemblance which we call truth — which can be inherent to a greater or less degree. It might be objected that there is a specific quality of falsity where there is no resemblance at all. But it is doubtful if this can be sustained. It might be said that there would be no resemblance if the bird suddenly fell to the ground. There might yet be greater resemblance — since the body of the bird was at least preserved intact — than if it was suddenly vaporized or transformed into an angel. From the dichotomy we derive the tautology that the image must be either true or false. A third alternative of 'meaningless' does not seem proper in this case. We can make any image we like out of the imaginative materials at our disposal. The word 'meaningless' does not seem to be usable in this connexion. 'Meaningless' is a secondary concept belonging to the logic of symbolism, rather than to logic proper.

I believe that the familiar word 'not' can be defined by saying that something is not true if, and only if, it is false. This would be to define 'not' in cognitive terms. I suggest that the application of 'not' to natural objects either carries an implicit reference to cognition, or is used analogically. Professor A. J. Ayer has recently made a penetrating study of negation.[1] He does indeed there treat the negative as being a property of natural objects. None the less there is a strong family resemblance between his doctrine and that here propounded. With him the positive is the more specific, and the negative the less specific. Similarly in the doctrine advanced above, the positive is what lies inside the arbitrarily defined limits of tolerance, and the negative all that is outside that boundary ; the positive is thus the more specific.

In modern symbolic logic much appears to rest upon truth tables. Since their precision is due to an arbitrary act of will, it is not surprising that a great edifice of precise deductions can be built upon them. But a warning must be given. Whereas

[1] *Philosophical Essays*, III.

the precision of the truth tables is the result of an arbitrary act of will, the properties of numbers *have precision in their own right*. It surely follows that there must be a fault in logic in any claim that the properties of numbers should be deduced from the properties of truth tables. We may admire the skill and ingenuity with which this deduction has been carried out ; we need not deny that the possibility of the deduction has a tremendous interest ; it points to something significant, although I am not sure whether anyone has yet told us what it is that it points to. But this interest and this significance must be despite the essential faultiness of the logic concerned. It cannot be the case that properties belonging to entities that are precise in their own nature, can be derived from the properties of entities that have only been endowed with precision by an arbitrary act of will-power. This alleged deduction has had a profound influence on twentieth-century philosophy. I am confident that in the long run it will not stand up to criticism. Many springs have contributed to this stream of thought. To take one case, Russell has told us that his own work sprang from his discontent with Mill's empirical treatment of mathematical truths. His discontent was well justified. It does not follow that his solution of this particular problem is correct.

Another pointer may be mentioned here. Small numbers are given ostensively. This means not only that they do not need to be defined in terms of other entities, but also that they must not be so defined. To define small numbers in terms of something else is to commit a similar fallacy to that involved in defining sensible colour in terms of wave-lengths. It is the most important, as well as the subtlest and most difficult, part of the logic of concepts, to discriminate between what is given ostensively and what is not. A mistake here can invalidate a whole system of thought.

Before proceeding to some very brief remarks about other categories of truth — hypotheticals, etc. — it is expedient to consider the nature of belief.

We may now substitute a rather more complicated example for that of a bird in flight. We may have a sensible impression of a man riding on horseback. Free of fancy, we may append all sorts of imagined (or symbolic) structures to the forward end of the specious present. Thus, if he is a sanctimonious individual, we may imagine him rising out of his saddle and ascending into heaven ; or, if he is pompous, we may imagine him standing up on his horse, or standing on his head on his horse, as though a glorified circus performer. Or, especially if he happens to wobble in his saddle, we may imagine his falling to the ground.

Or we may go further than this. In our imagination we may append any imagined attribute we choose (or the symbol for it) to our imaginative structure. Thus we may imagine the imagined form of the rider, ascending into heaven or falling to the ground, to become the colour of gold. Or we may endow this imagined form with another attribute, namely that of being a copy of sensible experience.

But as soon as we make this particular imaginative attribution, something else begins to happen. We can quite easily imagine the rider ascending into heaven ; but if we try to tack on to this imaginary picture the further attribute of its being a copy of sensible reality, we find this attribute strongly repelled. It does not agree with the imaginary ascent to imagine it a copy of sensible reality. These two elements in our imagination refuse to adhere together. If on the other hand he has a bad wobble and we tack on to the forward end of the specious present an imagined picture of his falling to the ground and we also tack on to that in turn the imagined attribute of being a copy of sensible reality, this further attribute may not be repelled ; on the contrary it may be strongly attracted, and we can express our state of mind by saying, 'I am sure that he will fall off'. Alternatively the imagined copy-attribute may not be either repelled or attracted and we can express this neutral state by saying, 'I wonder if he will fall off'.

I want to emphasize the difference between free flights of fancy in imagining structures without any thought of the copy-attribute and those same flights combined with an essay in attributing an imagined copy relation to them. By a free flight we may like to imagine his falling off simply because we dislike the man. But once we try to append in our imagination the copy-attribute we find ourselves subject to pressures. If the man is riding perfectly steadily, the copy-attribute is repelled ; if he seems to have lost his hold, it is strongly attracted.

I now have to make a digression. When we think of a particular sensible experience, we may do so by a mental image, which is its faint copy, or by a symbol (or group of symbols). Many symbols occur in a faint as well as a sensible form. Thus we may utter the word 'red' aloud or merely think the sound; we may write out the letters R E D or merely visualize these letters in our imagination. A symbol is initially constituted by an arbitrary act of will; as currently used, however, it may often have been accepted from others, the original act having totally disappeared from view; indeed the act is often quickly forgotten, as in the case of a nickname for a child which comes into currency no one quite knows how; none the less it must have been by the decision of someone and the acceptance of others that the special noise in question was applied to the child; a symbol may occasionally be onomatopaeic or otherwise resemble the thing symbolized, but is much more usually totally different from it. ' "Y" is a symbol of X' implies that an act of will has been made by the individual using the symbol, or by others, and accepted by him. It consists in a resolve to use 'Y' in thought processes in such a way that we attribute to Y the logical consequences that belong to X, and not those that belong to Y. When 'heat' occurs in a thought process, we do not regard what is entailed by or might be inferred from the presence of either the sound or visual appearance of the word 'heat'.

Symbols are notoriously useful for generic properties. If we want to think of a triangle by image, we imagine a particular triangle; if we want so to think of triangularity, we have to pass a sufficient number of images of different kinds of triangle in mental review and take note of their common property — a cumbersome procedure. If we can use a symbol such as the word 'triangle', that is much more expeditious.

We can presumably think of any particular sensible experience by means of an image; we can conjure up faint replicas of all its specific sensible qualities. But there is one attribute of a sensible experience which it seems that we cannot thus conjure up, namely its being sensible or lively as distinguished from imaginary or faint. Generally this does not matter, since what we are interested in are its specific features of shape, colour, etc., rather than that quality of liveliness which is

common to all sensible experiences.   But the obstacle becomes
serious, when we want to think of sensible experience, as such,
by contrast with imaginative experience.   I suggest that there
is no way of doing this by images alone, and that, if we want
to be aware of the contrast between sensible experience and
imaginative experience, we must put ourselves in the way of
having some sensible experience, *e.g.* by looking around the
room, and noting the difference between its liveliness and the
faintness of similar images that we can conjure up.   But if it
is inconvenient to do this, symbolism may come to our rescue.
At any moment of noting the difference between a variety of
sensible data on the one hand and a variety of imaginative
data on the other, we can ordain symbols for the qualities
distinguishing the two sets from one another, such as 'sensible'
and 'imaginative', and use them in our subsequent thinking.

In accordance with this reasoning, if we want to imagine
that an imagined structure is a copy of a sensible structure
outside the specious present, we cannot do so at all without
the use of symbolism.   By definition the sensible structure in
question is beyond the reach of our present awareness.   Therefore when we carry out the proposal of the foregoing paragraph
and seek by our imagination to assign to an imagined structure
the attribute of being a copy of sensible reality, we must use a
symbol for that attribute.   We cannot imagine a relational
attribute without adverting in our imagination to the other
term of the relation, but this is precisely what in the present
case we cannot do.   We cannot imagine a counterpart that
shall resemble an imagined structure in all respects except in
being something not imagined.   The difficulty is overcome
by our power to use a symbol for the unimaginable quality of
liveliness.   The interesting result follows that we cannot perform the most elementary of all thinking operations, namely
supposing that an idea that we have may be a counterpart of
sensible reality, without using a symbol.   This result, if correct,
is very notable, since it carries the corollary that there can be
no thought without will.

And what is the symbol we use when we want to say that
an imagined complex is the counterpart of a sensible complex ?
The word 'true' is available, but we do not normally employ it.
I said above that many symbols have both sensible and

faint counterparts. But by no means all have both, and
perhaps not most. The separate elements that go to make up
an imaginative structure must have sensible counterparts. But
it appears to me that in thinking we use many symbols which
have none. Permit me to illustrate. When as tyros, having
learnt the theorem of Pythagoras, we use it in another proof,
we may say 'By the theorem of Pythagoras', using full explicit
symbolism, even perhaps pronounced semi-audibly. Later we
may merely say, 'by Pythag'. But before long we shorten this
out of recognition, so that the mental event that constitutes
reference to the famous theorem is nothing more than what
might be called a mental click of microscopic dimensions.
The quality of the click is private and presumably different for
each person who employs a shorthand mental symbol for
Pythagoras. I confess that I do not frequently use this theorem
myself. My economic thinking requires the use in chains of
reasoning of such beliefs as 'an increase of the quantity of
money in the economy will tend to make interest rates fall',
or 'a sufficient condition for a devaluation of a country's
currency having a positive effect on its balance of trade is that
the sum of the elasticities of the country's demand for foreign
goods and of the foreign demand for the country's goods shall
be greater than one'. When these beliefs are employed in my
own mental processes, as they frequently are, I need hardly
say that they do not appear as long verbal rigmaroles but
simply as very rapid mental clicks, which, however, may be
clearly distinguished one from another. It would be quite
impossible for me to give sensible representations of these
clicks ; they are altogether illiterate, unutterable and private.

Some philosophers of pragmatic inclination have urged
that thinking is a kind of habit, like riding a bicycle, and that
we have no need to advert to the (logically) necessary steps in
an argument. They are simply by-passed. This is no doubt
true, if we have already established a train of reasoning for
proceeding from A to Z and take the intermediate links for
granted. But I doubt if this is correct where we have on hand
an essentially new train of reasoning, in which such beliefs as
those concerning interest rates and exchange rates have to play
new and independent parts in a new chain of reasoning. Yet
even when they do play some new and vital rôles, they may

only be present to the mind as quite illiterate specks.

The philosophers I have mentioned stress the point that when good reasons are available for believing in the truth of A, we often act as if A were true, without either adverting to the reasons or assuring ourselves that A is true. I do not challenge the possibility or importance of this. This facility of omitting the relevant arguments is a happy endowment, allowing great economy of time and effort. It may be that our physical brain does some reasoning for us, of which we are unconscious. But this account of the matter surely only holds when we are already habituated; it will not do for essentially new arguments. Alternatively I would urge that the logician cannot be satisfied if the chain of reasoning that ought to be there contains a link that could not in principle be there. Such a link in the case in point is the quality supposed to be possessed by an imaginative counterpart of being 'lively' or non-imagined. It is to serve as substitute for such a link that a symbol is indispensable.

I suggest that the symbol usually employed for 'copy of sensible reality' or 'true' is like that used for the belief about exchanges rates in being cryptic and private to each user. Since it is in continuous use and related simultaneously to many objects, it is not surprising that it should be reduced to the shortest of all conceivable mental short-hands. But it would be wrong to deny its presence. There is all the difference in the world between the mental state of idly imagining a picture of the rider falling off — perhaps out of sheer malice — and the mental state of trying to conjoin to that same picture the idea that it is a copy of reality, viz. that he may in fact fall off. This second state of affairs does not imply that we think he will fall off; on the contrary, we may decide that in all the circumstances he is unlikely to. When I say that we try to conjoin in our imagination to the picture of his falling off the symbol for the attribute of being a copy of sensible reality, I am describing accurately what could be popularly expressed by the words 'we give consideration to the real possibility of his falling off'. Please note that in all this passage I use the words 'the rider falls off' as shorthand for the observer having a sensible experience which we call seeing him fall off; no reference is intended to the alleged rider as an object with other properties of its own or to the alleged horse. I will not repeat this. Also I hope that I do not need to repeat what I said at the outset that when I use such an expression as having a picture of his falling off, symbols can be substituted in whole or in part for the 'picture'. In the case in point the bare symbol constituted by the words 'fall off' might suffice, or some private illiterate mental shorthand for 'fall off'.

If we find the copy symbol adhering very strongly to the image of his falling off (or its symbolic counterpart), we could appropriately express this by such words as 'I am convinced that he will fall off'. Or we may find the symbol repelled and say, 'I am sure that he will not fall off'. Or we may be in an intermediate position : 'I rather think he will fall off', or 'he may fall off'. Unless the position is one neither of attraction nor of repulsion, we may describe the state of mind of the observer by saying that he entertains a belief.

Belief is here defined ostensively by reference to psychological attractions or repulsions in specified cases. The mental event of believing that the rider will fall off must next be considered in relation to its environment. The tendency of the copy symbol to adhere or not to adhere to the falling-off image is not just an arbitrary fact, but is governed by surrounding considerations. If the copy symbol adheres strongly, it is because we have good empirical reasons for the belief. We may be guided crudely by simple induction, merely extrapolating forward the arc already made by the rider's body. More probably we rely on a sample of similar situations previously observed ; or, more grandly still, we may have in our minds a belief in some general laws of statics and dynamics, even if only unprofessionally formulated, and deduce that the rider cannot regain his balance.

Or we may conclude that he will not fall off. If our experience does not incline us in either direction, the copy symbol is neither repelled by nor attracted to the falling off image or symbol, and remains, so to speak, in neutral equilibrium. If the copy symbol is either repelled or attracted, there is also present, as well as the falling off image and the copy symbol, some mental reference to the relevant past experience.

The belief is said to be 'rational' if it conforms to the

principles of induction. It may be that the observer is very inept in assessing the logical force of the experience present to him, and that the evidence, which, when properly considered, should cause repulsion, in fact causes attraction. He may be a foolish man.

Unlike belief itself, rationality of belief is not here defined ostensively but by reference to the whole system of inductive logic. That system itself, however, rests on ostensive concepts, such as continuity, concomitance, repetition.

Having proceeded so far with the analysis of belief, I will revert to the subject of truth.

This volume is not concerned with the logic of symbolism, although the cardinal importance of symbolism in the thinking process is fully recognized. It is difficult at this point to abstain from referring to the profoundly unsatisfactory nature of sentences — and in what concerns us here, I believe that most of the professional symbolism of logicians is no improvement. Sentences are unsatisfactory in not specifying limits of tolerance in statements purporting to be true. Still more unsatisfactory is the fact that they give no indication of the degrees of probability attaching to the rational beliefs of which they purport to be the expression. Normally they just make flat statements as though conveying certainty. The word 'may' is sometimes used, but this indicates a bare possibility. Otherwise we can, if we are pedantic, resort to circumlocution such as 'it is probably the case that'; to do that at the beginning of every sentence — and almost all our speech is about probabilities — would be intolerable, and even that would not give an indication about the degree of probability, which is all important. Alternatively we may bring in an irrelevant reference to the speaker's private state of mind by such words as 'I think'. I only make a passing reference to these shortcomings because they come out clearly in the case of hypotheticals, and may be responsible for their unsatisfactory treatment in traditional logic.

I suggest that the disjunction can be defined ostensively and the hypothetical defined in terms of it. One may be a passenger in a car and come to a fork in the road. Alternative extrapolations (disjunctions) become possible. The driver may take the left fork or the right fork. Or, of course, he may take

N

neither, coming to a dead stop, or, losing his head and running off the road. Neglecting the possibility of neither, we
may consider the disjunction of left or right. Knowing something of the neighbourhood and our destination, we may even
assign probabilities, say two-thirds for the left and one-third
for the right — but of course they need not be so precise as
this. This done, the extrapolation may go further, ABCDE
for the left-hand alternative and MNOPQ for the right-hand.
A consists of the appearance of the initial piece of the left-hand
road, and BCDE may consist of the appearances of certain
shops, etc., with which I may be familiar ; NOPQ consist of
another environment, perhaps residential houses and gardens.
The probability of BCDE cannot be as great as that of A owing
to possible eventualities. After the driver's initial decision an
earthquake may occur, lightning strike the houses, or they
may catch fire, or may already be on fire. There is a bare
possibility of MBCDE, for instance if the car, having started
on the right-hand road, suddenly flew over the houses back on
to the left-hand one. In view of this, in order to be strict, we
may contrast with the probability of A, not that of BCDE,
but that of ABCDE. Let us denote probability by applying
the symbol p to the contents of adjacent brackets.

The fundamental relation with which we are confronted
here is that the ratio $p(ABCDE) : p(A)$ is independent of the
value of $p(A)$. The evidence for the occurrence of ABCDE at
the forward end of the specious present has two components :
the evidence for A and some further independent evidence
bearing only upon BCDE. The probability of ABCDE is
obtained by multiplication. We have a certain probability for
A, and, having gone forward to that position in our imagination, we have another probability — depending on the incidence
of fire, earthquake, etc., but quite independent of an evidence
for A — for BCDE. Therefore $p(ABCDE)$ divided by $p(A)$
is independent of $p(A)$.

We may set this out in the form of a hypothetical : if A
then BCDE. What this seems to say on the face of it is that
$p(A) = p(ABCDE)$. But this is owing to the unsatisfactory
nature of sentences generally. The equality just named would
only obtain if the hypothetical judgement was known for
certain to be true. But this is never so, where the judgement

relates to empirical matters. None the less there is something in the idea that the hypothetical form has a capacity lacking to the categorical form for conveying some certain truth. The certainty does not reside in what is said in either case. To claim certainty for any empirical belief of the form 'if A, then B' or '$p(A) = p(ABCDE)$' would be a piece of brazen effrontery. But there is a certainty wrapped up in the hypothetical. It is not the case that the ratio of p (protasis and apodosis) to p (protasis) is equal to one, although the hypothetical form of statement seems to be saying this. What is certainly true is that the ratio of p (protasis and apodosis) to p (protasis) is independent of the value of p (protasis). If the query be raised how we can be sure that there is no evidence that would make the ratio of p (protasis and apodosis) dependent on the value of p (protasis), the answer is that we cannot be sure that there is no such possible evidence, but that we can be sure, subject to the normal reservations about intellectual error, that the evidence we are using to justify our belief is not of that character. No part of the evidence that we are using in favour of the later parts of the road having a specific character depends on whether or not we turn into the road. In fine the certainty wrapped up in the hypothetical form is a certainty about the independence of two separate sets of evidence, to the extent that we are able to interpret them. Where the independent evidence about BCDE is such that p(A and not-BCDE) is exceedingly low, *i.e.* 'not (A and not-BCDE)' is a practical certainty, we have an approximation to the equality between $p(A)$ and $p(ABCDE)$. In that case what is actually stated in the hypothetical form is a practical certainty ; but categoricals can also have practical certainty in that sense. That kind of practical certainty is altogether different from the absolute certainty that is wrapped up in, but not stated by, the hypothetical form.

Hypotheticals and hypotheses tend nowadays to be thought about in different contexts despite their etymological resemblance. It is to be noted that the logical relation between a hypothesis and the conclusion reached on the basis of that hypothesis is similar to that between the protasis and apodosis of a hypothetical judgement.

New items of relevant evidence may alter the strength of

rational belief in the protasis A. But if this has no direct bearing upon BCDE, the probability of the hypothetical remains unaffected.

In the much-discussed unfulfilled conditional the protasis is implicitly denied, and thereby the conjunction of protasis and apodosis. But this denial has no effect on the truth, if it is true, that the ratio of $p(ABCDE) : p(A)$ is independent of $p(A)$. There is no reason why one should not express two separate but not contradictory statements, namely (1) that the conjunctive consisting of protasis and the apodosis is false, and (2) that the ratio of the probability of protasis and apodosis together to the probability of the protasis is, on the evidence available, independent of the value of the probability of the apodosis. (1) is a special case of (2), in which we happen to have evidence that the probability of the protasis and of the apodosis is zero. But the fact that we have the narrower piece of knowledge set forth in (1) does not invalidate the wider knowledge set forth in (2).

Nor is there any reason why we should not adduce further evidence affecting the content of the apodosis which only becomes available after the protasis is known to be false, *e.g.*, 'If you had taken the left fork you would have seen a terrible accident'. The temporal order of occurrence of evidence does not affect the probabilities generated by that evidence.

'All' may be defined ostensively within a specious present when there is a complete enumeration. 'I see a lot of balls on the billiard table and they are all white.' Imagination can enlarge the boundaries of an area and 'all' can be applied to a wider area in a similar sense. It is doubtful if this definition, and the validity of any other may be questioned, gives 'all' any meaning in relation to an area of undefined extent. Universal propositions of fact should be restricted by reference to a specified area.

The final question with which we have to concern ourselves is the nature of 'knowledge'. When, in opening the discussion on probability,[1] we sought to clear the ground by denying the possibility of gaining knowledge of facts or empirical laws by inference, it seemed extremely difficult to specify what it was that we were seeking to deny. If it is the case that empirical

[1] Chapter II.

knowledge cannot occur, then it would seem to follow that an ostensive definition of empirical knowledge cannot be given.

A distinction has been made, which becomes relevant here, between 'orders' of belief. There may be a belief about matters of fact and a belief about that belief; the latter is sometimes called a 'higher order' belief. This higher order belief belongs to the field of applied logic; if the lower order belief is an empirical one, then the higher order belief about it is within the field of applied empirical logic. It will be argued that a definition of knowledge can be given by reference to an instance of a special kind of higher order belief. But first it may be well to mention briefly certain other modes of approaching a definition of knowledge.

One such approach would be by using the mathematical notion of a limit. As a sample is enlarged, the probability of a proposed conclusion can, if the instances are favourable, be progressively increased. We have a convergent series with one as the limit. Knowledge might then be defined as the state of mind towards which rational belief tends. There may be value in this approach, but one is uneasy at having to take over a mathematical concept. Its proper scope has to be determined. From the point of view of the logician, all such concepts are explicanda.

Next an alternative approach by way of ostensive definition must be rejected. Reference was made in the passage already cited to instances of knowledge which are supposed to occur throughout direct experience; these consist in the mere awareness of the experience, provided that no attempt is made to interpret it. This seems unsatisfactory for two reasons. (1) The view that knowledge is inherent in direct experience, for example in the awareness of sense data, makes knowledge co-extensive with experience. Whatever experience one was undergoing, one would be said to have knowledge of the experience. Does this ascription of 'knowledge' add anything to the description of the experience itself? Surely not. Such a definition of knowledge would not seem to accord with the explicandum by reason of being too wide. (2) It seems to be required that the subject-matter of knowledge should be capable of being also the subject-matter of a belief that falls short of knowledge. But this would not be so under the definition here proposed. It is impossible to be in a state of wondering whether I am seeing an oblong red patch or having a pain — impossible, that is, on the assumption that no interpretation of those experiences is attempted. There is only wonder if an interpretation is attempted ; it is the interpretation that is the object of wonder ; but then that would in no circumstances become the object of knowledge. I may say that I believe I have a toothache, implying uncertainty. This would presumably mean that I do not know whether the feeling I have ought rightly to be called a toothache, or alternatively that I believe that a certain sensation I have is about to develop into a toothache. In neither case is the object of belief or wonder the same as the object of knowledge. If the word 'knowledge' is to be used in this connexion, it must be used to refer to the particular tone of feeling I have, whatever that may be. But then I cannot be wondering if I have this particular tone of feeling. Thus if 'knowledge' were to be used in this sense, it would not be a stronger form of cognition of an object that could also be the object of wonder.

In this connexion the classic definition of F. H. Bradley, whose other logical doctrines are widely out of accord with those of this volume, may be quoted. 'Judgement proper is the act which refers an ideal content (recognized as such) to a reality beyond the act.' [1] This definition is unexceptionable.

There is one kind of knowledge with which we are all well acquainted, and which is said to be much beloved by politicians and journalists — knowledge after the event. From some points of view this may be regarded as a completely useless form of knowledge ; yet it may serve a purpose in furnishing a method of approach to a definition of knowledge. Let us suppose in the example previously given that the rider does fall off. Provided that this occurs, as it well may, within the same specious present as that in which the observer believes that he will fall, we may say that he knows that his antecedent belief was true. Since this relates to the quality of a belief, it is 'higher order' knowledge.

At first blush it might be objected that the instance I have given is indistinguishable from those kinds of experiences which I have just condemned as not constituting knowledge,

[1] *Principles of Logic*, vol. i, p. 10.

namely so-called direct awarenesses of certain sensible data. (We are still assuming that the fall of the rider is taken to be no more than certain sensible experience occurring in the observer and is not interpreted in relation to alleged permanent properties of the rider.) This objection is not valid. There is all the difference between merely seeing a man fall off on the one hand, and on the other doing that and at the same time referring back to a previous state of wondering or belief. This reference back — 'I was right in thinking he would fall off' — is an event additional to the mere sight of the man falling off. If there had been no previous wondering, the reference back could not occur.

Such knowledge, although useless from the point of view of extending one's information, may not be entirely without subsidiary function. It might, for instance, be a source of pride that one had made a correct prediction. It might even be assembled with other evidence of one's power to predict, although once the specious present is passed, this item of knowledge is infected with the uncertainty that always pertains to memory.

It is to be observed that in this instance we have a case — unlike that of consciousness of a toothache — where wonder and knowledge can have the same object. In the early phase the observer may have wondered whether his attribution of the copy attribute to his image of the rider's fall adjacent to the forward end of the specious present was true ; in the later phase he knows it to have been true.

It is important to be quite clear about what we have been doing. We have defined truth and belief ostensively, the latter, as is proper, in psychological terms. We have defined rational belief by reference to the general principles of induction. We may entertain a rational belief, if the relevant evidence is present to us, without standing aloof from the belief and passing logical judgement to the effect that it is rational. We may, however, make a review of it, by adverting to the inductive principles involved, and pass the judgement, which constitutes a higher order belief, that the lower order belief is rational. Our higher order belief may of course be wrong owing to intellectual error. Now let the lower order belief relate to an alleged fact adjacent to the forward end of the specious present ;

if the fact occurs, the belief is not merely 'verified', in the sense discussed in connexion with the 'verification' of general hypotheses, but *fully* verified. The belief is in fact true. There is a privileged moment in the flight of the specious present when we can pass a higher order judgement on the belief to the effect that it was true and this higher order judgement is certain. We can contemplate the lower order belief and its full verification within the same specious present. We enjoy a very special state of mind in regard to this belief and its truth, which we can express by saying that we know it to have been true.

In logic it is our business to classify mental states. We can say in regard to the kind of state before us that in all states of this kind we have knowledge that our antecedent belief was true. Our generalization concerns a category of beliefs defined in a certain way, namely beliefs whose counterparts are realized within the specious present. The condition in virtue of which in this kind of case we have knowledge of the truth of a belief is the occurrence of a specified event in quick succession to the belief. Beliefs categorized in this way are always true. Knowledge that a given belief is true occurs as soon as it can be recognized as a belief so categorized. The full verification of the belief immediately after its occurrence is decisive evidence for the truth of the belief, and we are said to have knowledge because this evidence is present to us. Knowledge requires in this case that there be simultaneous apprehension of the belief and of the evidence which makes it true in accordance with the definition of truth.

We need to extend this idea of knowledge to a wider field. Of beliefs not categorized as above we cannot say that they are always true. But of certain classes of beliefs, namely those which are categorized by preceding events of a certain type having occurred, it is the case that they are more often true, or much more often true than not. The trouble is that we cannot have knowledge that these preceding events have occurred, owing to the fallibility of memory and records. We may, however, make the hypothesis that they have occurred, and, subject to that hypothesis, we have certainty that beliefs based on the evidence of these are more often true, or much more often true than not.

The circumstances in virtue of which beliefs can be categorized, namely evidence of a certain type, enable us to pronounce judgement on the beliefs thus categorized. In the case of one category of belief, namely that specified by the actual occurrence of the required type of succeeding event, we are able to judge that the beliefs are always true, and in the case of another category, namely that specified by the actual occurrence of certain types of preceding events, we are able to judge that they are more often true than not. The grounds of these higher level judgements have the same entailing quality in the two cases. If it is correct to say, as we do in the former case, that there is knowledge, it is appropriate to say that there is knowledge in the latter also. The example of the case of the fully verified belief pinpoints what is meant by knowledge. This knowledge is also exemplified in the judgement that other types of belief are more often, or much more often, true than not; and this last-mentioned kind of knowledge is by no means useless.

CHAPTER VIII

MEMORY

THERE are some who hold that memory is a kind of mental experience which by its intrinsic and internal character vouches for its own veridicity, that it is, in other words, a direct awareness of past events. This appears to me to be a very unsafe view. I do not attach much importance to the fact that we cannot always clearly identify our mental experiences as memories, as when we say, 'Do I remember or did I dream that so and so?' Nor do I regard as crucial the fact that some mental events which do clearly present themselves as memories are none the less deceptive. In cognition we expect exceptions. It would suffice for the intuitive theory if in the great majority of cases when we deem ourselves to be remembering we are in fact in direct awareness of past events.

I hold, on the contrary, that the events which we call memories do not carry within them a self-authenticating character, and that we are able to have very full confidence in the informative character of many of them because events external to the memories themselves provide evidence for that character.

There are those who plead vigorously from the apparent strength of certain memories that it is absolutely obvious that events occurred, for instance, that I know quite well that I entered yonder door a short time ago, that my friends usually call me by a certain name, that I was educated at a certain school, etc., and that it is scepticism run mad to challenge the directly intuitive character of such memories. If we have to acknowledge doubt here, they argue, we had better give up the game of knowledge altogether. Insistent pleading of this kind is always suspect in logic. The apparent obviousness of strong cases may be explained in another way.

The idea that there is something inside the mental event

called memory that guarantees its informative character is on the face of it dubious. Consider the case of dreams. If dreams almost always came true, or, when relating to the past, could often be verified by good evidence as replicas of waking experience, so that we could put our trust in dreams as usually informative, should we not come to believe that they were direct intuitions ? So far as their own intrinsic nature is concerned, they seem more, not less, convincing than memories. For, whereas in memory we stand in present detachment from the scenes supposed to be cognized, in dreams we actually seem to be doing those things or to be involved in the situations in question. If dreams were found by external evidence to be normally informative, we — or the unphilo-sophically minded among us — would certainly protest loudly that it was perfectly obvious that they were forms of direct intuition, carrying their own intuitive character on their faces, and that it was scepticism run mad to challenge this. In fact, when we review dreams in our waking hours we find that they do not usually come true and that they contain many features which are absurd and inconsistent with our general experience ; and so we reject them as un-informative. The reverse is usually true in these respects in the case of memories. This points to its being external evidence rather than their internal character that gives us ground for belief in their informativeness.

Before we proceed to consider this evidence it is necessary to identify memories. When I first treated of this subject,[1] I assumed that no definition of memory was required and that the phenomena called memories could readily be identi-fied — subject, of course, to doubtful cases. I no longer regard such an assumption as justified.

In the foregoing chapter belief was defined ostensively, while the adjective 'rational' in 'rational belief' was defined in terms of the inductive process ; a belief is said to be rational if it is derived by a correct argument from premises supplied by continuities, repetitions, etc. When we have beliefs about what will happen at the forward end of the specious present or in other locations specified by our present origin, we com-monly believe them to be rational, although they may not be,

[1] See *Mind*, January 1942.

as our inferential processes may be faulty and our reasoning capacity weak.

It is to be noted that belief *pur sang* was defined psychologically, namely in terms of the attraction or repulsion of the truth symbol when our imagination tries to bring it into relation with an imaginative structure. Once again we may recall that imaginative structures are taken to include structures consisting in part or in whole of symbols.

Now we find that there is a great class of imaginative structures to which the truth symbol attaches strongly, and sometimes very strongly indeed, for which, if we consider each case separately, we find that there is no inductive support whatever. It is true that in the case of many rational beliefs we may be conscious that the empirical evidence is rather thin ; normally in such cases the attraction of the truth symbol is rather weak. By and large the attraction of the symbol is in direct proportion to the strength of the evidence, subject to the believer's capacity to assess it correctly. But in the cases I have in mind there is no shadow and does not purport to be any shadow of evidence in favour of the beliefs, and yet the attraction of the truth symbol may in certain cases be tremendously strong.

The cases I have in mind are those in which we say that we remember something. The truth symbol attaches itself more or less strongly ; it sometimes attaches itself very strongly indeed, more strongly even than in those cases of prediction where a valid inductive argument gives near certainty. But what is peculiar to the memory is that there is no reason whatever for the attachment. That the structure contained in the memory has the character it does is a plain brute fact. If I go to the end of a path and discover a lake, which I had no previous reason for believing to be there, that is a brute fact of experience without rational support ; if I subsequently remember having seen the lake, that has the same quality of being brute fact. If we try to bring outside evidence in favour of there having been a lake at the place where I went, *e.g.* by consulting a map, that may give a rational ground for the belief that I saw a lake ; but to the extent that we try to reinforce the belief by such evidence, the belief ceases to retain its character of being simply a memory of having seen the

lake. It is of the essence of memory that it arises otherwise
than as the result of inference.

I submit that this account supplies all that is needful for
a definition of memory. A memory is an imaginative structure
to which the truth symbol adheres without there being any
apparent grounds for the adherence. Memories, in fine, are
members of the class of wholly irrational beliefs recognized
as such (definition).

This is not to say that it is irrational to trust to memory.
Quite the contrary. But it would be irrational to trust to any
one memory considered separately and in isolation. When
we have identified memories as a class, we can proceed to consider whether there are good grounds for holding them informative as a class. It is these grounds that have presently
to be considered.

When we come to examine memories *ab extra* and find
good ground for holding that as a class, but subject to exceptions, they tend to be informative, we also find that the proportion of informative memories among memories in which
the truth symbol has high psychological attraction is much
greater than the proportion of informative memories among
memories in which the truth symbol seems less strongly
attracted. This accounts for our sharp insistence that memories which, as we say, are very clear indeed must certainly
be true. The empirical evidence in favour of the smaller class
of memories, namely those in which the truth symbol has a
very high degree of attraction, may well give probability
amounting to 'practical certainty'. But in order to reach the
position in which we can give rational credence to memories,
more or less strong, we must first examine the credentials of
memories of varying degrees of strength *as a class*.

The position is opposite in the case of rational non-memory
beliefs. In these the rational grounds for credence belong
separately to each particular case. And in each case the
psychological attraction of the truth symbol arises in consequence of empirical grounds being apprehended, and has a
strength that is proportional to the cogency of the empirical
grounds in that particular case. In the case of memories, on the
contrary, we are entitled to give strong rational credence *because*
the psychological attraction is strong ; the psychological

attraction is itself our evidence in favour of rational endorsement of the belief.

In the foregoing definition of memory, which was not ostensive, but in terms of the psychological attraction of the truth symbol and the lack of empirical evidence in each separate case, it will have been noticed that no reference was made to the past. The past certainly cannot be defined ostensively. Nor is the notion that we have some prior innate idea of the nature of the past acceptable. Thus if we identified memories as being imaginative structures that somehow point to the past, we should have the arduous task of finding a definition of the past prior to the identification of memories. If we can identify memories independently, our task becomes much easier. The past is simply defined as the place where the lively counterparts of memories are — or, to use the conventions of our common speech, have been. The past is defined as the *lebensraum* of experiences remembered.

It has been suggested to me by Professor A. J. Ayer, a high authority, that it may be possible to define the past independently of memory. The specious present contains a time arrow, and it is within the power of the imagination, using this, to extrapolate backwards as well as forwards. If this contention is to be relevant to the identification of memories, it is implied that each and every memory contains some reference to the time arrow in the specious present. On whether this is so I reserve judgement.

If this view is accepted, I would none the less adhere to my definition, and merely add to it a reference to the past. For while my definition will, I submit, suffice to identify memories without any reference to the past, an attempt to define memory with reference to the past but without reference to the features I have specified will certainly not do, as can readily be shown. If we are able to conceive the past (with or without the aid of memory), then clearly we can locate the sensible counterparts of all sorts of wild imaginings in the past. In fact we often do this. The imaginative relegation of the sensible counterpart of a present imaginative structure to the past does not constitute that structure a memory ; there must also be a strong psychological attraction of the truth symbol to the imaginative structure. That is one element in my definition. Furthermore the attraction must be irrational ; we might indeed, on the basis of Professor Ayer's claim, extrapolate backwards by simple induction (or other modes of induction) and thus build up a network of rational beliefs about the past ; and this too we in fact do ; but the belief is not a memory if the psychological attraction of the truth symbol is associated with the inductive process. Someone might say that he must have seen All Souls College because his diary — of repeatedly proved authenticity — contains a water-colour sketch of that building. That is not a memory. The lack of evidential grounds for the adherence of the truth symbol is the second element in my definition.

Thus the inclusion of a reference to the past, defined in the manner suggested by Professor Ayer, does not make it possible to dispense with either of the two elements comprised in my definition. The only practical effect of Professor Ayer's amendment would be to allow us to take a more lenient attitude to second-sight and (apocalyptic) prophesy. On my original view, not diluted by that of Professor Ayer, any belief not purporting to be supported by any inductive argument whatever, would by definition relate to the past. Some may think it convenient to dispose of the claims of see-ers in this way. It would be perhaps a trifle arbitrary. They could be saved, however, by a little tolerance and the permission of exceptions, such as we usually have to allow in cognitive matters. If we say that the great majority of individually unsupported beliefs are memories, we can build up the notion of a past defined as the *lebensraum* of memory, and we can build up a notion of the future by forward extrapolation mainly based on evidence provided in memory (see below). In due course by ordinary inductive methods we people the past with a far greater number of experiences than those referred to in memories. And the more we are able to fill out the past, the more by simple induction can we enrich our idea of the future. Having taken a firm hold of these two concepts by these two methods, the past by attributing the counterparts of memories to the past and the future by using our memories for extrapolation forwards, we may then proceed, without jeopardizing the main structure of our notions about the past and future, to have irrational beliefs specifically relating to the future. But I do suggest that if, before this great sophistication was achieved, many people had had or had believed themselves to have many direct insights into the future, the human race would have been condemned to a welter of confusion, since it would have literally been unable to distinguish between past and future, and little progress towards an understanding of nature would have been possible.[1]

Most memories are complex. They are marked not only by the attachment of the truth symbol to the structure as a whole, but also by the violent repulsion of the truth symbol if the imagination makes any attempt to rearrange the pattern. I am perfectly free to form an imaginative picture of Tom Tower resting on the Post Office, which is on the opposite side of St. Aldates, Oxford; I may ponder upon the aesthetic qualities of such an arrangement, but as soon as I endeavour to imagine my picture having the quality of being a replica of a sensible experience of mine, this endeavour is violently frustrated. Similar repulsions would occur if we attempted to rearrange the pattern of beliefs about the future; for instance, I might imagine that, next time I visited St. Aldates, Tom Tower would appear on the Post Office side; this idea is repelled because it violates inductive principles which make such a reconstruction improbable. But the attractions and repulsions connected with a memory of what St. Aldates is like have no such inductive justification; they are brute facts; and it is this that identifies the structure as a memory.

So far the past has been considered only as a great region in which certain lively counterparts are located. But in the idea that we normally have of the past, there is a serial ordering. This may be accounted for in a number of ways.

We sometimes have memories the lively counterparts of which are specifically located as adjacent to the backward end of the specious present — memories of things that have just happened. These may be remembered as being (or having been) contiguous with elements still surviving in the specious present. Such memories, together with immediate predic-

---

[1] This is the kind of consideration that gives colour to Leibniz's dictum that this is 'the best of all possible worlds'. Some might think they could improve upon it by endowing us with an intuitive knowledge of the future. How then would they surmount the difficulty outlined in the text?

tions, provide, on the hypothesis that both are true, a somewhat longer series than that given by the specious present alone, and this series may make it easier for the imagination to extrapolate further in both directions. If we define the past as the location of the counterparts of memories, a part of the past is thus established as being backwards of the backward end of the specious present. For 'backwards of' we may substitute the word 'before' (def.).

The counterparts of memories, as of predictions, may contain faint as well as lively elements. (They may indeed consist exclusively of faint elements.) If the counterpart, B, of a certain memory comprises a memory of A, then the sensible counterpart of A is in the past relative to B. And if the sensible counterpart of B contains wonder about a forward extrapolation comprising the structure C, and if we also have a memory of C, B is in the past relative to C. Thus we may establish a serial order A B C.

One characteristic of memory is that by a specific effort of will known as concentration, we can extend the boundaries of an original memory structure without jeopardizing the strong adherence of the truth symbol. The memory as first occurring may not have any clue as to its order in a temporal series ; when by concentration we can enlarge the structure so that it comes to contain such clues, we are said to remember 'when' the thing happened ; this means that we have located it before one lot of counterparts and after another. By sufficient concentration we can get quite a large number of counterparts into one serial order.

Finding that many counterparts lie in one serial order we are tempted to form the hypothesis that all do. This is our normal way of thinking about our past. The fact that however much we concentrate, we cannot specify the location of certain counterparts is not a reason for denying that they have a place in the one serial order. If in addition to the main serial order A B C D, a separate serial order A^1 B^1 C^1 D^1 tends to build up — this might be, for instance, the past history of our philosophical reflexions — and if we can locate any one element that is between others in the secondary series, say C^1, as being in the main series, that enables us to locate the other items of the secondary series on the main

o

series within a range of indeterminateness. If we could not so locate any of the terms of the secondary series, that would be suspicious; but I am not aware that that often (or ever ?) happens. It must be admitted, however, that there are a great many floating counterparts that we cannot locate, whatever our effort of concentration, anywhere in particular. About the location of these some uncertainty must remain. The notion that all the events in the past of a sentient being *must* lie in one serial order is an unacceptable dogma.

Sophisticated man with his extended range of information about many things, has reasons additional to the clues provided by the contents of the memories themselves for believing that all counterparts lie in one serial order. He has reasons for believing (i) that our physical bodies have some connexion with those links between past and present that memories, if valid, constitute, and (ii) that, in accordance with certain physical laws, the events pertaining to our physical bodies all lie in one serial order. All this can never afford certainty. The notion that one single serial order is rigidly deducible from an *a priori* definition of the past I dismiss. This may do for some ideal or purely geometrical definition of the past; but the past with which we are concerned is an empirical phenomenon, to which such an *a priori* definition is inapplicable. It happens in this case, as in many others, that a broad generalization covering most of the phenomena is sufficient for our purpose, and that we cannot get beyond it. The mind has some tendency, by way of a tidying-up operation, to convert a generalization into a universal law. As a practical expedient, involving economy of mental effort, this may serve. But in logic we must be on our guard. And in philosophy too, where our mind is ranging among truths of no immediate practical import.

We must now turn to the task of supplying reasons for holding memories to be informative.

If most, or many, memories are valid, but not otherwise, the sensible elements in the specious present are the tail-ends, to date, of longer tracts of sensible experience. If these longer tracts have really existed, we may make short predictions on the strength of them of high probability value. If memories are invalid and these tracts did not in fact exist, we can get

little evidence for predictions of discernible length and substantial probability out of the experience of the specious present
alone, however generous a duration we may assign to it.

I call attention to the point that all our confidence in the
informativeness of memory must be derived from the experiences of one specious present. To adduce in favour of memory,
prior to any probability of its informativeness, evidence col-
lected from specious presents that have already disappeared
would be to argue in a circle, for it would imply that the
memory of those specious presents that have already disappeared was informative.

You might at first think it hard to collect from one fleeting
specious present strong evidence in favour of so momentous
a generalization as the veridicity of memory. But this is not
really so. Suppose an observer sitting quietly in a small room.
The room, as it figures in his sensible experience, may be
regarded as a collection of some ten thousand small patches.
Let him predict that all these patches will remain quite stationary in the specious present save for four, located on what he
calls the ceiling ; for these he predicts motion within the
specious present. There are some four hundred billion
alternative ways of selecting four patches out of a collection
of ten thousand. It was open to him to select any one out of
these four hundred billion sets and, if memory were illusory,
he would have had no evidence in favour of one rather than
another. Let us suppose his prediction correct, the four
patches selected being flies, which had been in incessant
motion before the backward end of the specious present.

He may also predict the kind of motion to which they
would be subject. He does not attempt to predict the motions
in detail, but he predicts a characteristic pattern and speed.
I do not know how many possible kinds of pattern, as distinctive
as that made by flies, the geometricians could devise for us nor
over what fraction of all discernible speeds the recognizably
characteristic speed of flies ranges. These considerations further
build up the odds, if memory were invalid, against the success
of the prediction.

Opposite the observer sits a man in a chair ; as he was in
the middle of a sentence just beyond the backward end of the
specious present, pausing only to take breath, the observer

predicts that within the specious present there will seem to issue from his mouth sounds of a highly peculiar character, namely spoken English. It was open to him to predict that such sounds would come from the vases on the mantelpiece or from any of the thousand books that line his walls. He does not predict what the man will say, but the general characteristics of spoken English must constitute but one of the many thousands of sound patterns of that degree of characterization. He also predicts the individual intonation, by which he could have identified the speaker, without seeing him, out of thousands of acquaintances, as we often do over the telephone.

By taking a few such simple matters I believe that we could get supra-astronomical odds against the truth of one combination of predictions, chosen out of all possible combinations of predictions within the range of the imaginable, if there were nothing in favour of one combination rather than another.

Evidence lying within a specious present need not consist only of extrapolations in accordance with experience immediately antecedent to the backward end of the specious present. I may notice that the hands of my watch, the reliability of which I remember, point to 9.5 P.M. precisely, and, recalling that I am within earshot of Tom Tower, predict the booming of a bell. All the 101 strokes that are sounded at that time cannot lie within a specious present ; but two or three can, and I may make an accurate forecast of the rapidity of the succession of strokes which is perceptibly greater than when Tom strikes the hour.

In using this evidence for the informativeness of memory, we need what may be called a guessing postulate. This is a variant of the ordinary sampling postulate and may eventually be dispensed with by the same logic. If a hundred pieces of paper lie before me, ninety-nine of which are white on the reverse side and one of which is black on the reverse side, and I have to guess without evidence which one is black, the guessing postulate in its strong form states that I shall only guess correctly once every hundred times. It follows that if memory is uninformative there are sometimes astronomical odds — even supra-astronomical odds — against having the success in prediction that one often does have in a single specious present. If, on the other hand, the memories used are indeed informative the successful predictions are quite probable. This presents the usual situation in which consequents have to be reversed. If my survey is comprehensive and I have success not only in positive, but also in negative predictions — *e.g.* that other objects in the room will remain stationary and silent — then it seems that no deflation is necessary. Even if some deflation is required, it will not be of much importance in relation to the huge improbability of success if memory is in fact uninformative.

In the first stage of the argument we can only establish probability in favour of the informativeness of the memories used. We can say that there is high probability in favour of the informativeness of most of the memories used for prediction in the specious present, and these can be taken as a sample of the wider class of all memories used and unused.

But as soon as we can say that there is high probability for most members of the narrow class of memories, viz. those used in the specious present for prediction, we are released from the cage of the specious present. For if these memories are veridical we have access, on the basis of high probability, to some past experiences, which may contain other examples of successful prediction. Thus the sample of memories very likely to be (or to have been) veridical is widened. We then proceed by ordinary sampling to establish high probability for a sizable proportion of memories generally.

We do not seek in this case to establish veridicity as a universal attribute of memory. The very arguments that supply high probability for the informativeness of a large number of memories also indicate that some are probably deceptive. In the case of a sample where all the P's have Q we are able to establish a specific probability for *at least* 99 per cent of the P's having Q ; we cannot establish any probability at all in favour of *at least* 1 per cent of the P's not having Q. If we seek to establish a higher ratio of P's having Q, the probability declines, tending towards total nescience ; there is never any positive probability on the other side so long as no P is found that has not Q. With memories the case is different. If only we were able to count up our successes and failures, we might have positive probabilities on both sides ; in fact we should be in the realm of statistical frequencies ; some area of total nescience would always remain. When we consider how impractical would be the project of counting up our successes and failures in predictions based on memory and also the number of unused memories, and when we consider also that almost all empirical beliefs rest in part on evidence supplied by memory, it is not surprising that precise probability numbers are seldom available for our beliefs. We have to be content with a rough idea, which is, however, essentially one of numerical frequency, about how reliable any particular memory is.

In this investigation we can, as has already been mentioned, subdivide memories into the more and the less clear ; it may be that in the case of very clear memories indeed we can achieve those tremendous odds in favour of almost all memories of that class being veridical which we have seen in very large samples in which all P's have Q. We may build up a very large sample of clear memories in which *all* are verified, so that the odds against any memory of so clear a type being un-veridical are supra-astronomical. We can in fine achieve that 'practical certainty' so strongly urged by those who would assign an intuitive character to memory.

The passage from used to unused memories is not a completely safe one. With that widening horizon that is due to a growing rational trust in memory, we may learn that an effort can be made on the occasion of a sensible occurrence to 'memorize' it ; we can perform some act of will which gains for memories relating to the sensible occurrences in question a higher score of veridicity than can be claimed for memories generally. We clearly must not include the score for memories in cases where such an act has previously been performed in estimating the reliability of memories generally. The difficulty goes deeper. It may well be that even in cases where no conscious act of memorizing has been performed, we are more likely to remember correctly when memory is useful than in other cases ; kind nature may provide that. Thus there may be a special danger in drawing on memories that are out of the normal run of use.

It will have been noted that in the foregoing discussion I have included false memories in the class of memories. Some might wish to exclude them ; this would mean that memories could not be recognized as such, as and when they occur. This is a purely linguistic point. It seems that popular discourse gives no clear guidance for correct usage. Some would hold that to remember X merely means to be in a mental condition in which the truth symbol adheres to the image of X. The other — more pedantic — view is that 'I remember X' implies that X was the case. On such a view it would be nonsense to raise the question whether memories are informative. For those who insist on such usage I should have to re-word this chapter, substituting for the word 'memories' the words 'states purporting to be memories' and for the words 'veridical memories' just the word 'memories'; the problem in fine would be how many of the states purporting to be memories are in fact memories. Some indeed might call for a still more astringent usage, holding it not to be a sufficient justification for 'I remember X' that X is true, but that if I am to say 'I remember X' I must know X to be true. This proposal may be ruled out as valueless, as by this usage there would be no memories at all.

It might be thought that one could secure an easy victory over the pedantic school of terminologists by pointing out that, since one never knows whether a past event occurred or not, then, if X's being true were a condition for rightly saying 'I remember X', one could never know one was right in saying 'I remember X'. *In every case* one would have to say 'I think I remember X', and this does violence to ordinary usage. Unfortunately this argument is not a good one, owing to the inherently unsatisfactory nature of ordinary language, which has already been pointed out. Most utterances consist of empirical statements not known to be true for certain. Yet an indication of this is seldom given ; we commonly make flat statements as though expressing, not beliefs in probability, but certainties. Thus it would be quite in conformity with general linguistic usage to say 'I remember X' when what I mean to convey is that 'I probably remember X'. Thus the claim of the pedantic school in regard to use of the word 'memory' cannot be rejected by an appeal to ordinary speech. I have adopted the looser usage simply for convenience of exposition.

The argument in favour of the veridicity of most or many

memories depends on a sampling postulate and is valid therefore only for the range from which the sample of used and corroborated memories has been drawn. It therefore has nothing to say in favour of the veridicity of memories that will occur in future. In their favour, however, we have simple induction. In this case simple induction may be used in its unconditional form, since we have relied continuously on the informative nature of memory from the first dawn of the thinking process. It is improbable that we are on the extreme edge of the great region in which that reliance is justified.

It is essential to observe that all this case in favour of the informative character of memory rests on the assumption that we have prior and independent grounds for regarding the inductive process as valid. If there was no prior probability in favour of extrapolating remembered continuities of relatively long extension up to the present, the success of the observer's predictions would be just as much a fluke, if memory was veridical as if it was not. Consequently his highly remarkable successes could not tell at all in favour of the veridicity of memory. We say that his successes support the hypothesis of veridicity, because, if this hypothesis is true, the truth of the predictions is probable, perhaps extremely probable, whereas, if it is untrue, there are supra-astronomical odds against their truth. This is our reason for believing the hypothesis. But if the odds against success in prediction were the same, whether memory was veridical or not, their success would not give any support for the hypothesis of veridicity.

I believe that there is a confused idea in the minds of some that the success of predictions based on experience somehow simultaneously both gives reason for accepting the principle of experience as a valid mode of reasoning and also gives grounds for trusting memory. In regard to the former claim I hope I have already said enough to dispose of it.

The success of predictions based on the principle of experience gives no evidence in favour of the principle. Nor, if we do not give prior acceptance to the principle, does the success of predictions provide evidence in favour of the veridicity of memory. If the principle is wrong, then predictions based on experience are no more likely to be right than guesses based on no evidence.   If memory is veridical, it provides a large amount of experience as data ; but, if the principle of experience is not valid, we are no better off for making predictions through having the aid of the data than we would be without it.   Consequently the success of predictions would provide no evidence in favour of the data being correct, *i.e.* in favour of memory being veridical.   But if we do accept the principle of experience as a prior principle, and then find that by using the data we get better results than we could expect without them, that provides evidence in favour of the genuineness of the data, *i.e.* of the veridicity of memory.

Thus the circle is completed.   First we must convince ourselves that the principle of experience is correct.   Then we find that by employing it we can use the data of memory to make successful predictions, against the success of which there would be supra-astronomical odds in the absence of true data.   This gives us reason for deeming the data true — that is for accepting the hypothesis that memories are often informative.

The vindication of the informative character of memory here set forth may reduce difficulties connected with its relation to the events remembered.[1]   So long as memory is regarded as a kind of self-authenticating knowledge of past events, vouching by virtue of its own internal nature for the predications made, some very queer relation between the memory and the past has to be assumed.   This relation seems out of harmony with the ordinary processes of nature known to us.   Now, though there is still more in heaven and earth than falls within our comprehension, and we could not refuse to postulate a quasi-mystical link between the present and past if the facts required it, it is proper to pause and re-examine the ground carefully before doing so.   The account which I have given dispenses with the necessity of assuming any such link. The memory may be regarded as a trace left by the lively event, a footprint in the sand, or the resuscitated pain of an old wound.   The human constitution reacts sharply to such an occurrence with the propensity to believe.   But the memory

---

[1] The concluding paragraphs of this chapter are taken verbatim, with only four minor verbal changes, from my article in *Mind*, 1942, vol. li, No. 201, pp. 66-7.

itself says nothing and knows nothing. A hypothesis may then be made that memory is informative just as a hypothesis might be suggested by the footprint that the island is inhabited. The hypothesis is found by experience to be highly probable. But long before this verification has been explicitly checked, man's instinctive equipment makes him get busy and think and act as though he knew that the memory was informative. A by-product of this instinct is that philosophers have been led to exaggerate the scope of our intuitive knowledge to the detriment of their own studies.

One more word should be said about the heedless credence given by common sense to memory. Man is endowed with a violently strong propensity to trust to memory, that is, to conjoin a symbol for liveliness in his imagination to the faint structures thrown up in the present by past lively structures. Trust in memory has been of immense biological advantage. And the instinct in rational man to impose such trust had to be especially violent precisely because, pending his full comprehension of the inductive principle, there was no reason whatever to do so. In many respects man has been much guided by the reason that is strong within him, but if in the early stage of its development he had been led by it to complete scepticism about his memories, he would have been lost. It is sometimes beneficial to have anti-rational impulses strong enough to resist the quiet and gentle but relentless voice of reason.

In the case of memory, the anti-rational instinct takes him to the same conclusion that reason reaches by a more circuitous and arduous route. And so there is no need for him to endeavour subsequently to shake off the instinct to believe memory informative, even if he could. Indeed he is fortunate in his endowment, for in the rough interludes of history the finer processes of thought may suffer eclipse. So long as the human constitution is conserved, this instinct will remain and, by its consilience with the processes of reason, serve in their stead.

CHAPTER IX

ONTOLOGICAL DIGRESSION

THIS chapter is called a digression for two reasons. First, the logical principles that I am endeavouring to expound are in no way affected by the answers to the questions raised in it. Secondly, I do not claim to be able to furnish the answers. Each of the other chapters professed to give positive solutions to the problems discussed ; I like to think that these together might serve as the foundations of a fully articulated theory of logic. This chapter will provide no such foundations.

Why, then, do I make the digression ? It will incidentally cover one point that still has to be cleared up, if the empirical system of logic is to give a satisfactory explanation of what common sense holds we are entitled to believe — namely in connexion with the existence of other sentient beings. We shall be mainly concerned, however, with rather different matters, which, though not necessary to an account of the logical principles which man has successfully used to date, seem to have a near-logical character.

Modern philosophy has been much concerned to show that some of the problems famous in the history of philosophy are essentially bogus and due to linguistic confusions. I would by no means disparage this line of thought. None the less, I would urge that traditional philosophy did concern itself with some very real problems, in regard to which we have become discouraged, not because they are in principle insoluble, but because they are so very difficult — notably those concerning the relation of mind to the external world. My reason for saying this is that the considerations I am about to bring forward do *look* so very like the clues to a soluble problem. To dismiss them as merely verbal would, in my opinion, show a great deficiency of intellectual discrimination. The trouble is that its solution may need not only the analytical faculty in which philosophers are traditionally strong, but also something akin to scientific genius, capable of wide-sweeping constructive hypothesis, in which the great philosophers have not so far excelled. This task may need someone who is greater than Newton, greater than Einstein. Such a man may yet arise. We do not want to be caught out by posterity as dismissing problems as insoluble, for no better reason than that they are quite beyond the powers of our own feeble imaginations.

I would open by drawing attention to the striking, and surely significant, family resemblance between two cases in both of which the choice between alternative interpretations was set aside as irrelevant to the logical validity of arguments. One case was when we affirmed that it made no difference to the logic entitling us to believe in the continuous (or nearly continuous) existence of common-sense physical bodies, whether we interpreted that as meaning no more than that certain hypotheticals — of the type, 'if a sentient being took certain action he would have certain sensible experience' — are continuously true, or as meaning that certain substances are in continuous existence. The other case was when we affirmed that it made no difference to the logic justifying many of our beliefs whether the sample of samples, constituting our total experience, was 'fair' or not.

The family resemblance is a striking fact, precisely because our grounds for disclaimer in the two cases were altogether different; it thus constitutes a pointer towards something that is unexplained, but perhaps ought to be explicable. It is certainly needful to consider the logical effects of the two disclaimers in relation to one another.

For this purpose we must first revert to the now rather painful subject of the Berkleian controversy. In a brief passage two reasons were given [1] favouring the Berkleian position. (1) Since the hypotheticals, if correct, give us all we want to know or could verify in making predictions about the future or conjectures about the past, without postulating continuous substances, and since entities ought not to be multiplied beyond necessity, these substances should not be postulated. (2) Since the intrinsic qualities inhering in these substances are unknown, and presumably unknowable, and

[1] See p. 82 *supra*.

since, so far as one can see, it would make no difference to any conceivable experience whether they exist or not, the question may be raised whether there is any meaning in postulating their existence.

It may be that both these reasons are over-stated. In regard to the former it is to be noted that we do postulate the continuing existence of such things as 'tables' in our thought processes about common-sense events. In the first instance, no doubt, the idea of a continuously existing table of constant shape is derived from a large number of different appearances arising in various perspectives and by tactual sensations. But once having framed the notion, our thought operates in the opposite direction. From the hypothesis of a continuously existing table of constant shape we deduce what sensations, visual or tactual, we are likely to have if we do certain things. This is more evidently the case when we are concerned with objects in a state of motion or change. We work out what is likely to happen in a certain time interval on the hypothesis that certain continuously existing things continue to operate in prescribed ways during the periods in which they are unobserved. These operations could in principle be described in terms of a series of multiple hypotheticals. But in fact they are not thought of in this way.

Tables, trees, motor-cars, etc., cannot be defined directly in terms of observables. In this they are analogous to the much grander physical concepts of mass, electron, etc. I suspect that, if Professor Braithwaite's arguments concerning definition are true of physical concepts in the full sense,[1] they are true of the concepts of 'chairs' and 'tables' also. These would then be defined in terms of the deductive systems in which they play their part — very humble little deductive systems, compared with the great schemes of physics — the functional equations consisting of the laws of perspective, etc.

This brings something to light in relation to the second reason for rejecting real substances. That reason is that the qualities of these postulated substances are unknowable. But in the light of the foregoing this must be an overstatement. For if they were altogether unknowable how could they figure in a thinking process? The plain fact of the matter is that

[1] Cp. pp. 135-6 *supra.*

204 FOUNDATIONS OF INDUCTIVE LOGIC

in that essay in realism implied in common-sense thought about external bodies only *some* of the qualities are deemed unknowable. A moderate realist would claim that some at least of the qualities of these alleged substances can be definitely specified. The alleged entities are deemed to have a *resemblance* to elements in sensible experience.

For this we have to go back beyond Berkeley to Locke and his distinction between primary and secondary qualities. His particular enumeration of these qualities has been discredited ; it can be reconstructed on better lines.[1] We are not here concerned with the history of the subject. In the Lockean system the primary qualities that are presented in experience belong to the world of external bodies, but the secondary qualities have only what I may call 'counterparts' in that world, which can also be regarded as 'causes' of the sensible experiences or 'powers' lying within the objects to cause sensations in us. The rejection of the continuous existence of the secondary qualities was not based on the general considerations that support a Berkleian position, but rather on certain special difficulties that arise in regard to them. In the case of tactual and kinaesthetic qualities no one would seriously plead for their continuous existence, since they consist of sensations that seem to be inside our bodies ; the most realist view must surely take them, in the form they are manifested to us, to arise from the interaction between our own bodies and the external bodies, the latter being deemed to have some counterpart quality which conditions our sensation when the interaction occurs. Similarly with tastes and smells ; noises are perhaps more doubtful. The most seemingly external of the qualities associated with one sense only are colours. In their case the decisive objection to postulating the continuous existence of visual qualities was — quite independently of and prior to Newtonian optics — the need for other external conditions, notably the presence of light, to be fulfilled. The external bodies should be deemed to have such properties that in the right conditions and on the occasion of the presence of sentient bodies also in a proper state of sensitivity, visual colours occur. Thus the rejection of these secondary qualities as continuous

---

[1] 'Solidity' was an important item in Locke's list of primary qualities, but is not included in my categories.

existents could be argued on the merits of each case rather than on metaphysical principles. But, of course, on a realist view, it has to be supposed that they all have 'counterparts' of some sort in the continuously existing external bodies.

In the foregoing account I have not brought in the argument derived from the 'illusions of sense'. This does not strike me as important. In all cognitive matters (*e.g.* memory) we expect many exceptions. We should rely on the nature of the majority of the phenomena in question.

When these various qualities are excluded from the ranks of those qualities, supposed, on a realist view, to continue to exist in identical form when unobserved, what qualities remain ? The primary qualities, which may, alternatively, be called structural qualities. They consist of number, spatio-temporal relations, such as between, greater than, and qualities manifesting themselves through time, such as rate of change of position.

It is to be noticed that in the account just given, although not perhaps in Locke's account,[1] the primary qualities are all essentially adjectival, or, to put it differently, they cannot exist without being conjoined with some other qualities complementary to them. If three is evinced in the empirical world, there must be three somethings ; if B, again confining ourselves to the empirical world, appears as being between A and C, B must have some quality or other, additional to that of merely being between A and C. Furthermore, the complementing quality must not itself be a primary. It does not complete the account of a sensible experience to say that what is between A and C is larger than either. In any sensible experience there must be at least one quality that is not primary. Similarly in the world of real bodies, every body must have at least one quality other than its primaries ; and, since the non-primary qualities are not identical with the elements of experience, every body must have at least one quality that is counterpart in character, its own intrinsic nature being unknown.

---

[1] Locke's inclusion of solidity among his primaries makes his position different in relation to what follows. For it appears to be that inclusion which enables him to regard the counterparts of secondary qualities as themselves primaries: *vide* Bk. ii, ch. 8, sec. 10. But cp. Bk. iv, ch. 3, sec. 11, where his expression 'yet more remote from our comprehension' suggests a view nearer to mine.

It may be held that the foregoing argument may also be applied in reverse and that no secondary quality can exist unless complemented by some primary quality. It might be said, for instance, that if there is a colour, it must be complemented by at least one primary quality, even if it be no more than that of being 'one' colour. It does not matter for our purposes whether the relation is reciprocal, whether secondaries need to be complemented by primaries just as much as primaries need to be complemented by secondaries. It suffices for the present purpose that primaries do so need to be complemented.

On a realist view it is accordingly necessary to postulate the existence of counterpart qualities, which do not enter into our sensible experience and are consequently of an unrevealed character in themselves, for two purposes, first to account for or correspond to all the variety in the experienced secondary qualities (various visual colours, etc.), the continuous existence of which we are debarred from postulating, and, secondly, to act as the necessary *carriers* of the primary qualities, the continuous existence of which we wish to postulate.

I hope that the broad distinction between primaries and secondaries here given may be accepted. It is not the same as Locke's, but it is based on the same *fundamentum divisionis*. The primary qualities are those which — waiving metaphysical considerations — we can postulate as continuously existing in identical form in our absence, while the secondaries are those which, for reasons special to them, we are unable to regard as continuously existing in identical form, and for which, therefore, we have to postulate counterparts in external nature of intrinsic character unknown. Modern physics does not disturb this critical dichotomy, for, although the primaries in our experiences do not belong to the ultimate entities which it wishes to postulate, they still belong to roughly demarcated aggregates of such entities — the macroscopic bodies which still survive.

It should be noted here that when, thinking in terms of a realistic ontology, we refer to external objects or entities, such as the bodies of common sense (tables, etc.) or the entities of physics (electrons, etc.), their nature is deemed to consist wholly of 'qualities'. These are divided into two kinds. The primary qualities specify their position relative to any origin, their geometrical configuration — if they are deemed to have any — and their behavioural properties as expressed in functional equations. When we speak of kinds of entities the question of position does not arise, and we may substitute for 'primary' the more modern and familiar term 'structural' in reference to this class of qualities. Whether it would seem natural also to call the position of a particular physical entity a 'structural' quality I am not sure ; it is certainly a 'primary' quality in the sense intended. All these primary qualities are expressible in mathematical terms. An entity cannot be a mere collection of primary qualities ; it must also have one or more qualities to which the primary qualities belong. In sensible experience these are the various qualities categorized by our powers of sensation, the visual colours, feelings of hardness, etc. In the external world they are the unknown counterparts of these. It will often be convenient to call them 'carrier' qualities, because we have to assume that there are some qualities that carry the purely adjectival primary or structural qualities. The carrier qualities and the structural together are deemed to exhaust the nature of the entities. This distinction between carrier and structural qualities is *not* analogous to the old metaphysical distinction between substance and attribute. In sensible experience the carrier qualities are colours, noises, etc. and these would not, I believe, be regarded in the old metaphysics as substances. Nature is deemed in this account to consist entirely of qualities, viz. primary and secondary, or structural and carrier, and the distinction between substance and attribute disappears. I do not know if that distinction has any validity ; it does not lie within the scope of our discussions here.

This dichotomy having been established, two very interesting, suggestive and far-reaching generalizations can be made. They are synthetic in character, and presumably therefore both empirical ; the one with which I shall deal second is quite clearly empirical, but as regards the former I reserve my opinion.

When we have an imaginative counterpart of sensible experience, whether in memory, prediction or otherwise, this

P

counterpart has by definition a resemblance to the sensible experience. It has already been observed that the structures that occur in our thought processes very often consist, in part or wholly, of symbols. In the present context I want to consider imaginative structures swept entirely clear of symbolism, save for the presence of the truth symbol itself, which cannot be dispensed with for reasons already given. In the instances formerly provided, that of the extrapolation of a bird's course of flight or of the prediction of a rider's fall, the content of the belief may take the form in its entirety of a mental image; while most memories contain a good deal of symbolism, it is possible to have a memory consisting exclusively of a mental picture. I may be in the room with a billiard table on which I remember seeing three balls, two white with a red one between them; this can be a pure mental picture. I may also predict, having regard to there having been no interference or commotion in the interval, that if I turn my head back in the direction of the billiard table, I shall have a sensible experience, comprising three balls, two white with a red between them; again, this prediction may consist wholly of a mental picture, save for the truth symbol itself.

These mental pictures resemble, but are not wholly identical with, the sensible experiences. In so far as concerns the secondary or carrier qualities they are similar only; no imagination, however vivid, can reproduce the feelings that occur when the eye rests on white and red balls. This is the basis of Hume's distinction between impressions and ideas; he uses the words 'lively' and 'faint' to draw attention to the distinction; the definition is an ostensive one and 'lively' and 'faint' must be regarded as terms of art used as instruments to provoke ostensive apprehension; it is not implied that in some other sense an imaginative idea may not be much more lively than an impression. It is lucky that this distinction occurs uniformly — or so we believe; for otherwise we should get into a hopeless muddle, being unable to distinguish present experiences on the one hand from memories and predictions on the other.

The imaginative complex also contains primary or structural qualities, and these can be *absolutely identical* with the primaries in the counterpart sensible experiences. (They are not always so, of course, if our memory is imperfect or the structure of primaries very complicated.) If we see three billiard balls on the table in our mind's eye, the threeness that then occurs cannot in any way be distinguished as regards its quality from the threeness that occurs when we look at the table. Similarly with the between-ness of the red ball.

And so we come to a striking generalization. As among the various qualities that occur in a sensible experience, the set which we are prepared to regard as continuously subsisting in identical form in the external bodies is the same set that can be reproduced in identical form in our imaginative experience; and the set which we are debarred from believing to exist continuously in identical form in external bodies is the same set that we cannot reproduce in identical form in our imagination. This can surely not be a coincidence. But what is its significance? One is tempted to say that the reason why we are willing to suppose the continuous existence in identical form of certain qualities in alleged unobserved bodies and not that of other qualities is *because* the former qualities are those which we can call up in identical form in our own imaginations while we cannot do this to the others.

The position is that the sensible experience stands, so to speak, at the mid-point of a system. Going one way, namely into our imaginative experiences of memory or prediction, we can reproduce certain qualities (primary) in identical form, but not others (secondary). Going the other way, namely into an alleged world of permanently existing bodies, we can suppose that the primary qualities of sensible experience are reproduced in identical form, but not the secondary qualities. Thinking man is not likely to rest content until he discovers the reason why this is so. I regard this as an instance of a clue to an unsolved, but soluble, problem. Until philosophy has put this clue to effective use, it may be judged to have worlds still to conquer. This is certainly not a merely linguistic puzzle; we have here a generalization in regard to matters of fact. One cannot exclude the idea that an attempt is involved to impose on an alleged external world a dichotomy that we know to exist in our own mental world. Perhaps I may be excused for characterizing the situation by the un-academic word 'fishy'.

But now we come to a still more remarkable fact. In this matter of what is deemed to exist in the external world we can discern a general trend. Primitive man, no doubt by too crude an analogy with our own bodies, regarded the external world of rivers, trees, etc. as largely animate. This hypothesis was later withdrawn. What may be called naïve realism endows the external world with all the brightness and sparkle that belong to our sensible experiences of it. Most people to-day and even philosophers, when playing backgammon or in other unphilosophical moments, are naïve realists in this sense. Sophisticated realism takes a more austere view. Continuous existence is allowed to the primary qualities, and for the rest there are certain mysterious counterparts of the secondary qualities of unknown intrinsic character. These counterparts must have sufficient inherent variety to account for all the variety in our sensible experience. Our own bodies, by changes in their nervous condition, may indeed contribute something to that variety; but these bodies are themselves part of the external world. In this progress a trend may be discerned towards diminishing the resemblance that the alleged permanent world of bodies is deemed to have to our sensible experiences.

Modern science has carried this trend forward to a notable extent. Its real world of continuously existing substances differs far more from our sensible world than did that of the relatively sophisticated type of realism described in the last paragraph. But note this aspect. In pre-scientific realism there was much vagueness in regard to the counterparts of secondary qualities. At that stage it was probably assumed, save to the extent that modern scientific ideas had already begun to filter in, that there were enough unknown counter-part qualities or 'powers' to match the secondary qualities of sensible experience. But now the situation is entirely changed. In the alleged world of real substances there has been a vast proliferation of primary or structural qualities and a great reduction in the number of *kinds* of unknown counterparts. Take the simple case of colour. Instead of a variety of unknown counterparts to match all the various shades of colour, we have only one counterpart of intrinsic character unknown, namely light itself, while corresponding to the various shades of visual colour are a number of new hitherto unsuspected primaries, namely the various frequencies.

The transformation has been widespread. The old primaries remain in being, as qualifying the various macroscopic objects — tables, trees, stars — which are aggregates with roughly specifiable boundaries. But in addition to these are a host of new primaries qualifying all the new microscopic entities. All that remain of the old unknown counterparts or carriers are a very small number of different kinds of entity — protons, neutrons, etc. These comprise natural kinds, that is entities believed to have uniform properties not entailed by their definitions, but discoverable by experiment. Their behavioural properties can be expressed by functional equations relating to them in which only primaries figure.

There was a phase in the nineteenth century when, according to the popular exponents of science, there was a real hope that the kinds of entity of intrinsic nature unknown could be reduced to one, namely uniform atoms, the ultimate bricks out of which the universe was constructed. All the features of the universe could, it was claimed, be specified in terms of these atoms, their spatio-temporal location in relation to some origin, and their behavioural attributes all expressible in terms of primary qualities, *e.g.* rate of change of relative position, as determined, *inter alia*, by the number and measured proximity of other atoms. The position has since become rather more complicated. But the main feature remains, namely the enormous multiplication of primaries by comparison with those which figure in sensible experience and the reduction of the different *kinds* of unknown counterparts of secondaries, *i.e.* carriers, to a very small number.

What is remarkable in all this is that the qualities which have been multiplied are those which are reproducible in the imagination in the identical form in which they appear in sensible experience ; while of the counterparts of those qualities not so reproducible there has been a great reduction in the number of different kinds postulated. It is as though the mind had been able to impose upon the external world a structure agreeable to itself ; of course it could not have done this unless the external world had been of a certain character.

It is to be noted that we have here an empirical generalization concerning the progress of thought. We start with the recognizable division of all qualities of sensible experience into those which can be identically reproduced in the imagination (primary) and those which cannot (secondary); we find, as a matter of hard fact, that in the development of science, which assumes, if only as a working hypothesis, a continuously existing real world of objects, the number of primary qualities supposed to exist has been greatly multiplied while the number of different kinds of counterparts to secondary qualities supposed to exist has been greatly reduced. Once again we are in the presence of a feature that looks extraordinarily like a clue. Once again the word 'fishy' almost irresistibly comes into the mind.

Dare we push the analysis a little further? It may be expedient at this stage to define primary qualities as those that are identically reproducible in the imagination; this gives something precise and subject to ready check. Any definition in terms of reproduction in the 'real' world is blurred by the uncertain and variable nature of the postulates required by a realist ontology.

Can we also say that the group of primary or structural qualities is identical with the group of ostensively definable qualities whose further properties can be established by a deductive process? This appears to be a constructive statement. It does not matter for our purpose whether the principles of mathematical deduction are or are not deducible from more general principles. To put the matter negatively, those qualities that are identically reproducible in the imagination are not natural kinds. In the common-sense world we normally think of natural kinds as total complexes; but the counterparts of secondary qualities can also be natural kinds, and thereby the secondary qualities themselves; if, for instance, wherever there is physical light certain other things can be counted on as (exceedingly) likely to happen in appropriate circumstances and these other things are not deducible from the definition of physical light, then physical light may be regarded as a natural kind; it is not, in other words, considered to be a contradiction in terms that we can ascertain properties of physical light by experiment ; if, whenever visual light happens, there is physical light, visual light must be regarded as partaking in the characteristic of physical light of being a natural kind. This would seem to be connected with the fact that visual light is not identically reproducible in the imagination ; if we could conjure it up at will, we should thereby have power to bring into existence by a mere act of imaginative will-power all those empirical properties that belong to light, many of which are unknown to us. If we reproduce three, we reproduce no additional properties other than those which being three entails.

The progress of science has consisted, then, in postulating the existence of an ever-growing number of primary or structural qualities whose further properties can be ascertained by deduction, while reducing the number of different kinds of quality the further properties of which can only be ascertained by experiment. We may appropriately call this a 'transformation' of unknown counterparts into primary or structural qualities. To the extent that this happens the subject of study becomes more deductive ; but, since no primary quality or group of primaries can have empirical existence save in association with at least one non-primary quality, the empirical element cannot be eliminated. It follows naturally also that in those fields of investigation, in which it has proved possible to do a greater amount of transformation, are also those in which deduction plays a larger part and laws can be more accurately expressed (the 'harder' sciences).

It may be asked whether it might prove possible at some remote time to carry the aim of nineteenth-century physicists one stage further and get rid of the last remaining counterpart quality ? We should have a universe conforming to Aristotle's idea that all properties, and thereby the progress of events, were demonstrable, by a deductive process ; we could then abandon empirical scientific research although we should still need a geographical conspectus (under which history would be subsumed) giving the spatio-temporal position of things relative to a given origin. This idea is in principle unattainable, since the primary qualities cannot exist in experience save as complemented by at least one secondary (or counterpart) quality.[1] Bertrand Russell does not appear to have given due consideration to this point.[2]

The reduction in the number of different kinds of these qualities is a notable achievement. We have not reached finality in the process. It may be that phenomena will occur making it necessary to increase once more the number of kinds of carriers postulated. Furthermore, I believe that scientists would agree that their present definitions of these carriers may later be changed out of recognition. The day may come when protons, neutrons, etc., will be heard of no more. It would not follow that the hypothesis of their existence had been incorrect. For what is this hypothesis? As regards their intrinsic qualities nothing is said, and indeed no interest is taken. Attention is concentrated exclusively on their rôle of being carriers of structural qualities, which figure in the functional equations that serve to define them. If these concepts — protons, neutrons, etc. — are ever dropped, it will be because new deductive systems, comprising new functional equations, will be established; the structural qualities figuring in our present equations will very probably be structurally related — although with modifications to take account of newly observed phenomena — to the structural qualities in the new set of equations. We shall probably remain indifferent to the intrinsic nature of the new carrier qualities. To put what has happened and is happening in a slightly different way, we may say that, since we can never know the intrinsic character of the carrier qualities, we are perpetually striving to take a view of the universe which makes that inevitable ignorance have as little importance as possible for prediction.

One is tempted to make an aside of a sentimental character. Some people are cross with scientists for having reduced the vibrant, variegated universe in which we used to think we lived, to a complicated, mathematical construction, comprising, however, nothing but a vast empty darkness peopled only

---

[1] Cp. *supra*.

[2] Bertrand Russell (*Human Knowledge, its Scope and Limits*, p. 461) writes: 'There are still natural kinds — at the moment there are electrons, positrons, neutrons and protons — but it is hoped that these are not ultimate, and may be reduced to differences in structure'. I should have supposed this hope to be based on a mistake and to entail a belief which is L-false.

by a few electric charges and centres of energy of tedious uniformity of behaviour. There is probably nothing in this idea. Scientists have concentrated only on certain aspects, endeavouring to fit as much as possible into the straight-jacket of structural qualities, those qualities being dear to them on account of a purely mental characteristic, namely being reproducible in identical form in the imagination, and thereby generating properties which can be handled by the precise tools of deduction. This gives power to their elbow. But we must be very cautious in supposing that their success has much bearing on what the universe is intrinsically like.

It may be well, before proceeding, to re-summarize certain features of the present scientific situation, if we assume a realist ontology.

1. In any spatio-temporal segment of the scientist's world there are far more structural qualities than would be experienced by an individual occupying it. On the other hand there are far fewer *kinds* of counterparts to secondary qualities or carriers than there are secondary qualities in the individual's experience. These two facts are linked. As the real world (which includes human bodies) must, on a realist ontology, have enough variety to match every element in the individual's sensible experience, the reduction in the number of kinds of counterparts to the observed secondary qualities of his sensible experience must be matched by an excess of primary qualities postulated as really existing over those present in his experience.

2. Any claim that there is a similarity between the secondary qualities of experience and their counterparts in the external world, has been completely discarded. Thus in a certain sense science may be said to have shown naïve realism to be false. On the other hand, the structural qualities of sensible experience retain their place in the external world of continuous existents, namely as the qualities of macroscopic aggregates. The statement that there are 'three' billiard balls on the table has its meaning in physics.

3. It has been claimed that the recent developments of physics involve a revolution in our ideas about the nature of physical entities,[1] ever since the attempt to decide whether an electron is truly a particle or a wave has been abandoned

---

[1] *E.g.* by H. Margenau, *op. cit.* chs. 16 ff.

as inappropriate. Hitherto, it is claimed, it had been possible to form a mental image of any physical entity and endow
that image with the structural qualities supposed to belong
to that entity. Thus the image would have a resemblance,
i.e. an identity in respect of structural qualities, with the
physical entity. It might be objected that there was not complete identity, since it was not possible to visualize a quickly
moving atom (old-fashioned type). But all that is required to
make the image structurally identical is a change of scale. It
is not presumably possible to form a mental image of any
object and endow that single image simultaneously with the
structural properties proper to a particle and those proper to
a wave. Thus it is not possible to 'visualize' an electron.
This is a fact of great philosophical significance, and it re-
enforces the suggestion in the last paragraph that science has
shown naïve realism to be false. But one must not exaggerate ;
it is to be remembered that, although one could visualize an
atom (old style), the carrier quality of the image of the atom,
say pale grey, which carried the structural properties visualized had no relation at all to the intrinsic nature of the physical
quality that served in that entity as carrier of its geometrical
properties and of its behavioural properties as expressed in
functional equations. That intrinsic nature remained totally
unknown. And even if we come to the common or garden
'table', which could not only be visualized, but also, in a
certain sense, 'seen', we must remember that its own carrier
qualities required to carry its structural qualities of shape and
to 'cause' visual and tactual sensations in us were also utterly
unknown. Thus from one point of view this aspect of the
quantum theory may be deemed simply to have brought into
the limelight what philosophers of the empirical school have
been teaching for a long time, namely the utter inability of
the mind to conceive what the intrinsic carrier qualities of
external bodies are like.

4. The few remaining kinds of counterpart or carrier
qualities are studied exclusively in terms of the laws that
govern their behaviour. There is no interest in what they are
in themselves. With one exception, all laws of behaviour may
be expressed in terms of structural qualities, namely in functional equations. The exception is when there is a belief in

regard to what will happen when some arrangement of these entities occurs within the sphere of observation of a sentient being, *e.g.* as when it is believed that a visual colour will happen on the occasion of the conjunction of certain light waves with the retina of a well-constructed organism that is a seat of sentience. It is a behavioural property of light waves that, if the retina and organism are of the right kind, the visual colour in question will happen ; but it is not a property that can be expressed in terms of structural qualities. It can hardly be denied that this exception is anomalous in relation to the general character of physics considered as a system. Anomalies are not inherently objectionable, but ought to provoke thought.

5. Although all the properties of the continuously existing counterparts or carriers of which we take cognizance are, waiving the exception, expressible in terms of structural qualities, these various kinds of entities cannot be regarded as mere collections of structural qualities. For in the case of each such kind of entity we make the hypothesis that it is a natural kind, that is, that its further properties can be ascertained inductively by experience and experiment. If we could regard an electron as nothing more than a constellation of the structural qualities figuring in the laws governing the known behaviour of electrons in various circumstances, we could ascertain *all further* properties of electrons by pure deduction. If this was also true of the other ultimates of physics, experimental physics would come to an end. All that would remain to do would be to get busy with telescopes and complete the geographical chart of the heavens.

6. It may be that the general notion of natural kind should be given a specific character in relation to such a science as physics. We regard repeating complexes as members of a natural kind, (*a*) if the repetition is 'strong' [1] and thereby (*b*) if it is regarded as likely to prove by experiment to be the seat of still more repetition. We may, of course, make the hypothesis that an entity defined in a certain way is a natural kind in advance of knowledge under (*a*) and (*b*) ; that hypothesis is then subject to test. We make the hypothesis that a certain physical entity exists by assigning it a rôle in a functional

[1] Cp. p. 128-9 *supra*.

equation in a deductive system. We are provisionally satisfied if the conclusions of this deductive system are in agreement with the relevant observables. Thus there was provisional satisfaction with the concept of ether. But if we make the hypothesis that the concept is a natural kind, we expect it to play rôles in other deductive systems also, or to be transferable to a rôle in a more comprehensive deductive system than the original one. If it fails under these heads and if we can reconstruct the deductive system in which it successfully played a part by introducing an alternative concept with a somewhat different rôle, which can also play a rôle in a wider system, we discard the original concept. It is generally agreed, I understand, that all the present-day concepts of physics are in jeopardy of being eventually discarded for the same reason. It does not follow that they are incorrect ; they are explicitly provisional. If they are discarded, other concepts — equally provisional — will have to be devised. They, like the old, will have a double rôle, namely (i) as carriers of structural qualities, that is, as the subjects of behavioural laws expressible in terms of structural qualities in functional equations, and (ii) as the objects of further experiment.

In one sense, it is true, though paradoxical, to say, that the real world of modern science is much more knowable than that of, say, Lockean realism. For this new scientific world is made up to a preponderating extent of structural qualities, which are old friends, existing with full explicitness in our sensible experience. The unknowable counterparts of secondary qualities, *i.e.* the carrier qualities, have receded further and further into the background ; their inherent nature is deemed to be of no importance ; they are mere carriers of the primary qualities expressed in the laws of their behaviour ; their definitions are constantly shifting. Yet they still exist, and can never be dispensed with.

Before proceeding further with these speculations about the universe of science, we must revert to the other disclaimer mentioned at the outset of this chapter. We saw that it makes no difference to beliefs of a predictive kind or otherwise bearing on actual or possible experience, whether the postulate that our sample of samples is fair (*i.e.* equiproportionally distributed on the sectors of their sample lines) is true or not.

If the postulate is true, we are justified in believing that a stretch of nature, which from the point of view of our interests is vast, has manifested certain regularities, and we can extrapolate forward by simple induction. If the postulate is not true, and it is not true that nature has had the regularity supposed, we are justified in believing that a stretch of experience, which from the point of view of our interests is vast, has been characterized by a large proportion of samples having had an enormous and consistent, but not uniform, bias towards the extreme right-hand ends of sample lines, and by simple induction we can believe that this consistent bias will continue and can extrapolate forwards on that basis. Since simple induction is no stronger in suggesting a continuance of a regularity of nature than it is in suggesting a continuance of a consistency of bias, it does not matter whether there has been a bias or not. Therefore no overall sampling postulate is needed to establish the validity of induction.

A curious point now arises. Our experience, to repeat, entails this dichotomy : either nature has been regular or our samples of samples have been biased in a consistent way. This may be stated as, either A or B ; we may for the purposes of this argument ignore the intermediate case of some regularity, though not as much as we suppose, and some consistent bias sufficient to account for the excess of apparent over real regularity. We have seen that it does not affect the validity of our beliefs, in probability, whether A or B is true. This can be inverted, so that we can say that nothing that ever happens can show us whether A or B is more likely to be true. Let us suppose that — against probability — we are on the extreme edge of a vast region and that from now onwards everything will behave much less regularly. No doubt the human race would rapidly be snuffed out in such an eventuality, but let us waive that. Should we then say that the former regularities of nature had been disturbed or that our sample of samples had formerly had a consistent bias that had now come to an end ? We might be psychologically disposed to prefer one or other explanation. But there would apparently be no method of deciding. We should know that in the new condition neither A nor B was true ; but this would not enable us to decide which of the two was true before.

There is a doctrine, with which I sympathize — I do not know whether it can be rightly said to belong to logical positivism — that, if nothing that can ever happen can affect our judgement about which arm of a disjunction, A or B, is probably true, A and B cannot really be two logically distinguishable alternative hypotheses; they must be saying the same thing in different ways, and it can only be by linguistic confusion that we suppose them to be saying different things. Yet on the face of it there seems to be a great difference between saying, 'nature has been regular and our sample of samples has been fair', and 'nature has been irregular, but our sample of samples has been consistently biased in being more regular than the populations from which they were drawn'. It can be argued that this difference, which seems so manifest and striking, is none the less in certain conditions illusory. Without committing ourselves to this view, it seems worth while to explore it. The tell-tale word in this case is 'nature'.

In simple induction, which is a case of direct argument from experience to experience, the problem before us does not arise. The problem is concerned only with those inductions using a sampling postulate. This refers to an unobserved population. It is the whole population, observed and unobserved, that we call 'nature'. What is this whole population? By an austere (Berkleian) ontology it is defined by a series of hypotheticals, of which the protasis always has some such form as, 'if a sentient being went to such and such a place . . .' or 'if a sentient being had an experience P . . .' Time passes and many, indeed the overwhelming majority, of the conditionals become unfulfilled; people cannot be everywhere at once. The unobserved members of the population are simply the apodoses of the unfulfilled conditionals. Now it may be felt that unfulfilled conditionals are only of academic interest. But this is not so. We need to build up high probabilities in regard to them in order to have leverage to get high probabilities by simple induction for the open conditionals of the future. That future presents a vast host of alternative possibilities; we may go this way or that; we may come across A or B or C or . . . or P. It is of the utmost interest what we are entitled to expect in each case as a concomitant set of experiences.

By a sampling method we build up beliefs about what would have happened in a given (past) stretch of time if we had adopted one or other of the many various alternative actions open to us. We cannot assume that each sample that comes before us is representative, for why should we not sometimes come across one or other of all the unrepresentative samples that exist ? But we do assume that our sample of samples has been fair, namely that the various samples we have come across were equiproportionally dispersed over their sample lines. By doing this we find that we have been living in a world which has much regularity, enabling us to entertain beliefs of high probability as regards what would have happened had we adopted one of the other alternatives. Now if we drop the sampling postulate and decide to attribute the seeming regularities to bias, we have to assume a widely pervasive and consistent bias. There must be some principle, analogous to Professor Williams's demon, which excludes us from the paths on which the irregularities of nature are exposed in their true light. But what are these paths ?

On an austere (Berkleian) ontology there are no such paths, nature consisting solely of the hypotheticals generated by the alternatives that are open to us. The so-called 'populations' are only guides to what is likely to happen to us in various cases. They have been projected from our experiences on the basis that our sample of samples has been fair. We might have chosen to project populations on any one of an indefinitely large number of hypotheses in regard to bias ; but since, by simple induction, we must assume a continuance of whatever bias we have chosen, we should, by deciding to assume some bias or other, merely be choosing a more devious method of arriving at the same beliefs (as to what we should have observed on alternative routes) that we make by assuming the fair sampling postulate.

It follows from this that the amount of regularity we believe to exist in nature is partly a function of the amount of bias — to the left or right — that we choose to assume in our sample of samples. If we were determined to make things difficult, we could assume a strong bias towards the right-hand end of the sample lines and project populations much more irregular in their characteristics than those of which we are accustomed to think ; that would not worry us as regards the future, because recalling the right-wards bias we assumed in making our projections of populations, we should be assured by simple induction that our future experiences would be much more regular than the alleged populations from which they were drawn. Or we might decide to have a nice tidy universe by assuming that our samples were strongly biased to the left-hand end of the sample lines and that irregular experiences were always exceptions to the rule — a common human propensity ; that would be a dangerous procedure if ever we forgot the way in which we had constructed our populations, and forgot that we were consequently likely, by simple induction, to meet in future with a quite disproportionately large number of exceptions. In all this it appears strongly that simple induction is our sheet-anchor, while sampling induction is an intellectual device, which is safe because supported by simple induction.

It follows that if our experiences became more or less regular than they have so far been, we could either continue to work on the fair sampling postulate and project differently constituted populations, saying that the 'nature' had changed, or we could re-interpret our old experiences by assuming that they had consisted of samples biased in a different way from those now before us, and that 'nature' was the same as before.

On this basis then, we should be able to conclude that A and B are not genuinely alternative hypotheses, but merely statements of alternative methods of regarding our experience with a view to facilitating our thought. So far the attitude of logical positivism — if I am right in so describing it ! — appears to be vindicated.

There may be mental resistance to this conclusion on the ground that we know quite well from particular experiences, *e.g.* when, having had a partial enumeration, we later get a complete enumeration of a certain population, what the difference is between a bad and a good sample, and that it is nonsense to suppose that we can make arbitrary assumptions, merely to facilitate thought, about whether our sample is good or bad. That is of course perfectly true. But there may be a fallacy involved in passing from particular samples to our whole experience, considered as a sample of samples. On no basis whatever can we deny that a particular sample may be good or bad, *i.e.* representative or unrepresentative, or that, pending further information, we cannot know which it is. We may choose to assume that it is one or the other, but must be prepared to reach erroneous conclusions if our assumption has been wrong. It is our uncertainty about where we stand in this respect, pending further information, that is expressed by the word probability.

But when we pass to our total experience, considered as a sample of a wider universe, the matter is different. In arguing outwards from our actual experience to future experiences or to newly inferred beliefs about the past, we base ourselves essentially on the principle of experience (simple induction). I have stressed throughout that this is a positive principle, vouchsafing beliefs, in probability, without extrinsic support. And I believe that weaknesses and fallacies in inductive logic and probability theory have been due to a lack of recognition of the importance of that principle *per se*, and a failure to explore it to the bottom.

Our actual experience is a funny mixed bag of odds and ends, pervaded, it is true, by many continuities and repetitions, which seem to be clues to some greater regularity than that contained in the experience itself. We accordingly build outwards from it a great world or population of unobserved events, which can be expressed in the form of unfulfilled conditionals, and which we call 'nature'. In this construction we have a certain amount of freedom. We choose to use a fair sampling postulate, not applying it to each set of items of experience, but to the experience as a whole. By that method we find that we can construct a fairly regular 'nature'; by other methods we might have been able to construct more or less regular 'natures'. Our choice of methods for building out 'nature' is free. It must, I suppose, be considered in some sense natural to take the fair sampling postulate as our first choice for the experiment. But we are bound in one respect. The principle of experience dictates that, whatever method we use in constructing 'nature', we must use that same method (viz. the assumption of a fair or biased sample of samples) in deducing from the 'nature' we have constructed what will happen in the future or what has happened (*e.g.* to other

Q

sentient beings) in the past unobserved by us.

Accordingly I suggest that it is not inconsistent to hold that, while in the case of particular samples we have to suspend judgement whether each is fair or not, in the case of the whole of experience considered as a sample of samples we can make what hypothesis about bias we like, always provided that we use the same hypothesis in arguing back from the 'nature' we have constructed to hitherto unobserved experiences past or future. From that again it follows that, if the whole character of our experience became more or less regular from now onwards, there would not be two alternative hypotheses we could hold, viz. that 'nature' had become more or less regular or that our sample of samples had become more or less biased to the right. The nature of 'nature', as it had previously been, depended on our previous assumption, open to our free choice, in regard to how we were to regard the sample that we then had. There would in the new situation be a choice before us, but it would not be a choice between believing in the truth of A or B; that alternative appears on this argument to be bogus. The choice before us would be whether to continue to assume our sample of samples was fair and re-describe 'nature' or to assume that our sample of samples had become differently biased, retaining our previous conception of 'nature' but modifying our notions of what was likely to result for us, in the form of future experiences, from 'nature' being thus constituted.

This conclusion is conveniently satisfactory, anyhow from the point of view of 'logical positivism'; but it seems to depend on the assumption of a Berkleian ontology. If my room is deemed to consist of continuously existing entities, what happens if visits to my rooms were grossly biased, say to the right-hand trillionth part of the sample line? My future visits to the room will be safeguarded by whatever force sustains the consistency in the bias of my sample of samples. But it does not appear that the hypothesis of continuously existing entities is so protected. If we cannot rely on our sample of samples not being grossly biased, no high probability can be established for the continuous existence of the room or other similar external bodies. Such continuous existence would not be impossible, but there would be a lack of strong evidence in support of the hypothesis. This seems to indicate that there exists a strong connexion between the postulate of a realist ontology and the fair sampling postulate.

We have, it must be confessed, violent prejudices in favour both of a realist ontology and of the view that our sample of samples is at least moderately fair. There seems little doubt that, despite the fact that our intellectual doubts about continuing external entities and those about the sampling postulate have quite different origins, the prejudices in regard to them have the same roots. Evidence favourable to a realist ontology, if there be any, rests on the assumption that the fair sampling postulate is true. If that postulate is thoroughly false and many of the paths in nature are not in fact as described in our account of nature, then the external bodies have not that continuing existence the urge to postulate which is the main ground for believing a realist ontology. If we take what I have ventured to call a logical positivist view of the fair sampling postulate, namely that it is meaningless to ask whether it is true or not, it would appear to follow that it is meaningless to ask whether ontological realism is true or not; and that violently offends the prejudice mentioned. If ontological realism is in fact true, but the fair sampling postulate false, the truth of ontological realism can be of no interest or satisfaction to us, since we have no means of acquaintance, even of an indirect kind, namely via knowledge of structure, with the continuously existing entities.

So far as the argument has taken us, the two prejudices, both that in favour of ontological realism and that in favour of the view that our sample of samples is moderately fair, seem to be without rational foundation and to play no essential part in the growth of knowledge. It does not follow that they are false. It is always wise to pay some respect to a strong prejudice, if it is really widespread and if it cannot be shown to have an ulterior motive — by Freudian or other techniques ! On a number of occasions in this study we have found that strong prejudices have been vindicated by strict analysis, even when these have run counter to prevailing philosophical opinions. In the case in point the prejudices are entertained by eminent scientists, who cannot be deemed to be completely lacking in intellectual sophistication. It would seem to be premature finally to dismiss these prejudices, since they are so closely linked with great unsolved problems concerning the relation of mind to matter. Accordingly I feel disposed to offer some further reflexions about the sampling postulate and a realist ontology. These will be provisional and inconclusive.

In referring to the possibility of a consistent bias in our sample of samples, I have spoken somewhat vaguely, saying only what was sufficient to support the logic of sampling induction, as re-enforced by simple induction. No precise definition of the nature of the 'consistency' was attempted.

First it must be remembered that even if our sample of samples had been as thoroughly deceptive as we can conceive it to have been, it would not follow that our universe was altogether irregular. For many notable regularities have lain inside our experience. There have been vast numbers of continuities, repetitions, and sequences conforming to simple laws. Where we may have been deceived, if our sample has been biased, is in supposing that our regular experiences are a part of a larger universe displaying similar, indeed greater, regularity. The universe in which we live is not Heracleitean ; we know that ; but it is possible that everything outside our own private field of experience is thoroughly chaotic.

What sort of bias must our sample have had to make this possible ? Reference has been made to the right-ward bias of our sample of samples. This must have been very vast indeed. But it would by no means suffice for our samples to have been uniformly displaced to a greater or less extent towards the right-hand end of the sample lines. A moderate displacement of this amount would not have much effect on our general notions about nature. Many of our most important beliefs, such as those concerning the continuous existence of common-sense bodies and many laws of physics and chemistry, rest on billion-fold or even supra-astronomically suggestive samples. While one or two of these may have been deceptive (cp. the earlier discussion on 'reversing the consequents'[1]), for them all to be deceptive there would have to have been in an immense number of cases a great displacement of samples to the right-hand billionth part of the sample lines or further. But there certainly has not been a *uniform* displacement

---

[1] Pp. 90-101, *supra*.

of this character in the case of *all* samples considered for their evidential value. I have seen a good many cats with tails and a certain number (commonly called Manx) lacking appendages properly answering to the description of tails. If there had been a displacement of this particular sample to the billionth right-hand part of the sample line, I ought to have seen either all cats with tails or all cats without tails. Thus the displacement, if it has occurred, must have been highly selective. If we have to describe the nature of the displacement that would have to be postulated to eliminate the regularities we believe to exist in the unobserved part of nature, we can only say, as I said in an earlier passage, that the pattern of displacements must be a mirror image of the regularities which, on the assumption that our sample of samples has been fair, we believe to exist in nature. This gives a systematic displacement, to the extent that we find by assuming the fair sampling postulate that nature has a systematic character. But it would by no means be a uniform displacement of all samples towards the right-hand end of sample lines.

A point may be noted here. In many cases we have been able to proceed from a sample to a complete enumeration. A curious enquirer might catalogue such cases. While he might find in the class of cases investigated some moderate rightwards displacement, I think that we may be confident that he would not find an undue proportion of displacements to the billionth, or even to the millionth, right-hand parts of the sample lines. One might be tempted to argue that, since, in cases where we have been able to proceed from samples to total populations, the samples have been found to be fair enough, we can infer that on average all samples, including those from which we have not been able to proceed to the total populations, have been fair. This, however, would be circular, since the argument would be applying to the character of samples the fair sampling postulate, the truth of which is under investigation.

None the less the result has significance. It implies something like fore-knowledge on the part of the demon, which arranges the samples maliciously — if I may revert to Professor Williams's metaphor—'I must not let this fellow have an undue number of deceptive samples in cases where there is any danger of his later being able to proceed to a complete or nearly complete enumeration of the populations in question.   Accordingly I must assure myself in advance about which populations he is destined to explore more thoroughly at a later date.'

Thus the bias that has to be assumed in our sample of samples is, although systematic, exceedingly complex. Furthermore, and this is an important point, it is not a bias that we could assume as a hypothesis in the course of our investigations. We could assume, as an alternative to the fair sampling postulate, a regular displacement, measured by some mathematical device, towards the right. On that assumption we should construct a nature not so very different from that to which we are accustomed. The kind of systematic bias that would have to be assumed to frustrate induction by sample is one which could only be discovered *after* we had built up our notion of a regular nature by assuming some less complex sampling postulate. Having done that we could job back in the opposite direction to discover what complex bias in our samples there would have had to be if nature outside experience was in fact altogether irregular. Indeed, if we suppose a person to exist who is a fervently dogmatic Heracleitean in regard to all nature outside experience, he would regard the work of scientists as a systematic attempt to discover the complex nature of the bias of our samples. And from the point of view of an austere ontology, there is no harm in interpreting science in that way, since the practical results, *e.g.* for predictions, are the same as if we assume a fair sampling postulate. The difficulty only arises if we wish — and I have not denied that we may have good reasons for wishing — to posit a realist ontology.

I will now confess that I am reluctant to have a query hanging over the fair sampling postulate. I must stress most strongly that the difficulty arises, not in the realm of logic, but in that of ontology, and that is why I have postponed it to this chapter. It is essential to recognize the irrelevance of the truth or falsity of the postulate for the validity of the inductive process.

But we are also interested in ontological questions, despite fashionable pleas to the contrary. This may not arise in science. It may indeed be meaningless to ask — although I would not dogmatically assert it to be so — whether those unknown carriers of structural qualities which we call electrons really exist or are merely devices for formulating the apodoses of conditionals, fulfilled and unfulfilled, of which the protases specify the acts of will in relation to a given 'origin' performed by sentient beings. There are some ontological beliefs of a totally different character — those concerning the sentient beings themselves. The vast gulf between the import of the question whether electrons really exist and that of the question whether other people really exist has already been mentioned.[1]

In the case of the electron we certainly want to say that all the structural qualities of all the electrons, namely the qualities specified in the functional equations that determine (or fail to determine !) the behaviour of particular electrons really exist, both in general and in each particular case. But all those structural qualities would really exist on a Berkleian ontology, because they would figure in full in the hypotheses of all the myriads of unfulfilled conditionals that one would have to draw up, if one wanted to give an exhaustive list of all alternatives open to sentient beings. The 'existence' would be defined as consisting in the truth of the hypotheticals ; *i.e.* they would be deemed to 'exist' if the relevant hypotheticals were true and not to 'exist' if they were false. Or, if these structural features did not figure explicitly in those hypotheticals, they would at least figure — this may, however, be deemed somewhat less satisfactory — as playing rôles in the deductive system or systems by which the formulation of those particular hypotheticals was achieved. But as regards the *carrier* quality (or qualities) of the electrons we do not claim to know anything, and indeed we do not think we can ever acquire any knowledge of them ; and consequently whether they exist or not could be deemed a matter of indifference.

But in the case of other people we are interested in the carrier qualities. We are not satisfied merely to think of these people in terms of the mathematical structure of their cerebral displacements : we posit the existence also of their carrier qualities, namely lively colours and other forms of sensation, to say nothing of hopes, fears, joys and sorrows, and when we

[1] Chapter V, pp. 141-2.

posit the existence of those carrier qualities we are not positing something unknowable. We know what we are positing, namely the existence of feelings qualitatively like our own. Whether they really exist or not is a matter of the liveliest interest, and common sense, which we should respect in this connexion, is quite confident of the answer. I say that we should respect common sense because time and again it has been shown to have great logical acumen, by comparison with the blundering and pathetic efforts of logicians to date.

It was argued in an earlier chapter that we have very strong evidence in favour of the view that organisms other than our own are seats of sentience. It is true that we have only one instance in which sentience and a certain type of physical structure are observed to be conjoined ; that is in our own case. But very strong probabilities can spring from a single instance, as happens so often in single laboratory experiments. The high probability deemed to be established from one instance rests on an enormous sample establishing the invariance of certain *types* of characteristic as between one member of a species and another.

The question we now have to face is whether our grounds for belief in the existence of other sentient beings are affected if the fair sampling postulate is false.

1. It has been seen that anything that can be established, in probability, by induction regarding our own (perhaps in this context I should say 'my' own) experiences, actual or potential, by assuming the fair sampling postulate to be true, can be established with equal force if the fair sampling postulate is false. This would seem at first glance to safeguard the sentience of people who come under my observation. But the matter is not quite so simple, because I have no direct evidence that even the bodies that I observe have sentience. It is necessary to call in simple induction to support sampling induction in this case.

By sampling induction we learn that there are certain kinds of property — circulatory system, respiratory system, nervous system, — such that if one member of a species has it the rest have it also. Sentience is a property of similar kind and we therefore credit it also with invariance, subject to suitable limits of tolerance, from member to member of its species.

If the sampling postulate is false, but a consistent bias exists, I shall still have confidence that any member of the species that comes before me will have the appropriate features of this type ; if I dissect, I shall find the heart and lungs there. The fact that the attribution of sentience has been based on one observation only does not alter the situation ; if I had a private opportunity of observing light rays in the neighbourhood of mass on some occasion, I should have complete confidence, subject to knowing how to conduct the observation, that I should observe a displacement of the light rays. This would be equally true if the fair sampling postulate were false, since I should be protected by its consistent bias. But in the case of sentience I am debarred in principle from making the (mental) dissection. This is analogous to the future which I am debarred in principle from observing now ; yet I have well-grounded confidence here in the present about a number of its features. If bias has consistently protected me from observing certain irregularities in the past, I may be confident that it will probably continue to do so for the time being ; I can hold that belief validly in advance of the future unfolding itself. Similarly in regard to beliefs about the present that I cannot verify. When people come before me, I have complete confidence that they have heart and lungs ; I could (in principle!) dissect them. But the fact that I do not do so and in practice could not do so, does not shake my confidence. The fact that I could not even in principle make a mental dissection to lay bare sentience does not shake my confidence ; and there is no reason why it should.

2. The main ingredients of sentience are present sensible experience, imaginative experience including memory and prediction, emotion, reason, purpose. There does not seem to be any reason to carve up this totality in this context. If B, who comes under my observation, has memories, he has as good reasons for believing his to be veridical as I have for believing mine to be. Therefore, if he exists, I have as good reason for believing his to be veridical as I have for believing my own to be. This gives me as good grounds for believing that he has had a past chain of lively experiences as I have for believing that I have had a past chain of lively experiences, and these are very good. It follows that the case for believing

in the sentience and continuing existence of the people of my acquaintance is good, even if the fair sampling postulate is false.

The position as regards people I do not meet is less satisfactory — indeed profoundly unsatisfactory. I have reports of large populations in India and China. I can judge by a large sample that testimony on this kind of topic is reliable. But if the fair sampling postulate is false, the reliability of verbal testimony and written records may be confined to cases that I am in a position to verify. This is an important point. If I have always found certain types of testimony reliable, I can believe by simple induction that they will continue reliable. If the fair sampling postulate is true (in some form) then the phenomena reported may be deemed probably to exist as reported. If the good confirmation I have had of such testimony is due only to a systematic bias in the sample of testimonies that I have happened to verify, I can still trust testimony, because by simple induction I can rely on the bias continuing. It makes no difference to me if testimonies which I shall never have occasion to verify are false ; it makes no difference in the sense that it does not affect my power to make correct predictions.

But if I am interested in the continuing existence of certain entities the position is different. The continuing existence of the carrier qualities of electrons, etc. makes no difference, because I shall never have access to those qualities in any case. The continuing truth of unfulfilled conditionals specifying the structural qualities of electrons, etc. makes no difference, provided that all fulfilled conditionals are true, *i.e.* actual experience is as predicted. But whether sentient beings have a continuous existence or not makes a great difference. In their case the truth or falsity of ontological realism is a vital issue for us. Although we can still retain good reasons for believing in the existence of some sentient beings, if the fair sampling postulate is false, the general position in regard to sentient beings would be profoundly unsatisfactory and do terrific violence to common sense.

I accordingly believe that it will prove possible to vindicate the fair sampling postulate, and that its vindication will be on very simple lines. My reason for the second arm of this belief is that in relation to the existence of other people the fair sampling postulate has always been used with great confidence ; my suggestion about the possible non-existence of inhabitants of the Far East will strike an ordinary person who has never been there as totally ridiculous ; I think it will be found that where a principle of this sort is used with complete confidence, its rational ground is usually implicitly understood ; if it is so understood, the principle involved must be fairly simple.

Examples are to be found in this book. The principle of experience, as stated in Chapter III, is really quite obvious, and is, I believe, perfectly well understood implicitly by everyone not confined for lunacy. So is the ground for preferring a simple explanation (Chapter VI). But people are unable to state in general terms the principles they imply in their ordinary thinking. That is the task of logicians ; but when logicians set out upon their task, they commonly become seized up in a terrible way ; their minds fly off to remote peripheries and they fail to observe the obvious. And in this I condemn myself, because I am confident that the vindication of the fair sampling postulate lies under our noses, and is indeed implicitly understood by everyone ; and yet I cannot present a thorough vindication of it.

Let us return to the case of dice and the very large class of similar cases where a roughly equal distribution of alternative events, categorized in a certain way, is confidently expected. We shall be entirely misled if we seek the key to this in our initial ignorance about which of the alternatives will eventuate. On the contrary, it will be found that in all these cases we have a considerable amount of prior knowledge. We certainly believe in the case of the die that its behaviour in the air and on its fall is in accord with certain simple dynamic laws well known to us. Our knowledge in regard to the physiological and/or psychological laws that determine the momentum imparted by the thrower is imperfect, but we think that we know what kind of laws hold and that these, together with the ordinary dynamic laws, give full determination of the path of the die each time. Similarly in regard to the fall of raindrops on a pavement of equal squares. It is important to observe that we have confidence *in advance* that there will be a roughly equal distribution. Reference was made in an earlier chapter to testing a die for bias by tossing. But we might assure ourselves of lack of bias by some other method, such as a minute physical examination, and thereafter we should be confident in advance of tossing of a roughly equal distribution of turn-ups. We do not in fact argue in this type of case by simple induction : this die has shown over a number of throws a roughly equal distribution and will probably therefore continue to do so. Rather, having by whatever method, of which prior tossing of the die is only one possible one, established that it has a symmetrical composition, we say that this is the *type* of case in which we expect a roughly equal distribution. The essential requisite seems to be a considerable knowledge of the laws which determine the precise result in each case, combined with a lack of any feature in those laws pointing to one or other of the alternatives.

There is a close analogy between this type of case and the fair sampling postulate. What samples we are confronted with depends on our sundry bodily movements from time to time ; or, in a more complicated case, on our arrangements with shops or contractors to supply materials for experiments. Here we have considerable knowledge about the reasons why we have moved in certain directions or gone to certain shops. Those reasons are sufficient to determine precisely our paths to places where we are confronted with samples. The fair sampling postulate is that on a run of experience our samples so reached will have a roughly equal distribution over the sectors of their sample lines. None of the reasons, which together may determine each confrontation quite precisely, have any bearing on which sector of its sample line the sample that we alight upon belongs to. What we have to note here is not absence of knowledge, but rather the full knowledge of our reasons for moving in certain ways, which are sufficient to determine in each case which particular sample we shall be confronted with. But those reasons have no bearing at all on which *kind* of sample we shall get.

If only we could specify precisely in general terms the conditions in which we normally expect *in advance* a roughly equal number of alternative outcomes, it seems probable that the fair sampling postulate would be covered by those conditions. The question would then be what kind of justification we can frame for that advance expectation. It must not assume the fair sampling postulate, since it is to be used in an argument for the truth of that postulate. Presumably the argument that justifies an expectation in this type of case must be L-true.

It may be that we are aiming too high in seeking in this kind of case for a vindication of the fair sampling postulate in its strong form. It will be sufficient for our purpose if we can assume that our sample of samples lacks systematic bias. What we should then be seeking for grounds for believing is that, if we know what determines the end result of a certain process and if, by knowing that, we know that the determining circumstances do not point to one or other of exhaustive alternative outcomes categorized in certain ways, then it follows that the distribution of the end results of a number of such processes among these alternatives will *not* be systematically biased. I feel myself *almost* within reach of showing that this is L-true.

It may be asked, however, how a nescient person could have the knowledge required for the premises of this argument. In the case of the dice and raindrops we have ample prior probabilities in the form of laws of dynamics that we believe to be true. *It is to be remembered that the probability of these laws does not depend on the truth of the fair sampling postulate.* I suggest that in the case of the nescient man the equivalent of such knowledge is provided by introspection. This is a form of knowledge regarded with much disdain even in such immature disciplines as economics and psychology.[1] It provides, however, rich data, of which full advantage should be taken. The almost nescient man may know that he proceeds on a certain path in order to reach a spring to drink from, that he proceeds on another path to take shelter from a storm in a cave, etc. He may observe various kinds of birds and plants on these different journeys. Even assuming the strong sampling postulate, he could at this stage argue from observed concomitances of characteristics in these to their regular concomitance only *within an area of equal distance from his origin*. Some of the samples he sees may be deceptive ; birds and plants

[1] In my own person I do not share this disdain, but regard introspection as providing the grounds for the most securely established general principles of economics.

otherwise rare in the district may happen to have congregated on those particular paths. But to deny that his experience gives any guidance as to the concomitance of characteristics in other parts of the limited area is to affirm that his sample of samples is grossly biased ; the bias implied may involve a concentration of his observed samples in the millionth or billionth right-hand end parts of their sample lines. This surely means that his paths are determined by the requirement that he be presented with billionfold deceptive samples ; that is inconsistent with what he knows, namely that his paths are determined by the quest for water, shelter, etc. It is in the inconsistency of this double determination that the vindication of the fair sampling postulate, anyhow in its weak form, may lie. This would also account for our prior assumption of unbiased distribution in the large classes of cases represented by symmetrically constructed dice.

It is crucial for the vindication of the fair sampling postulate — and I am confident that in the end we shall feel the need to vindicate it — that we should recognize that *the validity of induction is independent of its truth.* Once that is recognized, it is evident that *we can use all the knowledge that we have garnered in by induction, i.e. all the empirical knowledge that we have, to bear upon the question whether the mode by which we are confronted with samples is likely to give a fair sample of samples.* Just as it is our full knowledge about what does determine the fall of dice that gives ground for confidence that there will not be a bias in the upturn of facets, to avoid a double determination of the same events, so our full knowledge about the laws governing our bodily movements gives ground, on the same principle, for holding that we shall not be confronted with a grossly biased sample of samples.

Vindication of the fair sampling postulate is necessary to put common-sense views about other sentient beings on a really sound basis. It also seems favourable to the wider hypothesis — if it may be so called ! — of ontological realism. Having looked at this great problem, it is psychologically difficult to avert one's gaze without reference to matters metaphysical.

In this question of positing or not positing the continuous existence of physical entities, we are not truly indifferent —

save by escapism — but are subject to opposing intellectual impulses of terrific force.

On the one hand we are reluctant to posit the existence of entities which we cannot by any manner of means conceive. What does it *feel* like to be an electron ? If it is answered that it probably does not feel like anything, we are inclined to ask what is the difference between being something which does not feel like being anything and being nothing at all. 'We quite understand what you mean if you say that an electron is part of a chart cunningly devised on the basis of good evidence for specifying what *we* shall feel like in certain circumstances. Beyond that we cannot go.' We might add, on the lines of modern thinking, that it is meaningless to posit the existence of something of quality unknowable — for it must not be forgotten that when we posit the existence of an electron we imply at least one unknowable kind of carrier quality as well as its structural qualities, which are of a kind familiar to us.

On the other side we have to remember that it is impossible for us to imagine any qualities that do not figure in our experience. Therefore to bar all inconceivable qualities would be to take up the egocentric position that we should not allow the existence of anything that does not resemble some part of our own experience.

At this point Occam's principle may be appealed to. It can be argued that it is objectionable to posit continuously existing physical entities, because it is unnecessary, since all that we know or think we know can be expressed in the apodoses of a series of hypotheticals referring to possible experiences of sentient beings. But what is the ultimate authority of Occam's principle ? We certainly ought not to postulate entities, if we have no reason for doing so, out of fantasy or exuberant spirits ; that is not quite the same as refusing to do so save under necessity.

At this point we may refer to the admitted weakness of a link in a previous argument.[1] Would all the structural qualities of all the alleged physical entities be referred to in an exhaustive series of hypotheticals covering all possible experiences ? So long as we were dealing with a world of chairs and tables it seemed correct to say so ; all the structural

[1] Cp. p. 229.

qualities of such objects would find mention in an exhaustive list of hypotheticals concerning the experiences of sentient beings moving in proximity to those alleged objects. Would all the structural qualities of all the electrons get such a mention? Or would they not rather find mention only in the arguments supporting the hypotheticals, that is in the deductive chains of reasoning leading up to the specifications of what the observables would be on the alternative routes specified in all the hypotheticals? This provides rather a tenuous kind of existence for those structural qualities; they should surely be given a more full-blooded existence, if the fair sampling postulate is true. They cannot be given a more full-blooded existence save by positing the continuous existence of carrier qualities.

Where the carrier qualities are knowable — contents of the sensible experience of other sentient beings — the fair sampling postulate requires us to posit their existence. There are two objections to doing the same for the carrier qualities of electrons, etc., viz. (i) that they are unknowable, and (ii) that their structural qualities, which the fair sampling postulate *requires* us to regard as continuously existing, can be given suitable homes in the apodoses of unfulfilled conditionals. Doubt has now been cast on both these objections.

Then there is another ancient metaphysical principle which seems relevant here — *ex nihilo nihil*. About the status of this I make no pronouncement; it has undoubtedly been influential. It requires some kind of continuity. Newtonian gravitation seemed out of accord, and Newton was uncomfortable about that. I understand that this difficulty has now been put right in the General Theory of Relativity.[1] But meanwhile new trouble in relation to continuity appears to have broken out in the quantum theory.

It grossly violates the *ex nihilo nihil* principle to suppose that structural qualities are suddenly elevated, on the whims of sundry people as they walk about, from the tenuous character of being elements in a deductive system, yielding apodoses for unfulfilled conditionals, into elements in sensible experience.

---

[1] But I understand also that the General Theory has by no means so high an authority as the Special Theory. It may be tinctured by metaphysical prejudice.

On the other hand, it has to be remembered that the ontological realism of science does not save us altogether from a breach of *ex nihilo nihil*. For we still have some discontinuity in the sudden appearance, as people walk about, of the lively carrier qualities of sensible experience — visual colours and the rest.

No solutions have been provided for the problems discussed in this chapter. But I hope that I have shown that the subject is replete with *clues*, so that we are entitled to expect momentous advances at some future time. They are not likely to be achieved by the analytical faculty alone, but require that genius for bringing together various elements in a wide-reaching hypothesis that the great scientists have possessed.

R

CHAPTER X

FUNDAMENTAL PRINCIPLES
OF INDUCTION

No attempt will be made to present a catalogue of the various kinds of inductive argument, like Mill's celebrated *Methods*. It has not been the purpose of this volume to categorize arguments used by common sense or in the disciplines of the various sciences; the latter differ from one branch of science to another, in accordance both with the nature of the subject-matter of each and with the stage of development of each, that is, with the amount of prior information now available to serve as the premises of further arguments. Rather we have been concerned with certain fundamental principles, from which all the many special types of argument derive their validity. It is the purpose of the present chapter to draw attention once again to certain key points in the construction of our general system.

First, we will deal with the definition of probability. The notion that probability is an indefinable, directly intuitable, relation is rejected. Keynes sought to gain plausibility for the view that it is indefinable by referring to certain situations in which sophisticated man thinks it is obvious by reference to a variety of circumstances not definable in quantitative terms that a certain belief is probably true. In such cases there is apt to be a large mass of prior information not explicitly sorted, but used as premises by someone of well-trained habit, sometimes without even an explicit mental reference to it. It is dangerous to seek the essence of probability by examining such cases.

Probability is defined as present when what is taken to be the case in the premises of an argument has a character A, which is such that of all the times when A is the case there is something else that is often, or very often, the case. To this something else we give the general name X; the content of X will vary from argument to argument. If what has this character A is the case, X is said to be 'probably' the case (the specific content of X depending on the specific content of the premise or premises). It is claimed that this conforms to the popular idea of probability which is expressed in such terms as 'it seldom (or very seldom) happens for one to get evidence of this character in favour of something and for that something not to be the case'. We then say that that something is 'probably' the case. The difficulty lies not in the provision of the definition but in seeing how the premises of an argument can ever have the required character A. I have endeavoured in the course of this volume to show that premises of this character occur when we are confronted with continuities, concomitances of characters, 'strong' repetitions, or sets of observables whose measurements, considered as a function of time or of time and some other measurements, comply with a simple law. Such premises may also occur, when they are the conclusions of other arguments in the premises of which those continuities, etc. figure, or are the conclusions of a longer chain of arguments. It is not claimed that an exhaustive list has been provided of phenomena carrying the A character; those I have cited are certainly important, but there may be others. It might be desired to reach a more remote abstraction by finding a common character in these various phenomena which carry the property A; that might be done; it is not attempted here. We must build from the bottom upwards, for it is my contention that logic has so far hardly made a beginning. I claim that the character A is sufficiently widespread in our experience to account for all that we take to be probable in common life or science.

Probability is thus defined fairly and squarely in terms of frequency. But this is a strictly logical frequency, having no direct relation to alleged frequencies in nature. The logical frequency is the proportion of times that the conclusion from evidence of a certain character is true. This logical frequency sometimes, however, has an indirect relation to a frequency in nature. If, for instance, the premises of an argument consist (i) of an hypothesis (taken to be true) that of all the times that P occurs in experience it is shortly followed by Q one time out of three, and (ii) P has just occurred, then the conclusion that Q will now shortly occur has a probability of one-third. This means that of all the times that both premises are true, the conclusion is true one time out of three. In this argument the logical frequency (viz. frequency of the truth of the conclusion) is equal to the alleged frequency in experience. And if, begging many questions at this stage, we can identify frequency in experience with frequency in nature, we have here a case where a frequency in nature generates a logical frequency or probability in the conclusion of an argument.

Strictly speaking, however, the conclusion presented above is provisional only, since the hypothesis specified in premise (i) is said to be 'taken to be true'. There may be evidence for the hypothesis that is so good that it can be taken to be a practical certainty. In this case the statement of probability contained in the conclusion, which flows directly from the frequency in nature, may be taken to be a practical certainty. Alternatively we may decide to ignore the element of doubt in the hypothesis, to accept the conclusion and argue forwards from it. In this case the conclusion and any further conclusions reached by deduction from it are provisional.

The greater part of existing probability theory is concerned with deductions from premises of the above type. It has recently won *réclame* by proving useful in statistical mechanics, and in quantum mechanics. It is to be noted, however, that by far the greater part of the probabilities with which we are concerned in induction, both in common life and in science, do not conform to this pattern. One part of induction, but that itself by no means the major part, is concerned with the evidence bearing upon the probability of hypotheses of this type — upon the probability *of* the hypothesis, not the probability stated *in* the hypothesis. It need hardly be observed that the probability of an hypothesis affirming a statistical frequency in nature is not itself a statistical frequency in nature nor a reflexion of one. Most of induction, however, is not concerned to establish statistical frequencies, but to establish uniformities, laws or particular facts.

It is a point of cardinal importance that evidence pointing to the probability of an hypothesis H does not usually or even frequently have any independent evidential value for the hypothesis not-H. It is a first-rate fallacy to suppose that one can

find the probability of not-H by subtracting the probability
of H from 1. The evidence available which validly establishes
a finite probability for H may have no bearing at all on the
probability of not-H. An easy illustration may be given from
simple induction. This uses continuance to date as evidence
for the further continuance of a continuity ; but continuance
to date provides no evidence as regards termination ; to derive
the probability of termination by subtracting the probability
of continuance from 1 would be to ignore the possibility that
the continuity will have infinite duration. The bare fact that
the continuity has continued for a certain time cannot be taken
as evidence that it will eventually cease. There is a popular
adage that 'it is a long lane that has no turning'. But we do
not know this to be true. We certainly have no evidence that
the laws of physics, such as we now take them to be, will continue to be in operation for ever ; but I believe that we have
no evidence that they will not. We are totally ignorant on this
point, with no probabilities either way. This is not inconsistent with there being a strong probability that they will
continue for some time into the future.

To safeguard the truism that either H or not-H is true,
where the evidence establishes some definite probability, call
it p, for H, but has no bearing on not-H, we should say that
the probability of H is *at least* p. As most probabilities are of
this kind, the mathematical development of probability theory
should be mainly concerned with *minimum* probabilities. Sometimes there is evidence for not-H, but not sufficient to make the
probabilities of H and not-H add up to 1. If these probabilities
add up to an amount very nearly equal to 1, it may be convenient for further calculations or deductions to split the
difference. But there is no logical foundation for splitting it
in the proportions $p(H)$ and $p(\text{not-H})$ and, as a safeguard
against fallacy, this should never be done ; it should be considered mandatory to split the difference in such a way as to
get the nearest round numbers.[1]

In the chapter on probability it was stated somewhat

---

[1] This is slightly analogous to a rule very familiar to economists ; when
an aggregate is found by adding some precise returns, perhaps stating pounds,
shillings and pence, to estimates only supposed accurate to the nearest
thousand or million pounds, the aggregate should be stated only to the
nearest thousand or million pounds.

dogmatically that, when the premise yields a conclusion that can only be stated in loose quantitative terms, such as 'probably' or 'very probably', a precise number is always implicit, although not present to the mind of the arguer, and is in a quite different category from other evidence with which he might have acquainted himself but did not in fact; and an analogy was given from observations of an incompletely full tank and a flight of starlings. The reasons behind this can now be stated. We have to examine the various situations that generate a probability relation.

First, we take observation of a continuity. Here the relevant numbers are the length of the continuity already observed and the length it is proposed to predict. Vagueness arises because we may not in fact have measured the continuity, because the probability of our memory being true may not be accurately assessed, and because, in cases of simple induction, we may not be interested to formulate closely the precise length of the forward extrapolation we wish to make. We may be interested in some rather loosely defined period such as 'our lifetime' or 'that and those of our children and grandchildren'. But we may none the less be sure that the supposed length of the continuity to date is great compared with the forward period in which we are interested, and that our memory is so clear and the testimony we have so good as to endow their contents with high probability. Multiplying the probability obtainable by simple induction for the forward period by the probability of the veridicity of the memory and testimony, we may get a high probability for the forward extrapolation. The probability is known to be 'high', but a precise number cannot be inserted because the evidential data have not been counted or measured.

Where an inductive argument is based on observed concomitances or strong repetitions, two numbers are involved, (1) that provided by the theory of Combinations, and (2) the rate of frequency of the occurrence in our general experience of phenomena of similar evidential structure. In both cases these numbers are in principle precise; none the less we may only have vague quantitative estimates in our mind. We may not have counted the number of items in our sample (some of which may be subject to the uncertainties of memory or

testimony) ; except where, in applying the theory of Combinations, we assume an infinite population — which entails an *at
least* in the consequential ascription of probability — we may
be vague as to the size of the population. At this point, however, if only we could find means for counting our sample
and if we assumed an infinite population, we could get precision for the first of the two numbers wanted. A far more
serious limitation is our vagueness in regard to the rate of
occurrence in our general experience of samples of similar
logical structure — of which more will be said presently. This
is an essential number for the precise evaluation of the probability of the hypothesis or of the belief that we seek to infer.
The rate of occurrence is an absolutely precise number, but
how far indeed we are from knowing what it is. A little care
would not suffice to obtain it. We should have to make simultaneous counts of the various properties of all the phenomena
that come to our attention — an impracticable proceeding.
But it must not be assumed that we know *nothing* about this
number ; if that were so, most of our inductive arguments
would be invalid. We have some notion of its order of magnitude, and this may suffice to establish rather high or very high
probabilities for our conclusion. But the precise measure will
be lacking. Where, as so often in common life, there are
supra-astronomical odds in favour of a conclusion prior to
'reversing the consequents', the value of the 'deflator' involved
in that process will not matter much.

Again, in the case of laws precise numbers are implied. It
is required to find the number of possible sets (of a given size)
of observations that would comply with *any law of simplicity
ranking equal* to that with which the observations before us
comply. I do not know whether, when we have a law with
several adjustable parameters, mathematicians could in practice
discover this number ; there is clearly an actual number
involved. Then we have to take the ratio of this number to
the number of possible sets of observations if the Heracleitean
hypothesis (of lawlessness) were true ; here there is the question of the range within which on the Heracleitean hypothesis
we ought to assume the magnitudes in the possible observations to lie ; we may take some conservative hypothesis as to
that range, which at once introduces an 'at least' into our

probability estimate. In the case of laws, too, the value of the 'deflator' has to be established, if a precise probability is to be given to the hypothesis that the law holds.

Thus it appears that in all the kinds of case which we have shown to generate a probability relation, precise numbers are implicit, and from these the precise value of the probability could be calculated ; but it is also apparent that to perform the counting and measuring operations required to ascertain those precise numbers is usually impracticable. I would further add that I do not believe that there is any kind of case generating a probability relation in which a precise number is not implicit ; that is no doubt a dangerous negative generalization ; but I would suggest that the *onus probandi* is on the other side ; let someone cite such a case.

It is now necessary to review briefly the kinds of situation giving rise to probability.

First and foremost we must take the case of the continuity. The analysis of the probability generated by a continuity specifies precisely what we mean by the Principle of Experience.

This Principle lies at the base of the whole system of principles of induction. It is constituted by the belief that, when we are traversing an expanse of unknown size, we are not likely at any time to be on its extreme edge. The word 'unlikely' is to be interpreted rigorously in terms of a frequency theory of probability. To say that 'we are unlikely to be on the extreme edge' means that 'if we continuously believe that we are on its extreme edge, it is certain that we shall be wrong much more often than we are right'. Thus if we believe that we are not on its extreme edge, we shall certainly be right much more often than we are wrong ; thus we shall certainly be right in deeming that we are probably not on its extreme edge. It is implicit in the meaning of 'probable' that we may none the less be on its extreme edge.

In quantifying this probability, or frequency of being right, by a precise number, regard must be paid to the fact that beliefs regarding continuance already entertained at a certain point are irrelevant to the probability of future continuance at that point. This difficulty is overcome by the theorem illustrated by the square diagram on page 56. The problem is to find a mechanism for subtracting from the class of beliefs to be used in determining each probability ratio the beliefs already entertained, and therefore to be excluded from the present probability estimate, on the analogy of excluding balls already drawn and not replaced from the estimate of the probabilities of future drawings of balls from a bag. This subtraction is achieved by positing that the ratio of true to false answers must be considered from every point on the line of travel over the expanse. One way of putting this is to say that we successively assess the ratio of true to false answers on a line that is ever becoming shorter, until it finally comes to an end, and then take the average of the assessments. Since the traveller never obtains information about how far he has proceeded until the very end, the formula based on these successive assessments has to be settled at the outset and applied throughout. Since probability is essentially a relation between evidence and conclusion, there can be no re-appraisal of the probability as the journey proceeds, since no new relevant evidence arises. This is but one of many illustrations of how important it is to adhere strictly to the principle that probability is relative to evidence available.

In the general formula we give equal weight to each ratio of true to false answers as seen from each point of view on the line between the beginning and end. This is not an application of the Principle of Indifference. That Principle asks us to assume, on the basis of ignorance, that an equal number of each of a variety of exhaustive alternatives would occur ; there is no proper basis for any such assumption. But in the case of the journey under consideration there is a basis for the assumption of the equal probability of the different assessments ; for it is perfectly certain (by definition) that the traveller will in fact be for an equal period in each aliquot part of the line. This justifies giving equal weight to the ratio of true to false answers pertaining to each length of line, as it is diminished from the whole line to zero, and accordingly justifies us in taking the arithmetic average of all the ratios as the ratio appropriate to the nescient traveller.

Since the Principle of Experience is so fundamental in the whole story of the acquisition of knowledge, it is quite proper to use the situation involved in having experience, that is essentially travel on a continuity, for a definition of probability.

Probability may be defined as the frequency represented by the number calculated in the manner prescribed in the square diagram. From this definition the general theory of probability can proceed by way of logical entailment, and the only remaining question is whether this definition gives a meaning to probability that conforms with what has been called the explicandum, that is the meaning that we give in our own minds to the idea, when we use it in our common or in our scientific thinking. I suggest that this definition does in fact conform with the explicandum. It would be in conformity with the ordinary use of language and the ordinary modes of thought to say that if an individual does not know how far he has proceeded across an expanse, it is 'improbable' that he is on its extreme edge. And it is quite acceptable that the notion of 'improbable' should be explained in terms of frequency, namely as meaning that if one entertains the belief that one is on the extreme edge, one will be much more often wrong than right. What the individual would not readily recognize, but it has been the purpose of this volume to explain, is that from this notion of probability defined by reference to these circumstances, viz. position on an expanse, all the other applications of the notion of probability can be derived.

Thus the Principle of Experience, as such, is a first principle and a universally sustaining principle of all induction, and consequently of all our positive knowledge.

We next proceed to the case of sampling, in the widest sense of that word. This may be otherwise named as induction by simple enumeration. This principle lies at the basis of all arguments where we infer from the characteristics of a limited set of phenomena the characteristics of a larger unobserved universe. It is on the basis of the generalities that we can establish as probable by simple enumeration that we can proceed to other methods of discovery such as by a single laboratory experiment. No fallacy could be more absolute than the view that nothing is gained for the advancement of knowledge by the mere repetition of instances.

There are two cruxes in establishing the validity of inference by sample in the broadest sense. One is the problem of deflation when we take the critical step of 'reversing the consequents'. The other is the problem of the fair sampling postulate. The former of these is of much greater significance in inductive logic ; the interest of the latter is for ontological rather than logical study.

First we may consider the approach to this problem recommended by Professor Williams. Phenomena considered as a sample give rise to a probability situation owing to the fact that more samples resemble the populations from which they are drawn within certain limits of tolerance than do not. This is subject to the sampling postulate, which will be considered presently. If we classify samples by their size, the majority of resembling samples becomes progressively greater as their size increases, and we can at the same time reduce the limits of tolerance. Thus if we entertain the belief about a sample that it resembles its population within limits of tolerance, we shall be more often right than wrong — much more often right, if the sample is large. There is clearly a close family relation between this situation and that which arises from one's position on a homogeneous expanse, and there need be no hesitation in applying the same word 'probability' to the two situations.

It is not to be denied that Professor Williams's theory constitutes a significant and important approach to the general theory of induction. This remains subject to the problem concerning the fair sampling postulate, which will presently be considered. But the trouble about this approach is that we only get, save in the case of samples of vast size, rather low probabilities. The tremendous amount of experience one would have to have in order to get rather meagre returns does not seem in accord with our common-sense notions about what we believe of nature with very high probability. And if we stop here, we are making no use of certain very salient facts in our experience which improve our situation out of recognition.

The all important point is that the binomial theorem vouchsafes that there are far fewer samples of the kind 'all P's have Q' and 'no P's have Q', when the composition of the populations differs from these ratios (all and none) by a certain proportion, than there are samples of the kind 50 per cent of the P's have Q or 80 per cent of the P's have Q, when the composition of the populations differs from these ratios by a like proportion.

It is essential that we should use the logical leverage provided by this all-important fact. Owing to this, we are justified in attaching much more importance to a sample of reasonable, but not vast, size in which all P's have Q than we are to a sample of the same size in which 55 per cent of the P's have Q. In the former case, but not the latter, we can establish immensely high probabilities that the population does not diverge by more than a narrow proportion from the composition of the sample.

With this in mind, it is not enough to rest content with Professor Williams's very general proposition that samples resemble their populations. We cannot accordingly rest content with having for the premise of our inductive argument 'samples in general resemble their populations to such and such an extent'. We need to give special consideration to the samples of the 'all P's have Q' kind. But as soon as we do this, we need a further premise for our argument. Under the more general (Williams) type of argument, we only need for our premise, 'this set of phenomena may be considered as a sample of a certain size, and all samples of that size have a certain proportion which resemble their populations within certain limits of tolerance'. We now go over to the situation in which we are confronted by a sample of a special kind, e.g. 'all the P's have Q in this set of phenomena'; we then have to consider samples of this kind, not merely as instances of all possible samples of the same size, but as instances of all samples of this size having this type of composition, namely 'all the P's have Q'.

On the basis of the theory of Combinations, we get the fact that samples of substantial size in which all the P's have Q are tremendously rare in populations in which it is not true that almost all the P's have Q. Unfortunately this tremendous rarity does not, in and by itself, give us logical leverage. If it is in fact a tremendously rare event for us ever to come across a sample of a certain size in which all the P's have Q, then the appearance of such a sample has no evidential value at all; it gives no grounds for inferring that it is probable that almost all the P's in the total population have Q in the case before us. Thus we need for this type of argument a further premise, namely that the occurrence of sets of phenomena in which all the P's have Q is not 'tremendously rare'.

In fact in our world we do not find that such an occurrence is tremendously rare ; on the contrary, it is extremely common. This fact justifies us, by strict logical entailment, subject to the fair sampling postulate, in holding it to be highly probable, that in the populations in question probably almost all the P's have Q. We may say that if in each case we believe that almost all the P's have Q, we shall certainly be much more often right than wrong.

This imports into our logic an element of paradox and untidiness. They both have to be accepted. A sample of fair size in which all the P's have Q may be regarded as *prima facie* evidence for, or, to use our earlier terminology, suggestive of, the view that almost all the P's in the total population within the range of observation have Q. But it does not provide good evidence, or even weak evidence, for that, unless we have some notion of the frequency within our general experience of the rate of occurrence of this type of sample, viz. samples of a certain size in which all the P's have Q. It is this reference to our general experience that is paradoxical; we have certain specific evidence E_h relating to a specific hypothesis H and what we are saying is that certain other phenomena E_a, E_b, E_c, etc., which have no direct bearing whatever on H, but have a specific bearing on quite different hypotheses, A, B, C, etc., affect the evidential value of E_h in relation to H. This paradox must be accepted. And, if we think of the matter very carefully, we see that there is no paradox at all, but that the reference to the hypotheses A, B, C, etc., is implicit in the notion of probability. When we say that H is probable on the evidence E_h what we are saying is that out of all the times that we have evidence of the logical character E (*e.g.* a sample of a certain size in which all the P's have Q), the hypothesis to which it points will be true a high proportion of times. In other words, 'H has at least 9/10 probability on evidence E_h' means that if we have a number of cases of evidence of this logical character, namely E_h, E_a, E_b, E_c, etc., etc. at least nine out of ten of the hypotheses H, A, B, C, etc., etc. are true. Thus in the statement that H is 'probably' true, there is already a reference to the hypotheses A, B, C, etc., etc. There is of course no reference to the specific contents of these hypotheses, but only to the logical structure of the sets of evidence in their favour. Thus the reference to matters which seemingly have no connexion with the specific argument concerning H, with which we are concerned, is implicitly contained in the word 'probable'. Consequently it should cause no surprise, nor be regarded after reflexion as paradoxical, that a reference to E_a, E_b, E_c, etc., viz. a reference to the rate of occurrence in our general experience of E type evidence, should have a logical bearing on the evidential value of E_h in relation to H. The reason why E_h has strong evidential value for H is that if not-H were true E_h would be a *rarissima avis* in the hyper-population of samples of which it is a member. But if an occurrence of logical structure E is a *rarissima avis* in our general experience, then the occurrence of E_h has no evidential value in favour of H.

This principle is at the very heart and centre of inductive logic, and I would say that, after the Principle of Experience, *i.e.* of Simple Induction itself, it is the most important principle with which we are concerned. These two principles are far removed from the ordinary ways of thought of the theorist of deduction ; firm grasp of them should be regarded as the hall-mark of the competent theorist of inductive logic.

The principle of Deflation imports an element of untidiness into our logic, because the rate of occurrence of samples of a given logical structure is extraordinarily difficult to assess accurately — impossible in practice outside the laboratory. But in ordinary life we may have a sufficiently rough notion of its value for our purposes. This untidiness may give an impetus, especially to those who think logic ought to be tidy, to renew the quest, in the manner of Carnap, for initial prior probabilities, which might be thought to rescue us from dependence on Deflation. It is to be remembered that the premise specifying the rate of occurrence of samples of a certain logical type does the logical *work* that could be done by the assumption of initial prior probability, if only that assumption were warranted. Now suppose that logicians were convinced that Carnap's *m*-function, defined with such wonderful precision and expertise, were acceptable. It would then be possible to establish definite probabilities for conclusions of sampling arguments, without any reference to the rate of occurrence of samples of similar logical character in our general experience ; and the hearts of the tidy-minded would rejoice. They would be wrong to rejoice. For the rate of occurrence of samples of similar logical structure *is* relevant in each specific case. The assumption of initial prior probabilities can lead to the establishment of a definite probability for a conclusion on the evidence of a sample, without reference to the rate of occurrence in our general experience of samples of similar logical structure. But this would involve leaving out a relevant piece of evidence. If we subsequently tried to bring this in, we should find the probability of the conclusion over-determined or find ourselves involved in contradictions. In fine, the assumption of initial prior probabilities has to be rejected, not only because it is unwarranted in itself, but also because it is redundant, and liable to lead to mutually contradictory conclusions.

We may now pass to the fair sampling postulate, which is required both for the Williams approach and for the approach that takes advantage of the distribution given by the binomial expansion. No postulate is required, or could be creditably maintained for a moment, that any given sample is a fair one. The postulate is that our experience as a whole is a fair sample ; being fair is defined as the fact that the various samples are equi-proportionally distributed over the aliquot parts of sample lines. If we could rely on particular samples being fair, we should have certainty about the composition of unobserved populations. It is the fact that we allow that any particular sample may quite well be unfair that compels us to say that our inference in regard to the composition of the population is probable only. But it would at first seem that this probability would itself disappear unless we assumed that the sample of samples, constituting our experience as a whole, is fair.

It is at this point that simple induction is brought in to support sampling induction. Without simple induction, the validity of sampling induction could not be sustained. So far theorists of induction appear to have ignored simple induction, and I would suggest that this is the reason for their failure. By the fair sampling postulate we can measure the amount of bias there would have to be in our sample of samples, if nature was altogether lacking in the regularity ascribed to it, *e.g.* if my room was often not there on occasions when I did not happen to go to it. It would not be enough to defeat induction for samples to be regularly and uniformly biased to the right-hand end of sample lines. If they were, nature would be less regular than we suppose it to be, but it would still retain much regularity, and that regularity would have a uniform structural relation to the regularity that we normally suppose. For induction to be frustrated it would be needful for our sample of samples to be biased in a very peculiar, but systematic, way. The best method of describing this way is to say that if nature were altogether irregular, the biasing of our sample of samples would have to be a mirror image of the regularity in nature that we have inferred by assuming one sample of samples to be fair. By simple induction we can hold that if this bias does in fact obtain, it will continue for the time being. This being so, we can validly believe on strictly logical grounds that such phenomena as we should be led to expect by assuming the sample of samples to be fair, and inferring thereby certain regularities in nature, will occur just the same, even if our sample of samples has been biased in such a way that nature has in fact no regularity at all. The same result would hold if nature had some regularity, but our sample of samples had been biased in a special way, leading us on the fair sampling postulate to infer greater regularity than exists. Accordingly the fair sampling postulate is not necessary for the validity of the inductive process. But even if it is not true in fact, it is an essential tool of thought ; for it enables us to infer what the bias in our samples has been (if nature has had in fact no regularity), and that enables us to make valid predictions, in probability, as regards our future experiences.

Thus simple induction renders the fair sampling postulate otiose for induction by simple enumeration, *i.e.* for sampling induction. The postulate is not required to sustain logical arguments. But it becomes relevant as soon as we consider ontological problems. In our daily life and in science we are not interested in these save for one point, and that all important, namely the real existence of other sentient beings. The great confidence that common sense has about this and the fact that common sense usually has a greater sureness of touch than logicians in its implicit logic make me believe that it will be possible to vindicate the fair sampling postulate. My ideas about an approach to such a vindication were set out in Chapter IX. We must resolutely eschew resort to the principle of 'equal distribution of ignorance' which has proved so detrimental to inductive theory. Rather I would say that we could formulate a principle of 'equal distribution when there is complete knowledge'. It would probably only be possible to vindicate the postulate in a weak form, *i.e.* as laying down absence of systematic bias; but that would be sufficient for our ontological problems. If we have complete knowledge about the development of a type of process, yet that knowledge does not specify which among a set of alternatives, so categorized as to be exhaustive, the end item of the process will be, then, if the end items were required to have systematic bias as between the alternatives, the end items would be overdetermined, viz. first by the known laws governing the process and, secondly, by the requirement of bias. If it be asked how this knowledge about the laws determining the end items of the type of process is to be acquired, prior to rational grounds for belief in the fair sampling postulate, I would remind the reader that *inductive knowledge does not depend on the fair sampling postulate.* Only ontological knowledge so depends, and thus we may garner in all the fruits of induction to indicate the cases in which the equal distribution of outcomes may be appropriately assumed.

In the case of dice the relevant knowledge is that concerning dynamic laws governing their flight and physiological laws affecting the thrower. In the case of the fair sampling postulate, which would figure simply as one kind of instance where lack of systematic bias could be assumed, much of the relevant knowledge would flow from introspection, by which we know why we move in this direction or that from time to time. Thus despised introspection may prove to be a king-pin after all.

Argument by analogy has been shown not to be, as Keynes, for instance, supposed, an arm of empirical reasoning independent of, and to be contrasted with, induction by simple enumeration. Its principles are to be derived from the more fundamental principles of induction by simple enumeration. The existence of repetitions, within boundaries roughly deter-

S

minable, enables us to use an argument of the following type. Let there be two or more regions, within roughly determinable boundaries, of similar pattern. Locations within the regions may be defined as correspondent if they bear the same specific relation to the boundaries. These locations may or may not be occupied by features that are similar from region to region. If only a small number of the total locations have similar features, it is improbable (by the fair sampling postulate) that in an over-all but incomplete inspection I shall find all the features similar. If I do find them all similar, that may be taken as evidence that the regions have a substantial number of similar features. This establishes a probability that can be applied to each of the unobserved features. The structure of the argument is clearly quite identical with that used in proceeding from a sample to a population. In this application of the sampling principle the 'population' is nothing less than all the features of the regions in question. The 'sample' consists of the features of those regions that I have observed. To enlarge the positive analogy is merely to observe more similar features, and thus render the 'sample' larger. This type of argument may be applied not only to the spatially related features, but to features otherwise connected within a region, such as the behavioural properties like specific gravity, melting-point, etc. If it be held that such regions have an indefinitely large number of behavioural properties, this method of analogical induction can still be used by assuming the 'population' to be infinite, and yield good probability if the number of similar features observed is fairly large. The number of features observed plays the same logical rôle as the number of items observed in an ordinary sampling enquiry. In the case of analogy, we can make the same use of the fact that the share of the sample line occupied by various samples tends to stability, as the population increases to infinity. Therefore we can establish a definite probability in favour of a behavioural property of a certain region being similar, even if this is but one of an indefinitely large number of behavioural properties.

The genus-species relation is of fundamental importance for scientific induction. Within a genus certain kinds of characteristic may be found to be invariant from member to member of each species, but not between members of different species of the genus. This invariance may be exemplified in a very vast sample, so that the probability in favour of these kinds of characteristic being almost always invariant from member to member of each species of the genus, may be tremendously high. This property of invariance from member to member of each species is to be regarded as a property of the genus, and may be ascribed to it with high probability. Accordingly there will be a high prior probability that characteristics of a species not hitherto examined in respect of those characteristics will be invariant, within the limits of tolerance specified, from member to member of that species. This is the basis of the single crucial laboratory experiment. Its existence and importance is by no means inconsistent with the view that all knowledge of unobserved nature springs ultimately from induction by simple enumeration. The belief in the invariance of the characteristic from member to member of the species of the genus may rest on a very vast sample. This establishes a high probability of invariance, so that when we come to a new species, we may assume invariance as a prior practical certainty from the beginning. What physicists now regard as the ultimate constituents of the material world may be considered as a genus ; there is prior practical certainty as regards invariance from member to member of each constituent — though it now seems that this invariance must be taken to cover the case of compliance with a given statistical law.

This is the limited sense in which the uniformity of nature may be said to have been established by empirical methods. The uniformity only relates to certain types of property, and the practical certainty only relates to the region that lies within the range of observation and, by simple induction, to the near future. Thus circumscribed, the uniformity of nature may be ascribed as a property of nature ascertained by empirical methods ; it can in no case be accepted *a priori* ; and it is by no means a pre-condition, as is sometimes urged, for the validity of any principle of inductive argument whatever. But the existence of such uniformity, as and when established *a posteriori*, may give scope for further particular inductions that would not otherwise be possible. Indeed it gives large scope. A vast number of inductions rest on the assumption, as applied to the type of property in question, that there is a uniformity.

It is this fact, no doubt, that has given rise to the fallacy that inductive principles require uniformity as a presupposition. The high probability of certain types of uniformity, as established by an immense simple enumeration, gives much logical leverage. If these uniformities had never been established, induction would lack much of the scope that it has in our world. Once again it is necessary to draw a distinction between conditions necessary if induction is to have good scope and conditions necessary for the validity of induction. The existence or non-existence of uniformity has no bearing whatever on the validity of the principles involved in induction.

We may refer back to the three stages in the development of inductive reasoning that were specified in the first chapter. Reasoning which can assume a high prior probability for invariance in the kind of properties it is investigating belongs to the third stage ; many branches of science are in that stage and the triune scheme of hypothesis, deduction and verification gives a good description of the pattern of argument normal in that stage. This volume has been mainly concerned with the forms of arguments available before that stage can be reached.

In the consideration of the general theory of sampling induction, in the widest sense, and notably in the crucial step of 'reversing the consequents', the concept of rarity plays an important part. We have the fact that substantial samples in which all the P's have Q are very rare, except when in the populations from which they are drawn almost all the P's have Q. The fact that this sample would be extremely rare, except on the hypothesis that in the population in question most of the P's have Q, inclines us towards that hypothesis in every case when we come across such a sample. But it has been shown that if samples of this kind were very rare in our experience, the movement of thought towards accepting the hypothesis that most P's have Q would be without logical warrant. We have to know the rate of occurrence of samples of this logical type within our experience to judge what evidential value the occurrence of any one sample of this type has in favour of the hypothesis to which it points. Subject to this, we say that the hypothesis in question is very probable. This probability rests on the rarity of the sample, within its own hyper-population of samples, if the hypothesis were not true.

In using the rarity of a sample on the hypothesis not-H in order to establish the probability of H, a further principle is involved. A sample that is rare on the hypothesis not-H has no evidential value in establishing H, if all other samples on the hypothesis not-H are equally rare. There are two points of view from which we can regard samples of the type that all P's have Q. It may be that, if in fact the population has a sizable number of P's lacking Q, there are many types of sample, such as '50 per cent of the P's have Q', that are not nearly so rare as the sample of the type all P's have Q. But there is a further point here which is distinct. We are free to consider samples from various points of view. One of these is in relation to the characteristic of uniformity. From this point of view to assess the importance of the relative rarity (on the assumption that a certain proportion of P's in the population lack Q) of a sample in which all the P's have Q, we do not need to assess its rarity compared with the rarity of each other particular kind of sample, e.g. '95 per cent of P's have Q', '94 per cent of P's have Q', but its rarity compared with all other samples having less uniformity than it has, i.e. all the samples to the left of it on the sample line. Thus the sample is rare in two respects. It is rare in respect of embodying the particular ratio of frequency of P's having Q that it does — in this case 0 of P's lack Q ; in this respect each of the other kinds of sample, 100, 95, 90 per cent, etc., have their own degrees of rarity which can be compared with each other. But it is also rare in respect of its uniformity. We may, in fact, grade all samples by their degree of uniformity, as in the sample line furnished. We are free to make any kind of grading that we like in our attempt to get logical leverage. In respect of uniformity the sample before us has a rarity which all the others lack. We are therefore entitled to assess its rarity on the basis of the ratio of uniform samples to all samples less uniform in the hyper-population to which it belongs. If we assessed rarity merely on the basis of the proportion of P's lacking Q being a certain number, then we should have to compare this rarity with the rarity of each of all the kinds of samples in which the proportion was a certain number. In fact we can do better than this. We can measure the rarity of samples having a certain degree of uniformity against the rarity (which, unless there is considerable uniformity in the population, is in fact a high frequency) of all the samples having less uniformity.

This principle comes out strongly in relation to simplicity. Here we are concerned with a set of observations each of which contains two (or more) magnitudes, and we have in mind that these magnitudes may have some regular relation expressed in general terms as $y=f(x)$. On the hypothesis that in fact the two magnitudes have the Heracleitean relation to each other, viz. that each number for one is in the total population paired with every number for the other, within limits, a roughly equal number of times, then all different sets of observed pairs of numbers will be equally rare. Therefore the fact that the set of pairs of numbers in the observations before us is very rare on the Heracleitean hypothesis, is no evidence against that hypothesis. The mere fact that phenomena on a certain hypothesis are rare endows those phenomena, when they occur, with no evidential value against the hypothesis if all other phenomena on that hypothesis would be equally rare.

Just as we are free if we wish to consider samples from the point of view of uniformity, so we can consider sets of pairs (or of trios, etc.) of observed magnitudes from the point of view of the simplicity of the law connecting the magnitudes throughout the set under observation. We no longer consider the phenomena simply as exemplifying a particular set of pairs of numbers, but as exemplifying a law of a certain degree of simplicity connecting the numbers in the pairs. We are thus entitled to assess the rarity, on the Heracleitean hypothesis, of the phenomena that exemplify some law or other of that degree of simplicity, relatively to all observables on the Heracleitean hypothesis not exemplifying any law of that degree of simplicity. It is on this basis that the preference shown by scientists for a simple law over a complex one can be shown to be not an ultimate prior preference, but derivable from the more general characteristics of inductive argument.

At the expense of repetition we may reiterate. The probability of a simple law is based on the rarity, if no law is operating, of the sets of observables obeying this law or *any other law of equal simplicity ranking*. The reference to other laws of equal simplicity ranking is absent in logical treatises. In practical working it may often be ignored, since when in the presence of simple laws we are usually concerned with very high probabilities, and the deflation due to the necessary reference to other laws of equal simplicity ranking would not be of significant magnitude. But, if my reasoning is correct, this reference to other possible laws of equal simplicity ranking is clearly one of the most fundamental principles of induction. Failure to observe the logical leverage given by this reference may account for the lazy-minded lapse into the assumption that a prior preference for simple laws is required to account for the actual preference for them that is rightly shown by scientists. Preference for simplicity is not an ultimate principle, but is deducible from the more general principles of induction.

If the foregoing principles of induction are correct, a high probability can be ascribed to the informative character of memory.

It is claimed that all the principles of induction set out in this book are, in the terminology of Carnap, L-true. They are applicable in every possible case. If we apply them correctly, the results of our reasoning, which however will assign probability only, not certainty, to our empirical beliefs, will invariably be correct. The principles of induction have equal logical status with those of deduction.

If our universe did not have those characteristics, which happily it manifests, of continuity, repetition and observables complying with simple laws, the principles of induction would not thereby be rendered invalid ; but there would be lack of scope for their application. And in that case we should no doubt not be at pains to discover what they are.

CHAPTER XI

BEYOND EXPERIENCE

MODERN thought contains two opposite tendencies. On the one hand, using inductive methods, it has achieved a vast extension of actual knowledge about our universe; the area of its domain and the precision of its detail would alike have astonished our forefathers; we confidently expect this progress to continue. By contrast, when we assess the utmost limits of our potential knowledge our notions have suffered a contraction, in which two stages may be distinguished.

There was a time when philosophers or savants hoped that, whether by using general metaphysical conceptions or a supposed intuitive power to apprehend the essential nature of material bodies, we should succeed in demonstrating the immutable properties of the whole universe, even if we had to regard it as of infinite extent. These claims must be reduced if we accept the view that we can only obtain knowledge of our environment by its impact on us through our limited organs of sense. There may be many things to which we have no access in this way; they may neither have a direct relation to our sense impressions, nor be capable of being inferred from those impressions. Thus we cannot deny, but rather may be more disposed to accept, Hamlet's dictum: there is more in heaven and earth, Horatio.

The arguments of this volume carry the matter a stage further. Not only may the aspects of the universe that we can glimpse be but a small selection of all its aspects, but our right to extrapolate outwards from the aspects actually glimpsed in our neighbourhood is seen to be severely restricted. It rests solely on the principle that we are not likely to be on the extreme edge of a region having the characteristics we have noted. In principle we are in the same position as those lower forms of life the limitations of whose range of vision are apparent to us. Even what we claim to know must be taken for probable only; we may awake to-morrow to find that the reign of the vaunted laws of physics is over; if we attempt great extrapolations we cannot even claim high probability; we wander about on our own little surface, pleased with our knowledge only because we cannot see the edge of its domain.

It has been the purpose of this volume to give rational grounds for the beliefs we have, to strengthen our logical foundations. In this regard it claims to be constructive. I see dangers in prevailing tendencies in modern logic, by the doctrines of which, if only we were quite frank, we should have to confess that there were no better reasons for accepting the findings of modern science than any chance fairy tale. But this provision of a foundation, which should be welcome, has its price, namely the repudiation of all claim to gain knowledge by empirical methods of an area of infinite extent, of all claim to universality, and the imposition of a strict limit to our right to extrapolate far from our own here and now.

It is natural to us to wonder what may exist over and above those things which make their sense impressions on us, directly or indirectly, and beyond the surface, if it be not infinite, on which we are moving. We shall be told at once, and rightly, that we can make no judgements as to the probabilities of the case. I accept this, subject to one reservation. Probability is a logical relation arising within experience, requiring for premises certain types of experience and pertaining to conclusions about potential experiences in the vicinity; when we have fully explored the ambit of those conclusions we have exhausted the potentialities of the probability relation. About what lies beyond the region covered by this relation there can by definition be no probability. And that, I fear, is the end of the matter.

I would suggest none the less that there is just one belief that we can hold for probable in regard to things beyond the range of inductive argument, and that is, simply, that there are such things. In this context the use of the plural has no special significance. It is obviously possible that there are such things; but I suggest that we can go a little further than that. The argument would be as follows. If a universe — or, in this connexion, should we call it a super-universe? —

contains sentient centres with varying ranges of observation, and if these centres believe that what lies within their own respective ranges of observation is all that exists, they will more often be wrong than right. In other words, a totally egocentric point of view is unlikely to be right.

This is certainly as far as argument in probability will carry us beyond the world of our experience. None the less, if we take it for probable that something lies beyond, it is natural to us to wonder about it. Now if in these days we are tempted in that direction, a host of governesses descend upon us, to shoo us off. 'This sort of thing', they say, 'is a sheer waste of time, and therefore most reprehensible.' Both the premise and the inference here are open to challenge. There is a puritanical strain in this attitude. Wonder about the invisible world might possibly be pleasurable and is therefore to be condemned out of hand. There is a utilitarian element — in the popular and wrong sense of that word. Activities are to be condemned that cannot be shown to be 'useful' for some purpose outside themselves. This is analogous to the hoary fallacy in economics, which distinguished between productive and unproductive labour. What is this veto? To speculate upon the invisible world [1] has become in our latter day theology something like the forbidden fruit of ancient theology. Why should we bow to this impertinent restriction on our liberty? If it is probable that there is something beyond, why should we not wonder about it?

Even from the narrow utilitarian point of view, the veto may be wrong. It is possible that such wondering may increase our fortitude in dealing with the affairs of this world. This is an empirical question subject to test.

I must not go too far. No doubt these modern governesses have their case. We must keep our sense of proportion and pursue the golden mean. What the governesses fear is that, once any liberty is allowed, these speculations will be carried to excess, that owing to the great gullibility of mankind, false creeds will be strengthened or new ones spring up, carrying

[1] I shall use the familiar expression 'invisible world'; it would be pedantic to insert each time that this means what is neither seen nor capable of being inferred from what is seen, and still more pedantic to refer each time to its lack of impact on our organs of smell, touch, etc.

also false maxims in regard to conduct ; 'otherworldliness' furthermore may provide an alibi for neglecting the palpable duties of this world ; there is enough to be thought and practised within the empirical sphere to absorb every ounce of human energy. In a slightly different strain they may argue that it is a positive insult to the empirical world, with its inexhaustible beauties and splendours, and its varied challenges to thought and purpose and creative effort, to deflect one's mind to a vague wondering about something different. I need not re-sing the praises of the Renaissance which turned the central thoughts of men back to our own world ; I take them for granted.

The appeal, however, to be up and doing about this glorious world of ours may in some cases be unrealistic. This has its application in all sections of society and among members of all income groups. In our complex social pattern the interplay of opportunity and the inherent capacity of the individual may be such as to impose a restriction. No doubt social reform and psychological therapeutics should be strenuously addressed to enriching the phenomenal lives of all. But it is vain to hope for complete success. The lives of most will not be so full of successful achievement as to allow no room for enrichment by speculation about the invisible world ; and I believe that even the lives of the successful and the mighty could sometimes gain thereby.

The real difficulty is what content or form to give to this wondering. If we can know nothing for certain or probable about the nature of what lies beyond experience, it may well be so different as to be unimaginable. Are we then brought to a halt, before we even begin ?

It is relevant to recall that we do not have to go beyond the range of our experience to be confronted with the unimaginable. The carrier qualities of electrons and protons, or of chairs and tables, if they exist, are unimaginable. If we seek for mystery, we have unfathomable mysteries under our very noses, indeed in our own bodies and brains, the structural qualities of which, if they have more than a shadowy existence in the apodoses of unfulfilled conditionals, must have unimaginable carrier qualities to sustain them. We may reject their existence, in the manner of Berkeley, holding that only consciousness in its various forms exists, and, if we did this, we should presumably apply the dictum in our wondering about what lies beyond experience.

We are not greatly interested in the nature of these alleged carrier qualities, because the entities in question seem to be so fully defined by their structural qualities. In this respect they are entirely different from the carrier qualities of conscious being. While the discovery of these structural qualities of matter has been the most exciting achievement of mankind, once known, they strike the mind as a little monotonous. In wondering about the innumerable possibilities of the mysterious unknown, it would be natural to select what i sinteresting.

A word, however, must be said about the monotony of matter. We are baffled by the problem of scale. Relatively to ourselves an electron seems very small ; this has no absolute meaning ; each electron may be a vast theatre of rich entertainment. Light is a quick mover, and the fact that it takes a million years to traverse only part of the astronomer's universe would certainly be discouraging, if we felt we had to look in a physical sense beyond it for something more interesting. This thought has in fact, I believe, discouraged some people. But from another point of view this astronomer's universe may seem as small as an electron seems to us. These questions of scale, where absolute size is merely an appearance generated by introspection, have no relevance for our wonderings about the world beyond experience.

The only form of existent with which we have full acquaintance in the empirical world is conscious being. It might be objected that it should not in that case be possible to discriminate between consciousness and existence. The reason why we can make the discrimination is that we are asked, in consequence of a process of inference of an inductive character, to postulate the existence of material bodies having unimaginable carrier qualities. Great perplexity must still beset this point ; it has been discussed in our chapter on ontology ; I do not claim that the difficulties have been cleared up.

When we say, on the basis of the improbability of an egocentric view being correct, that there are probably things beyond experience, the argument entitles us to regard those things as forms of conscious being. On general grounds it is probable that there are conscious beings which do not directly or indirectly impinge on our senses. To deny this is to take an egocentric view of an extreme form.

It may also be the case that there are many things beyond our range of experience that are unimaginable and these may be the more important things. But even if this is so, it is not wrong to wonder in terms that we can imagine. Furthermore, it is possible that our thoughts about the imaginable can be translated into thoughts about the unimaginable by an intellectual operation unknown to us.

Before advancing it may be proper to take a passing glance at theology. The main trouble about theology in its most familiar forms is that it is dogmatic, and this is of course totally unacceptable. While not intending to be entirely negative in my attitude towards theology, I must bring two further charges. One is that in its struggles with its subject — difficult enough in all conscience — it uses words, like eternal and perfect, which trick the mind by purporting to mean something, but which in their theological context mean nothing whatever. Here it seems that the criticism made by proponents of linguistic analysis is appropriate. The question whether we believe certain theological dogmas to be true or false just does not arise ; for we are asked in such cases to affirm or deny something that makes no sense. Another criticism brought from quite a different point of view is that when theologians depart from abstractions that are meaningless in the literal sense to tell some stories, these are often of a tawdry and tinselly kind. They bring a blush to the cheek. When one thinks of the wonderful and beautiful creations of poets and story-tellers in the historic period, it is sad that theologians who profess to be directing our minds to what is most sublime and elevated can sometimes be content with such poor stuff. I refrain from giving examples.

These various weaknesses stem from the same root, which is the attempt to make general or particular statements of the type that could flow from empirical evidence, about a world about which by definition empirical evidence can give us no guidance. Let us suppose that contrary to all reasonable expectation we were able to get empirical evidence — say, by tapping a table — about a world of 'spirits' ; then every-

thing that could be said about those spirits would lie within
the empirical world. But I am here concerned with what lies
beyond the empirical world, and I am assuming that that is
the proper province of theology. If theologians repudiate that
definition, no matter. From the logical point of view the
fundamental distinction is between what can be inferred from
actual and possible experience and those things that lie beyond
that realm of inference. If we could really make good judgements in probability about these alleged 'spirits', they would
be brought within the ambit of empirical knowledge, which
would thus be unexpectedly extended. Table tappers would
be quite wrong if they supposed that if they ever achieved
success — and that would no doubt have its own interest —
they would be gaining access to the sphere with which theology
and, I would add, religion are concerned.

How, then, are we to proceed ? In high philosophical discussion the word 'immanence' has been used. This has the
right aroma. We may derive an analogy from the progress of
science, that is, of inductive methods. Instead of proceeding
by framing a definition of a solid body and seeking to deduce
what qualities a solid body must have, we examine the behaviour of so-called solid bodies. This method of approach
may serve us, even when we seek to extend our speculations
beyond the empirical world.

In our thoughts about our own world we find various
matters of interest. In some cases the interest is independent
of any fact. The things that have for us an interest of this
kind would still be interesting even if every one of our beliefs
about the facts of our empirical world or the laws obtaining
in our world were false. Thus the interest of these things is
in no wise dependent on the success of our empirical enquiries.
When I speak of 'our empirical world' I do not refer merely to
that world of which we believe ourselves to have knowledge at
present, but to any world larger (or smaller) by comparison
with that, about which we might gain knowledge by inductive
methods. Our empirical world might shrink through the
appearance of new phenomena discordant with existing hypotheses and not suggesting new hypotheses ; we hope and
believe that it will continue to expand. Such a shrinkage or
expansion would have no effect on the interest of the things

in question. Thus the domain of interest of those things is not coterminous with that of our empirical world ; it has no relation to the boundaries of that world. The factors inherent in induction that impose limits to the realm of our knowledge have no relevance to these things. Thus, when we are in contemplation of such things, we may deem ourselves in touch with the world beyond experience.

And what, pray, are these things ? In this concluding chapter of a book on inductive knowledge it is only proper to make a few brief notes and jottings. Disclaiming originality I would say that these things have some relation to the time-honoured categories of truth, goodness, beauty and love. It is a redeeming feature in theologians that they make not infrequent references to love.

I began by using the word 'interesting', and this strikes me as fundamental in this context. It is connected with the great differences that exist between people. Out of certain ingredients, an inherited complex of emotions and capacities, and experience, a character is formed. The capacity for variety is amazing. It is a matter of universal experience that the more closely one knows people the vaster are the differences from person to person that become apparent. From the universality of this experience we may infer that comparable differences exist between the people one does not know. One may visit a new country or continent and view seething masses of humanity ; one is tempted to think of them as mere repetitions of the human species, but a little reflexion surely suggests that on closer inspection they would prove as different one from another as our close friends. All faces appear utterly different from one another on close knowledge ; how much more so do characters. It is in the difference that 'interest' lies ; mere repetition is not interesting. When one turns up a stone and sees crawling life, one may be more doubtful ; on the other hand, our doubt may be due to our lack of intimacy with the subject-matter ; we have to suspend judgement.

Mere difference as such is not interesting. It is necessary that each complex should have a quality, different each from each, that exhibits some aspect of the aforementioned categories of truth, goodness, beauty and love. These traditional words are not fully adequate instruments of thought. Once again it is a universal experience that each person, if closely known and understood, does exhibit some unique aspect of these categories. (It cannot of course be known to be unique ; there may be a fully identical twin within the wide universe. But no competent observer has yet reported a case.)

The words 'character' and 'personality' may be used in this connexion ; but they are both a little too restricted. The old-fashioned word 'soul' is a good one. I am not suggesting its use in any sense such as could give rise to an argument about whether there is such a thing as a soul. What I would designate is something utterly palpable and obvious — the personal and different contribution by each separate individual within the field of the four categories. It would be proper to speak — with exceeding brevity — about each.

Truth is not quite in line with the others. Truthfulness of utterance belongs to the second category — 'goodness'. We come nearer to a separate category if we think of the quest for truth. Among modes of search we find great variety. It might be argued that this manifestation is confined to intellectual people, even to scientists and humanists of genius. I am not sure. The zeal for truth may take many forms according to the varied circumstances of the truth-seeker. The interest inherent in the quest depends upon the knowledge already available, rather than in the content of the truth when established. To an outside observer who knew the whole story already the most sublime discoveries of science would have no interest ; it is in the methods used by poor nescient man to reach that point of vantage that the interest lies. That applies, too, to the unlettered observer making his own way forward with the means at his disposal.

Reference to the quest for truth inevitably suggests a reflexion about dogmatic theology. The gravamen against it is not only that it sometimes asks for the acceptance of positions which, if not meaningless, are most unlikely to be true, but, worse, that it finds merit in the acceptance as true of beliefs quite apart from the grounds for them. This is to stab true religion to the very heart. If we would dwell on the great mysteries of the invisible world, if, to use traditional language, we would enter that holy place, then we must surely first pledge ourselves to the service of truth. We must devote ourselves utterly and unreservedly to its quest. There can be various occasions in our phenomenal life when we can wisely pursue customary paths or when the question of truth is not relevant to our endeavours. But if we are to turn aside to think about what lies beyond, then we must resolve not to deviate from our quest for truth by a scintilla. Otherwise what is the point of turning aside ? Better to get on with our ordinary job, to follow the advice of the governesses, and not to think about these mysteries.

In the face of all this, theologians have come forward and alleged merit in the acceptance of tenets even when the grounds for them were not decisive. Where can the merit lie ? In the religion of truth doubt is as holy as belief. And what manner of religion dare divide itself from the religion of truth and still hold up its head ? Perhaps no better definition could be given of a lie in the soul than to believe on authority what at the deepest level of one's intellectual being one finds grounds for doubting. When it was added that if one did not accept doubtful matters on authority one would be condemned to eternal torture, that was carrying blasphemy against the religion of truth as far as it was possible to go. No doubt modern Christian theologians of the better type have long since discarded such doctrines.

I now pass to the second category, the domain of ethics. Before considering this in relation to the invisible world, I will seize the opportunity to make some observations, which properly belong to our general subject of inductive logic, on the logical status of ethical judgements. The tide is running out and I can but summarize my own views. At the risk of being presumptuous I shall be exceedingly brief about the philosophical problems involved. I suggest that it is conformable with the time-honoured usage of mankind, in other words with the 'explicandum', to hold that in ethics we are concerned with kind, unselfish, or, to use a less pleasing word, altruistic, conduct. The major premise of all ethical judgements, general or particular, might be expressed as 'one ought to be altruistic', this premise constituting a definition of 'ought'. In conjunction with various facts about human (or animal) needs and pains and laws of nature, etc., this premise yields a variety of conclusions, general and particular, containing the word

T

'ought'. The 'ought' in these conclusions is accounted for by the 'ought' in the major premise. Since this is a definition there is no meaning in asking why one ought to be altruistic. In other words, to say that something 'ought' to be done means that it conforms with the code of altruism to do it. The ethical system is an elaboration of all that flows from the idea of being altruistic. And that, subject to a supplementary point considered below, is my summary of the philosophical aspect of ethics ! [1]

In many cases it is quite clear which action as between two alternatives is selfish and which unselfish. These are when the proximate or nearly proximate effects are all that are likely to be of quantitative significance. In other cases we may have to take more remote effects into account — 'be cruel to be kind'. Here we have to adduce our general empirical knowledge of nature and our conclusions may not have high probability. The debate should be conducted on fully rational and empirical lines, bringing to bear all relevant facts and assessing probabilities.

There has recently been creeping into general speech and notably into the subject of economics the expression 'value judgement'. I believe that this expression is commonly used to cover absence or gross confusion of thought. Economics and ethics are mutually relevant at many points, but I do not judge that the expression 'value judgement' serves to elucidate their interaction. It seems to be implied that a value judgement is merely the personal expression of an opinion, which is not objectively true or false. But unless the so-called opinion is a meaningless conjunction of symbols — but this is not, I think, usually suggested — it must be either true or false.

Ethical opinions, indeed, are either true or false, although, since in many cases they depend upon the facts of the empirical

---

[1] In general speech 'ought' is very frequently used without any ethical implication. It occurs when action is considered in relation to a purpose. 'You ought to add a pinch of salt' is an appropriate expression even when the cook is expected to consume the soup himself and when, accordingly, to impart flavour to it cannot be deemed an act of kindness. In economics the word occurs very frequently, the purpose there being to make scarce resources that can be applied to alternative uses yield as much of what people want as possible. The context usually makes it plain whether the 'ought' has an ethical significance. The word 'good' has a similar ambiguity.

world, we often do not know which they are. Pure economics is in similar plight, so that the fact that some conclusions in economics depend on ethical premises does not in general tend to bring them onto a different plane of validity.

The supplementary point referred to above is concerned with moral obligation.[1] Here, again, I claim to be proceeding in line with time-honoured usage and thus to be supplementing the elucidation of the 'explicandum'. There are many cases in which it is considered morally obligatory to choose one out of alternative courses of action, although its consequences, including the most remote that can be assessed, are on balance hurtful. There are cases in which it is appropriate to consider the situation in question as one of the wider class of all similar situations, and assess the effects not of one's taking a given choice on the particular occasion, but of every one taking the same choice on the similar occasions. Kant understood this, but gave the wrong reason for it. Pedants have arisen to protest that no two situations are identical. It will at once occur to the judicious reader, however, that in assessing similarity we need here, as in other cases, to specify limits of tolerance, which will rule out irrelevant differences.

Kant held that to act wrongly was to act on a principle, which, if universalized, could be shown to involve a contradiction. This account of 'wrongful' does not yield the required result. There would be no self-contradiction in having a rule never to do anything the foreseeable consequences of which were on balance hurtful. The real reason for the requirement for universalizing is that it is often the case that the harm done by n acts of a certain character is much greater than n times the harm done by one such act. The classic instance is the lie. Confidence in the truthfulness of neighbours is a prime instrument of human welfare. n lies uttered within certain limits of time and space may have far more than n times the effect of one lie in undermining general confidence in the truthfulness of communications. Hence arises the moral obligation to speak the truth on each occasion, even although on each of a number of occasions among these, when considered separately, the pain given by speaking the truth outweighs any good effects of doing so (which might be nil).

[1] See also 'Utilitarianism Revised', by R. F. Harrod, *Mind*, April 1936.

T 2

The obligation is not, however, absolute. It may be outweighed on a particular occasion if the direct harm done on that occasion is sufficiently great. It is a fallacy to suppose that it is morally right to tell the would-be murderer the truth about which turning his victim had taken. There is a right and wrong on each occasion, although it may often be impossible to assess. The situation is analogous to the presence of uncountable numbers in our evidence which would make our estimate of probability precise, if only we could count them.

The matter may be schematized thus. We take all the occasions on which telling truth would cause, say, a thousand units of pain and have no good effects and assess what would be lost (impossible to do within fine limits) by the weakening of confidence in the spoken word if lies were told on all those occasions. We might make a rough judgement that the loss of confidence would not be substantial and that the lie was therefore justified on each such occasion. Then take all occasions on which a truth would cause one unit of pain and do no good and assess the consequences of the loss of confidence due to lies being told on that far greater number (n) of occasions. If it seems that the loss causes more damage than n units of pain, then it is obligatory to speak the truth. We can only expect the roughest of rough assessments. The final judgement would in fact be either true or false. In this respect it is quite unlike the alleged 'value judgements' which are supposed to be purely subjective. A man who combined a deep sociological understanding with a good power of assessing the quantitative importance of factors would be more likely to get the answer right than one lacking those attainments.

It is to be observed that what has to be set on each occasion against the avoidance of pain due to the lie is *not* the loss of confidence due to the lie being told on that occasion, but the loss of confidence due to its being told on that and all similar occasions. Any loss of confidence due to the particular lie is part of the foreseeable consequences of that particular lie and therefore not a consideration which relates to the specific quality of moral obligation. Thus the fact that it was known, as it might be, that on the particular occasion the lie would not be found out would have no relevance to the moral issue. The plain man's view that a lie is usually wrong, even if the truth causes some pain and yields no direct benefit and even if the lie will never be discovered, is correct.

Similarly the wrongfulness of an act in this class of cases is quite independent of its effects as an example. These are included in the sum of the foreseeable consequences of the particular act.

It has further to be observed that action in accordance with a certain rule is only morally obligatory, if the rule is commonly observed in the society. If there is no confidence in the truthfulness of communications anyhow, it is not incumbent on the individual to tell the truth in a particular case, if to do so would give pain and yield no advantage. It is the requirement of this further condition for the presence of moral obligation that constitutes the element of truth in the view that the content of moral obligation depends on the evolution of society. This fact was blown out by some writers into undue importance and made the basis of hazy metaphysical doctrines of the state. Hume understood the point quite well, but kept his sense of proportion ; what he has to say about the social contract is superior to what is found in the philosophers more commonly recommended for reading on this subject.[1]

Observance of a commonly observed rule, which is of such a kind that observance of it on n occasions yields more than n times the advantage to others than observance on each occasion considered separately yields, is a moral obligation. This is a definition of moral obligation. Since this kind of observance serves the general purposes of an ethical (altruistic) system, it is appropriate to use the word 'ought' in recommending it.

The common use of language, which so often achieves the higher virtue of subtlety at the expense of the lower one of tidiness, applies the word 'ought' (in its ethical sense) to moral obligations generally, but to cases of straight altruism only where the pleasure given to or the pain averted from others is rather great. 'Ought' has varying degrees of strength. We have already seen that the 'ought' in a moral obligation can be overruled by the straight altruistic 'ought' where the damage done to others on a particular occasion is sufficiently

---

[1] Hume, *Treatise of Human Nature*, Bk. III, Pt. II, secs. III and V-VIII and Pt. III, sec. I.

great. In cases of straight altruism the 'ought' takes into the reckoning the pain which the deed may inflict on the agent ; one would not say that a man ought to do something (otherwise than in observing a moral obligation) if he thereby caused himself much pain but only slight benefit to others. In this respect the common use of 'ought' corresponds to the utilitarian code. But the strength of the 'ought' does not measure the ethical quality of an act ; the time-honoured assessment of this (the explicandum) is not in accordance with the utilitarian code. If in performing an act conveying moderate benefit to others the agent inflicts much injury on himself, this injury is subtracted in assessing the strength of the ought (and may serve to eliminate it), but added in assessing the ethical quality of the act if performed.

It has been the purpose of this digression to show that, given ethical major premises which conform with time-honoured usage (the explicandum), the detailed contents of ethical beliefs depend on empirical knowledge and may be the subject of rational discussion ; there is nothing subjective about them. And this conclusion also accords with time-honoured usage and suggests that the ethical definitions here supplied satisfactorily elucidate the explicandum. There is, however, something more to be said about ethics, which must be reserved. We must now return to our central theme.

In what theology has to say about the relations of man to the invisible world, ethical goodness plays the supreme, if not the sole, part. This strikes me as greatly mistaken emphasis. This is not for a moment to disparage ethical goodness ; a man who leads a good life in hard circumstances and does not compensate himself in indirect ways at some one else's expense is a rare and precious phenomenon indeed. None the less I would say, to speak in wild metaphor, that, while goodness is a *sine qua non* for admission into heaven, it is not the main ground of entitlement. For that entitlement must be more intimately connected with the unique contribution of the individual soul.

My third category is beauty. Despite the splendid connotations of that word, it is nevertheless inadequate. The public exponents of beauty are the creative artists. I would suggest that any one of the greatest of these brings us into closer touch with the invisible world than all the dogmatic theologians put together. A great work of art has the two-fold qualification that its individual quality is unique, and that its interest is independent of whether the beliefs we have about the facts or laws in our empirical world are true or false.

However, this argument is not primarily concerned with the artist. His rôle is to give public representation, in forms that can be understood by others, to patterns of emotion, purpose and apprehension that exist in each separate soul. He selects out of the vast wealth of material at his disposal, contributing, too, from his own soul. What he succeeds in offering for public inspection is but a tiny fraction of the beauty that exists locked up in the breast of each separate person, perhaps known only to a few friends, perhaps to no other person.

I have referred to the artist as giving public expression to aspects of beauty. There are also those who have the opportunity of impressing themselves by their careers in action. One may think of eminent statesmen ; unhappily the majority of those who strut across the stage do not make very good impressions, as they lack sufficient capacity to do justice to their occasions. In more moderate walks of life, the manager, the doctor, the foreman may achieve a more adequate pattern ; and so also the operative or peasant who also has his opportunities in the common relations of daily life. When a man dies we realize that something unique is lost and cannot be replaced. We may comment that no doubt there will be another like him to fill his niche. This is purely superficial ; we know quite well that there will not be another like him within very wide limits of tolerance indeed ; so far as we are concerned that unique pattern of emotion, purpose and apprehension is gone and lost for ever, save for such memories as we may retain.

That may strike some as a good riddance. They could glimpse no pattern of beauty in the person in question. There will usually be some, and those they who had more intimate knowledge, who are more appreciative.

The soul has its phases. In youth there may be a wide range of aspiration. Expression is fluid and a variety of potentialities may be observed. Usually later the expression becomes more adequate, but the range more limited. The pressures of the environment restrict development ; many aspirations have to be jettisoned. In some cases the pressures and practical handicaps are so great as seemingly to crush and kill the spirit ; I believe that even in those cases, if only one could penetrate to the core, some pattern of beauty would be found to survive.

Some observers are more concerned to notice faults and failings. In the ethical code wrong and bad have their specific reference as determined by the empirical premises. In the case of beauty, in the wide sense now under discussion, I do not believe that there is any quality that may be held to be its opposite. There is deficiency in the strict sense, that is lack of adequate endowment. Out of his endowment of passion and apprehension a man may succeed in making an interesting pattern, which constitutes his character or his soul ; or he may have very poor success, so that little of interest emerges. There is then an unsatisfying pattern or an absence of pattern. I see no positive quality to contrast with beauty in this sense. The pattern has a unique quality ; there is no corresponding unique quality in the jumble constituted by the complete failure, if ever there be such, to be an adequate human being.[1]

I take a religious attitude to be a tending to dwell on the belief — which is probably correct — that one's aspiration is occurring in a larger universe than that of which we gain knowledge by induction. The aspiration may not find adequate expression, so that its quality is hidden from our fellow mortals. It is sometimes said that, while busy and successful people have no need of religion, it is valuable for the weaker brethren or the less successful. This, it must be confessed, sometimes goes with the thought that any old nonsense is good enough to stuff them up with. This is an insufferably patronizing attitude. But it is not unnatural or in any way contemptible that those whose aspiration is largely unfulfilled in this life may derive a greater measure of consolation from the thought of a larger universe.

I have used the over-all term 'beauty', the inadequacy of which must already be apparent. I cannot forbear to mention

---

[1] There is some family resemblance between this doctrine and the definition of truth supplied on p. 167.

one special aspect of the soul's pattern, which is a most precious one. There is no adequate word for it, perhaps because it is too gossamer for the crudities of common speech. If a man praises another for having a sense of humour, one may be inclined to guess that they are both bores — markedly lacking in any beautiful pattern. Humour is a dreadful word. Other words of similar purport have special twists. The best one can do is perhaps to refer to the quality in question simply as what tends to make for laughter. This has the property of uniqueness in high degree. Its interest is also independent of the truth or falsity of all inductive inferences. It is a curious fact that it is felt to be alien and inappropriate to those solemn times and places — we call them 'solemn' and that very word seems to banish the possibility of laughter — where man seeks to place himself in relation to the invisible world. I would not dare to assert this to be wrong; but it is peculiar, and seems to point to something artificial and sectional in religion as ordinarily conceived. We surely do not wish to banish laughter from the invisible world.

We may now give fresh consideration to ethics from two points of view. Its essence is altruism and with the aid of empirical data rules of conduct are generated. If one considers the various ways in which one man may help another, one can think of handing over a cheque or helping a blind person across the road; one may also think of honourable dealing, etc. But the sum of all such actions by no means constitutes the full picture. The most frequent way, taking the exigencies of life as they are, by which one person can benefit another, is by bringing him good cheer. But this cannot be done by rote or by any copy-book rule whatever. It can only be done if the would-be benefactor has some beauty in himself. His friend is despondent; he must have sensitiveness and power of comment that avails to dispel the clouds of gloom. He can only do that if he is himself an integrated character. If he lacks beauty of soul, as I have perhaps too pompously called it, the mere disposition of benevolence cannot achieve the objective of altruism. It might be that in such a case the power to represent the situation in a funny light would be the crowning grace; or that might be inappropriate. Whatever the quality is, it is something additional to the pure will to do good, something more akin to the gift which the creative artist exercises for more public purposes. In the actual task of doing good it is the pattern of the soul, unique in each individual, and not the mere will to be altruistic, that achieves the altruistic intention. The content of any code of ethics is determined by empirical facts ; the fulfilment of the purposes of that code often depends upon qualities, which would be of interest whatever the shape of the empirical world.

In the late nineteenth century there was a tendency among some influential minds towards a rebellion against ethics. This is to be distinguished from a rebellion against particular ethical codes, which was also present. All such codes are empirical and provisional and in cases may tend to obsolescence in relation to new circumstances. On matters of sex notably new thought was then desirable. Such codes may be the matter of rational debate on normal empirical lines. A word of warning, however, is necessary to the effect that time-honoured codes, especially those concerning moral obligation, often have subtle reasons that can easily be ignored by starry-eyed reformers.

The revolt I have in mind went deeper, tending to criticize the major premise of altruism itself, and to set in its place some seemingly alternative criterion ; this might take various forms, but may be conveniently recalled by some such term as 'self-expression'. The burden of the foregoing has by no means been to belittle self-expression. Rather goodness in the ethical sense and self-expression are complementary. Self-expression may be regarded as the development within the soul of some unique aspect of beauty. Without self-expression the scope for good conduct would in practice be greatly reduced. Furthermore, a world in which each person complied fully with the ethical code but achieved no self-expression would be one of endless repetition. But, in general, repetition is not interesting. The great value of repetition in our empirical world is that it gives leverage for inductive argument, and thus makes it possible for us with our limited cognitive resources to acquire knowledge. If we are to think that what we achieve in an empirical world has interest from a wider point of view, it must be on account of variety, and because each soul achieves its unique pattern. In this sense it is right to hold that self-expression is more significant than compliance with an ethical code.

It does not follow that we should countenance the overthrow of ethical codes for the sake of self-expression, as was perhaps implied by those nineteenth-century thinkers. The ethical code supplies the framework within which the pattern of beauty is to be achieved. Why ? Why should we reject the pattern of self-expression achieved by the a-moral man ? I do not suggest that we must do so in every case, but only that we should tend to do so. We are seeking for what is of general interest. A pattern imbued with selfishness has a different appearance to others from that which it has to its contriver, the self. Even within this empirical world the fact that a pattern contains a selfish element makes it lose much of its interest for others. *A fortiori* if it is viewed from a wider horizon. To summarize the case, may I revert to my previous metaphor ? Goodness is the *sine qua non* for admission into heaven, but not the main ground of entitlement. The latter consists in the achievement of a unique pattern in the category which, for want of a better word, I have called beauty.

One must not, however, be too severe with a-moral people. Dogmatism is certainly out of place here. In the push and thrust of life it often seems that people who, to judge by their professions and many of their actions, are quite a-moral are the very ones most able to bring joy and light into our lives. One is sometimes even tempted to toy with the paradox that those who achieve most altruism in practice are those least consciously addicted to the code of altruism. Explicit profession does not of course matter in this connexion. It may be that many of these apparent a-moralists are imbued with altruism at a deeper level. These are questions of immense subtlety not to be readily answered. We dare not condemn unconditionally even the most deep-dyed a-moralist.

There remains the category of love. I said above that if a man dies, one has the sense that something unique has been lost that cannot be replaced. If a close friend dies there is a double loss. There is that loss, but there is also something over and above that ; one feels that part of oneself has died and can never be revived. By his stimulus one was able to achieve a certain pattern of thought and feeling, to view events in a certain way. Those old jokes are gone for ever. It is not simply his comment and his attitude that are lost ; it is also one's own power to comment, one's own power to see things, as one could under his stimulus, which is lost too. Each soul has its unique character ; but in the interplay between two souls something can emerge that is different from either. Death is not the only terminator. If a new friendship or love occurs, a vast new field of aspiration arises ; a new world seems to open up ; then often tiresome circumstances intervene and clutter up the ground and the potential is never fulfilled. Yet one may be sure that potential was not illusory, as when a poet has the conception of a poem still to be written out.

> When I have fears that I may cease to be
> Before my pen has gleaned my teeming brain . . .

Can we seriously doubt that there was a potential there which would have been fulfilled, if only he had survived ?

I have twice made reference to death. This is only because that event causes thought to focus upon certain matters which are always sufficiently obvious, but to which common speech does not give adequate expression. There is a reason for that. In relation to beliefs about empirical facts and laws language has means of referring to thought at the two levels that have already been mentioned, the beliefs themselves and our (higher level) categorization of the beliefs. Language is also the vehicle of expression, in the common round of daily life, of the unique patterns of beauty. But we lack language for the higher level categorization of those patterns. Not only are there difficulties in achieving such a categorization, but there would be no point or purpose in it. In empirical matters we need the categorization to aid thought in achieving its proper purposes in that field. Explicit thought is much influenced by language and, where forms of linguistic expression are absent, explicit thought tends to be absent likewise ; what thought there is has to use private, illiterate symbols of a kind not usable for communication. It does not follow that thought about the unique patterns within the categories of beauty and love is rare ; on the contrary, it is the daily bread of the conscious life of all people.

The preciousness to us of these things by no means depends upon the existence of an invisible world. None the less it may sometimes serve a purpose to bring our thoughts about them into relation with our thought about the invisible world. There is a natural relation, because these are things the range of interest of which is not co-terminous with the empirical world. If we give this turn to our thought, that may nourish the impulses within us tending towards beauty and love ; it may even in favourable circumstances fortify our resolve to be good in the ethical sense — as is so often reiterated in pulpits. It may, in fine, strengthen — I will not say it always does — our will to creation in the fields here discussed. Furthermore, such thought may bring to many a consolation in distress, which is by no means to be despised. The verdict of public opinion and the arbitrament of success in life are not always, or perhaps even usually, just and valid. It is natural for a man frustrated in his aspiration to regard the invisible world as a court of appeal and find comfort therein.

Total obliviousness of the invisible world marks what seems to be meant by the use in common speech of that lamentably ambiguous word, materialist. Such obliviousness is an intellectual defect. Since a world beyond our ken probably exists round the corner, so to speak, it is wanting in intellectual energy never to give a thought to it.

To think sometimes, or even often, about the invisible world does not, I suppose, by itself constitute a religious attitude. For that what is called faith is also required. This is to be distinguished from belief, whether rational or irrational, about empirical matters, which has been analysed in the foregoing pages. I would suggest that there are two essential articles in religious faith. (1) Where a unique pattern has been achieved in the categories of truth, goodness, beauty and love, and has been lost in the empirical world, whether by death or because the practical difficulties of daily life have smothered it, it will retain some place in the wider world. (2) Where there has been aspiration and an unfulfilled potential for a unique pattern, this will somehow be fulfilled. These seem to constitute what is essentially meant by the idea of personal survival.

It is natural to man to speculate upon such things. He will benefit, if sustained by tradition and by the garnered wisdom of past and present times ; for unaided he will lack strength, all the more so because it is impossible to provide any detailed content for such speculations, such as the mind is used to in its thought about empirical matters. It is not inappropriate that there should be certain rites and places set aside and consecrated persons devoted to such speculation. It is quite natural, as has happened in established religions, that the same persons should discharge the function of drawing the mind to dwell upon the invisible world and of recommending ethical precepts. While such institutions could have no interest for the pure materialist in the sense defined above, there seems no reason why they should not be accessible both to those who have and to those who lack 'faith' ; perhaps it is also possible in such a case to be betwixt and between.

When I was young some attention was still paid to men of an earlier time who favoured forms of corporate expression for what might be called the religion of a modern man. Renan and Matthew Arnold had widely different outlooks, and one might find much to object to in both ; but they had that in common. It seemed possible to some that the Church of England, nurturing its great tradition of latitude and purged of dogma by some modern Luther, might serve as a vehicle of expression for the religion of modern man, linking it with Christianity which has, after all, despite its failings, played a central part in making our civilization, and with a continuing veneration for its Founder. We can surely not doubt that this development would accord with the wishes of the Founder. But interest in such matters seems since to have fizzled out. Indifferentism has grown ; it is often said that subscription to dogmatic beliefs has also grown, although about this I have doubts.

A most unnatural situation has arisen. The man who, not content with materialism, seeks association with others in his religious aspiration, is confronted by the obstacle of the obsolete dogmas that are propounded, at least at the official level, by the established religions. He may make the mental reservation that the dogmas are not to be taken at their face value ; none the less they constitute a barrier, and a greater one for those who would wish to be ministers of religion, than for laymen. Thus the ordinary thoughtful man is thrown onto the resources of his own private religion ; but for the majority these may not suffice, and the consequence is a spiritual impoverishment. This has its dangers in our modern world of increasing pressures and tempo of change.

There are some who contend that a religion cannot exist, unless it is dressed out with hard and fast statements of fact, taken to be certitudes, and with a definite story having its time and place in the empirical world. The religion of modern man, it is claimed, would make no appeal and win no adherents. Yet we may doubt this when we recall to mind the Founder of the Christian religion. He brought to his aid no facts, no story, no hard and fast dogma, no creed. With parable and imagery he preached the simple gospel of love, fortitude, faith in a good outcome, and consolation for the unhappy of this world. In view of what has happened in the last two thousand years it is rather difficult to argue that he had not the remotest idea of what were the necessary ingredients of a viable religion. Of course there are those who claim that the success of Christianity has not been due to its Founder, but to the St. Pauls, the interpreters, the myth-makers, the miracle-mongers, the creed-writers, church-founders and dogmatists. One must not accept this too readily. It is just possible that the opposite may be true. It is possible that the authentic words of Jesus, which may be found among the sayings attributed to him, have struck deep into the hearts of ordinary people, generation after generation, and have caused his religion to survive, despite all the subsequent accretions.

I have now strayed rather far from the subject of inductive logic. Having endeavoured to define the nature and limits of our thinking about the empirical world, it seemed proper to give some indications, however scrappy and disjointed, about other types of thinking which also have their place.

INDEX

PRINTED BY R. & R. CLARK, LTD., EDINBURGH